Martial Ros
Tel: 01962 8

WITHDRAWN FROM
THE LIBRARY

UNIVERSITY OF
WINCHESTER

D1422438

KA 0400589 9

WRITING PERFORMATIVE SHAKESPEARES

This innovative study offers a genuinely groundbreaking approach to Shakespeare in performance. Six chapters work like case studies, each highly creative in terms of visual form and structure – including puzzles, comics and pinboards – inviting the reader into playful engagement with the performative dimensions of Shakespearean production. The case studies include discussion of training and rehearsal processes; the materiality of the performance event and its various embodiments; the intertextual citations through which productions make meaning; and, in response to all of this, the multiplicity and variety of audience perspectives and interpretations. Conkie's production choices range from original practices to politicised adaptations, small-scale workshops to multi-media spectacles, offering inventive analyses of what Shakespeare might mean, or can be made to mean, at particular times and in specific places, at the start of the twenty-first century.

ROB CONKIE is Senior Lecturer of Theatre and Drama at La Trobe University, Melbourne. His research integrates practical and theoretical approaches to Shakespeare in performance. He is the author of *The Globe Theatre Project: Shakespeare and Authenticity* (2006) and has published articles in journals including *Shakespeare, Shakespeare Bulletin* and *Shakespeare Survey.*

WRITING PERFORMATIVE
SHAKESPEARES

New Forms for Performance Criticism

ROB CONKIE

UNIVERSITY OF WINCHESTER
LIBRARY

CAMBRIDGE
UNIVERSITY PRESS

CAMBRIDGE
UNIVERSITY PRESS

University Printing House, Cambridge CB2 8BS, United Kingdom

Cambridge University Press is part of the University of Cambridge.

It furthers the University's mission by disseminating knowledge in the pursuit of
education, learning and research at the highest international levels of excellence.

www.cambridge.org
Information on this title: www.cambridge.org/9781107072992

© Rob Conkie 2016
Chapter 4 © Rob Conkie and Bernard Caleo 2016

This publication is in copyright. Subject to statutory exception
and to the provisions of relevant collective licensing agreements,
no reproduction of any part may take place without the written
permission of Cambridge University Press.

First published 2016

Printed in the United Kingdom by TJ International Ltd. Padstow Cornwall

A catalogue record for this publication is available from the British Library

Library of Congress Cataloguing in Publication data
Names: Conkie, Rob, author.
Title: Writing performative Shakespeares : new forms for performance criticism / Rob Conkie.
Description: New York : Cambridge University Press, 2016. | Includes
bibliographical references and index.
Identifiers: LCCN 2015049381 | ISBN 9781107072992 (Hardback)
Subjects: LCSH: Shakespeare, William, 1564–1616–Dramatic production. |
BISAC: LITERARY CRITICISM / European / English, Irish, Scottish, Welsh.
Classification: LCC PR3091 .W75 2016 | DDC 792.9/5–dc23 LC record available at http://lccn.loc.gov/2015049381

ISBN 978-1-107-07299-2 Hardback

Cambridge University Press has no responsibility for the persistence or accuracy
of URLs for external or third-party internet websites referred to in this publication,
and does not guarantee that any content on such websites is, or will remain,
accurate or appropriate.

The authors and publishers acknowledge the sources of copyright for third party material and are grateful for the
permissions granted. While every effort has been made, it has not always been possible to identify the sources of all
the material used, or to trace all copyright holders. If any omissions are brought to our notice, we will be happy to
include the appropriate acknowledgements on reprinting and in the next update to the digital edition, as applicable.

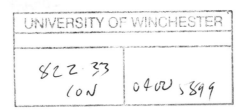

UNIVERSITY OF WINCHESTER

822.33
lon   04025899

Contents

Acknowledgements

I am very grateful to all of the people who have helped me with this book. It all started when I was working at The University of Winchester. I am grateful for the research grants I received whilst in Winchester and for discussions and interactions with many dear colleagues, including: Synne Behrndt, June Boyce-Tillman, Jude Davies, Tony Dean, Helen Grime, Stephen Hall, Mick Jardine, Eve Jeffrey, Nick Joseph, Annie McKean, Ronan Paterson, Charlotte Purkis, Geoff Ridden, Nick Rowe, Marianne Sharp and Carol Smith. At La Trobe University, my current workplace, I have been extremely fortunate with both collegial and financial support. Much of the work in this book has been supported by either the Centre for Creative Arts (thanks especially to Norie Neumark, Hugh Davies and Jan Brueggemeier) or, under the inspirational and generous leadership of Sue Thomas, the Disciplinary Research Program for English and Theatre and Drama. This support aided me with a research assistant and Peita Collard has been invaluable on the home stretch. My departmental colleagues have contributed in big ways and small to this book and they include: Julie Andrews, Angie Black, Owen Dalton, Alexis Harley, Sue Martin, Tegan Marshall, Mike Nolan, Alison Ravenscroft, Hannah Schurholz, Terrie Waddell and Becca Waese. And my Theatre colleagues have been supportive and inspirational: Kim Baston, Christine Burns, Kim Durban, Emily Dutton, Saumya Liyanage, Damien Millar, the late, great Geoffrey Milne, Julian Meyrick, Meredith Rogers and Peta Tait. A special mention is reserved for my unbelievably supportive friend and colleague, Loretta Calverley, who always kept an eye on the book and me, too.

Colleagues from other institutions, of course, have also shaped and supported this book (or me) and I think, hoping not to forget too many of them, of: Pascale Aebischer, Susan Bennett, Jim Bulman, Maurizio Calbi, Christie Carson, Ralph Alan Cohen, Bill Dunstone, Carla Della Gatta, Alison Findlay, Kate Flaherty, Penny Gay, Stuart Hampton-Reeves, Diana Henderson, Barbara Hodgdon, Romana Huk, Scott Maisano, Rob Ormsby, Joan Pope, John Ray Proctor, Peter Reynolds, Elizabeth Schafer, Robert Shaughnessy, Joanne Tompkins, Don Weingust and my regular collaborator, Penelope Woods. I am especially grateful to those scholars who agreed to gather round the discussion table (on p. 103): Christian Billing, Bridget Escolme, Pete Kirwan, Steve Purcell, Sarah K. Scott and Sarah Werner. And Carol Chillington Rutter offered the idyllic surrounds of Camp Crimscote for a summer sabbatical: without her I may never have finished my introduction.

I owe a great deal of thanks to the various theatrical companies and institutions that have assisted in the production of the book (and some of the theatre that features in it). At the Victorian College of the Arts I am extremely grateful to Tanya Gerstle and Bagryana Popov (also a colleague) for allowing me into their rehearsal rooms and for making suggestions about Chapter 1. I am also very much indebted to Ann Reid for offering me access to VCA archives and for help with follow-up enquiries. At the Globe, Farah Karim-Cooper has always pointed me in the right direction and the research library staff – Jordan Landes, Victoria Northwood and, more recently, Ruth Frendo – have been immensely helpful. At Toneelgroep Amsterdam, Loes de Graf and Marlene Kenens were kind enough to assist with performance texts and at the University of Western Australia, Bob White, Erika von Kaschke and Pam Bond have been enormously supportive: indeed, the work of Chapter 5 of this book would not have been possible without the support of the Australian Research Council Centre of Excellence for the Study of the History of Emotions, 1100–1800.

At CUP, Sarah Stanton and Rosemary Crawley have been patience sat upon monuments, and I am also thankful to the three anonymous readers of the book at proposal stage: it is very much improved for their input.

The creative practitioners who are the subjects of this book are listed in appendices at the end of each chapter but I am especially thankful to Oliver Coleman, Sam Duncan, Rachel Perks and Rani Pramesti, all of whom agreed both to be interviewed and to provide me with access to their rehearsal journals. My Winchester colleagues and collaborators, Richard Cuming, Alexandra Hoare, Sian Radinger and Olu Taiwo, were fabulous to work with, as are my current company, Nothing but Roaring: Tom Considine, Tom Davies, George Lingard, Bob Pavlich and Chris White.

I still can't quite believe my luck in having met Bernard Caleo, my co-author on Chapter 4. That collaboration was truly rewarding from start to finish and I look forward to further adventures. I'm also grateful to Arj Barker, Jeff Busby, Michael Ray Charles, Currency Press, Remi D'Agostin, Olivia Glynn and Leah King-Smith for their kind permission to reproduce their respective texts and images.

I have mentors spread across the globe and I owe them more than most. Peter Holland has supported me from my days as a postgraduate student and is always unfailingly generous and inspirational. Paul Salzman has nurtured me back me in Melbourne and put up with my ungenerous assessments of performances he has quite liked. And Stevie Simkin, PhD supervisor, movie-going and, almost as important, heart-to-heart buddy, continues to read and shape my work. To all of you, thank you very, very much.

Of my nearest and dearest, thanks to my long-suffering parents and to Stuart, Julieanne, Jamen and Madeleine, who endured significant radio silence when I lived overseas but have never seemed to resent it. And finally, thanks to my little family. Una Clemens, who introduced me to my favourite performative text, *The 13-Storey Treehouse*. And Rachel Hughes, with whom many a productive study date has been enjoyed, and much more besides.

Chapters 2 (Sudoku Shakespeare) and 3 (Red Button Shakespeare) of this book had previous lives, respectively: 'Sudokothellophobia: Writing Hypertextually, Performatively', *Shakespeare Survey* 60 (2007), 154–69, and 'Red Button Shakespeare', *Shakespeare Survey* 62 (2009), 123–40. And I am thankful to Elizabeth Schafer for permitting 'Remember Me', *Australian Studies* 4 (2013), 1–21, to evolve into chapter 6 (Ghosting Shakespeare) of this book.

The authors and publishers acknowledge the sources of copyright for third party material and are grateful for the permissions granted. While every effort has been made, it has not always been possible to identify the sources of all the material used, or to trace all copyright holders. If any omissions are brought to our notice, we will be happy to include the appropriate acknowledgements on reprinting and in the next update to the digital edition, as applicable.

INTRODUCTION

Writing performative Shakespeares

When the project that has become *Writing Performative Shakespeares* was just beginning, some time before it knew or had named itself, the (writing) practice definitely preceded its theorisation. Therefore, this introduction – which will attempt to explicate what is here meant by that slippery and ubiquitous term *performative*, what is here practised as performative writing, and what is here defined and theorised as writing performative Shakespeares – will be, to some extent at least, retrospective and revisionist.[1] What turned out to be this first instance of writing performative Shakespeares, a revision of which features as Chapter 2 of this book, came about because of my incapacity to provide a linear account of (Shakespearean) theatrical meaning-making as contingent upon each of its various materialities, discourses and practices. Thus, in attempting to analyse a production of *Othello* that I had directed, and being unable to repre-sent (in linear form) its discursive effects as a productive coalescence of, for example, the text used, the rehearsal processes, its various contexts, theoretical, cultural, historical and pedagogical, the finished production itself and its recep-tion, I eventually opted to allocate equal and post-structured space to each of those elements via the form of a Sudoku puzzle. In order to publish that article I was required to frame it with an introduction – which began with an exhor-tation to skip straight to the puzzle – which was also a retrospective theorisation of writing practice subsequently labelled performative.

Why then, apart from attending to explanations of this book's specific under-standings and deployments of performative writing, continue reading this introduction, and not go straight to the collection of puzzles, creative and in-novative forms – the writing of performative Shakespeares – that follows? It is certainly possible, of course, to consider any of the following case study chap-ters without having read this overall introduction, each of which is framed by its own contextual and, to some extent, discrete (and, in some cases, retrospective) introduction. On the other hand, the chapters are ordered in such a way as to offer a developing argument – which is outlined below – about types of written performative engagement with Shakespearean production, each designed to intervene in methodological debates about Shakespeare in performance criti-cism. And, irrespective, or perhaps because, of my claim above that the practice of this book preceded its theorisation, especially given the authoritative inser-tion of 'definitely', such a claim begs (of me, self-reflexively) a deconstructive scrutiny that usefully, on at least three counts, illuminates this project. First, *Writing Performative Shakespeares* is consistently motivated by disentangling and reintegrating binaries such as practice and theory, process and product,

1. In 'Performative Writing as Scholarship: An Apology, an Argument, an Anecdote', *Cultural Studies ⇔ Critical Methodologies* 5:4 (2005), 421, Ronald J. Pelias writes, performatively: 'With his proverbial hand slapped against his face, he slowly moved towards this form, a form that did not for him at that time have a name but a form that held promise for the central question he was struggling with: How can we write about performance in our reviews and essays that evokes the spirit of perform-ance? He knew that to call for an exact representation was a fool's folly, but he wanted more than a record of what happened when. He wanted to be reminded of why we go see performances in the first place, that is, he wanted to encounter genuine renderings of human exper-ience. What he is now most comfortable calling "per-formative writing" offered such a potential.'

A note on notes. The notes for this introduction, and for the separate introductions for each chapter of this book, are deliberately placed on the same page in order to fore-ground the citational nature of the project. There isn't space, though, for notes to the performative sections of each chapter – the columns, boxes, puzzles, etc. – on their actual pages. These notes, what I am calling Performative Notes, will feature at the end of each chapter alongside Appendices providing details of the performatively written productions.

2. "'I have not chosen performance autoethnography as a method,'" writes Claudio Moreira in 'Tales of Conde: Autoethnography and the Body Politics of Performative Writing', *Cultural Studies ⇔ Critical Methodologies* 11:6 (2011), 590, "'it has chosen me.'"

3. Della Pollock, 'Performing Writing', in Peggy Phelan and Jill Lane, eds., *The Ends of Performance* (New York University Press, 1998), p. 75.

4. Carol Chillington Rutter, *Enter the Body: Women and Representation on Shakespeare's Stage* (London: Routledge, 2001), p. xiii.

5. Bridget Escolme, *Talking to the Audience: Actors, Audiences, Selves* (London: Routledge, 2005), p. 11.

6. H. R. Coursen, *Reading Shakespeare on Stage* (Newark: University of Delaware Press, 1995), p. 27. Coursen's 'countervailing [to new historicism] force of scholars [comprises] J. R. Brown, John Styan, Bernard Beckerman, Marvin Rosenberg, Philip McGuire, Alan Dessen, Cary Mazer, Michael Goldman, Stanley Wells, Jay Halio, Peter Reynolds, William Worthen, Anthony Dawson, Thomas Clayton, [and] James Bulman'.

critical and creative: I may not have (realised that I had) read any performative writing until almost all of the chapters of this book were conceived, but subsequent engagement with such writing has enriched my understanding of the things I was attempting to achieve. Second, a deconstructive querying of my assertion that this practice preceded its theory focuses the important performative notion that discourses and practices mobilise almost imperceptibly: in other words, that I may have appropriated various strategies of performative writing without being entirely cognisant of the process; indeed, that performative writing might have appropriated or interpellated me.[2] Third, and following on from this, a deconstructive reversal prioritising theory above and before practice emphasises the important genealogical dimension of this project: what processes and practices underpin the production of performances, of identities, even of books – indeed, the act of reading itself?

Performative writing has often been labelled needlessly obscure – indeed, it has been characterised from within as a 'difficult intervention'[3] – but it is the intention of *Writing Performative Shakespeares* to address the kinds of questions posed above in an accessible style; thus, here follows an attempt to articulate the two major ways by which this book deploys the practice and theory of performative writing. First, the writing contained in this book is performative in the sense that it endeavours – to cite Carol Chillington Rutter (to whom I will often return) – to 're-perform' Shakespearean (mostly theatrical) performance for the reader.[4] It addresses questions such as: What happened in the theatre? What happened on the stage? What were the features of the design? How did the audience respond? What was the atmosphere of the theatrical event? This is fairly standard Shakespeare in performance critical practice, which, this book will argue, requires further specifically performative augmentation. Second, the writing contained in this book is performative in the sense, already alluded to in the previous paragraph, that it endeavours – to cite Bridget Escolme (to whom I will also often return) – to make 'evident the work behind the illusion',[5] to trace, reveal and demystify the genealogies underpinning, informing and shaping Shakespearean performance. It addresses questions such as: How does Shakespearean theatre make meaning/s? How is Shakespearean production and the meanings it generates shaped by alternative types of actor training, by rehearsal practices, or by various contexts, historical and contemporary, local and global, social and political? What kinds of (theoretical) histories and geographies underwrite this practice? What kinds of (rehearsal) histories undergird this performance? What kinds of (production) histories underlie this canon? What kinds of (subjectivity) histories undermine this identity?

In the next section of this introduction I will establish a framework for performatively addressing these kinds of questions via Della Pollock's seminal essay 'Performing Writing' (1998) and with reference to other articulations of performative writing, and to the several Shakespeare in performance criticism heroines who inspire this book. H. R. Coursen's 1995 list of venerable Shakespeare in performance critics are all male,[6] but the authors who impel the critical energy of this project are, for the most part, female, feminist and predominantly, at least when these books were published, near the beginnings of their respective careers. The Shakespeare in performance critics to whom this book owes its most significant debt, and who will repeatedly illuminate the following discussion, are (in chronological order of publication): Carol Chillington Rutter;[7] Pascale Aebischer;[8] Bridget Escolme;[9] Roberta Barker;[10] Kim Solga;[11] and Kate Flaherty[12] (several of these critics owe their most significant critical debt to Barbara Hodgdon's fabulous ground-breaking work; Hodgdon is not cited here but features throughout the book). These critics, along with others such as Stephen Purcell, W. B. Worthen, Robert Shaughnessy and John Russell Brown,[13] have led the recent reinvigoration of Shakespeare in performance and production studies, a vigour (and rigour) *Writing Performative Shakespeares* seeks to emulate and extend.

Writing evocative Shakespeares

The first of Della Pollock's 'Six Excursions into Performative Writing', articulations which, predictably, resist definitiveness, is that 'Performative writing is *evocative*'. Pollock writes of such writing that

It operates metaphorically to render absence present – to bring the reader into contact with 'other-worlds', to those aspects and dimensions of our world that are other to the text as such by re-marking them. Performative writing evokes worlds that are otherwise intangible, unlocatable: worlds of memory, pleasure, sensation, imagination, affect, and in-sight.[14]

This description is exemplary of the project attempted here in its attempt to evoke the absent other-world of Shakespearean theatrical performance, to re-presence it, and resonates with recent examples of Shakespeare in performance criticism. In the preface to *Enter the Body: Women and Representation on Shakespeare's Stage*, Rutter asks, 'how does the body play on Shakespeare's stage … and how can I account for it, bring it on stage within this text'?[15] One of the answers she provides is to write about Shakespearean performance with 'a body-conscious language attentive to feeling, to the itch and pleasures of desire, and to pain',[16] an echo of Pollock's formulation above. Rutter's evocation of the final moments of the 1990 RSC *King Lear* is demonstrative of this method. She writes the scene almost as a novelist, describing the dead Cordelia 'like a broken doll, her head flopped on the twisted neck, her arms akimbo, legs and feet at bizarre angles, her history written on her body'.[17] The questions asked of the action described – such as 'out of the air (or out of his mind?)' or 'Kent howled, but was he addressing Lear's heart or his own?'[18] – lend weight to the author's prefatory claim that her writing 'is provisional, contingent, never definitive',[19] although I will have more to say about this below. Rutter's final chapter remembers Emilia – her specific phrase – from the 1989 RSC *Othello* and similarly begins with powerfully evocative prose, its clipped rhythms suggesting the tragically inevitable momentum that the play will enact.[20] Later in this analysis, Rutter's prose becomes even more poetic, figuring Desdemona's dropped handkerchief as 'tantalizing, innocent, a piece of litter, a time bomb' and describing Emilia's surrendering of it to her abusive husband thus: 'She turned her gaze up towards

7. *Enter the Body.*

8. *Shakespeare's Violated Bodies: Stage and Screen Performance* (Cambridge University Press, 2004).

9. *Talking to the Audience.*

10. *Early Modern Tragedy, Gender and Performance, 1984–2000: The Destined Livery* (Basingstoke: Palgrave Macmillan, 2007).

11. *Violence Against Women in Early Modern Performance: Invisible Acts* (Basingstoke: Palgrave Macmillan, 2009).

12. *Ours As We Play It: Australia Plays Shakespeare* (Crawley: UWA Publishing, 2011).

13. These texts, respectively, are: *Popular Shakespeare: Simulation and Subversion on the Modern Stage* (Basingstoke: Palgrave Macmillan, 2009); *Shakespeare and the Force of Modern Performance* (Cambridge University Press, 2003) and *Shakespeare Performance Studies* (Cambridge University Press, 2014); *The Shakespeare Effect: A History of Twentieth-Century Performance* (Basingstoke: Palgrave Macmillan, 2002); and *Shakespeare and the Theatrical Event* (Basingstoke: Palgrave Macmillan, 2002).

14. 'Performing Writing', p. 80.

15. *Enter the Body*, p. xii.

16. Ibid., p. xv.

17. Ibid., p. 24.

18. Ibid., p. 25.

19. Ibid., p. xiii.

20. Ibid., p. 142.

Iago, standing ramrod straight, staring like a basilisk, like Milton's Satan gazing on Paradise. The kiss lingered. Iago glanced sideways, found Emilia's eyes. The emptiness between them was a wasteland'.[21] On the next page, Rutter evokes the intangibility of 'illicit' and 'unbearable' spectatorship, or, more accurately, auditor-ship, as she hears and reports that (Zoë Wanamaker's) Emilia's 'voice suddenly cracked':[22] here is the 'body-conscious language attentive to feeling' and 'to pain' the preface promises, and the metaphorical rendering of absence that performative writing seeks to make present.

Pascale Aebischer's *Shakespeare's Violated Bodies: Stage and Screen Performance*, which develops Rutter's preoccupation with embodiment, also considers the evocation of absent performance and the difficulties that lie therein. Thus, having noted that theatrical performance is 'characterised by its ephemerality, spontaneity, productive interaction between spectators and actors, and the subjectivity of its reception', Aebischer further argues that in 'writing about performance, a physical, three-dimensional medium is flattened into two dimensions, leading inevitably to distortions and misrepresentations'.[23] Aebischer's attempts to address these problems include, to take examples from her opening chapter on *Titus Andronicus*: scrutiny of other texts, such as memoirs (34, 46), biographies (41) and even novels (32), which contextualise the chosen productions; consideration of rehearsal process (34); critical sampling of theatre reviews (39); the application of critical theory (40); the recording of personal response (43); textual analysis (44); stage manager's show reports (46); private conversations with practitioners (50); descriptions of audience members' physical or vocal responses to on-stage moments (51); discussion with audience members (52); and, of course, detailed descriptions of on-stage action (36–37, 45–46, 50–51). Further considered within various social and political contexts (57), the combination of these various strategies offers a compelling methodology for the articulation and representation of (Shakespearean) theatrical performance.

Performative writing regularly deploys innovative form[24] as an investigation, interrogation or evocation of intangible content, something *Writing Performative Shakespeares* seeks to do in each of its case study chapters. Rutter's deployment of novelistic and poetic form within academic analysis might thus be described as performative, especially given her stated desire to re-perform performance. Likewise, Aebischer's evocation of absence, a three-dimensional grappling with the ephemeral, spontaneous, interactive and subjective nature of performance, depends upon a form 'Reconstructed self-consciously from a variety of sources'.[25] This writing might be described as performative, especially given its stated ambition to ameliorate the flattening effects of two-dimensional print, according to several of Pollock's descriptors: it is 'subjective' and reflexive; it 'crosses various stories, theories, texts, intertexts, and spheres of practice'; and it is 'citational' in its 'accumulation of quotations'.[26] Moreover, Aebischer maintains, echoing Rutter, that her methodology must acknowledge 'the fragmentary and contingent nature of the [assembled] evidence' and that the 'subjectiveness of the approach preclude[s] determinacy';[27] I will have more to say about this last claim below, too.

Kate Flaherty's 'accumulation of quotations' in *Ours As We Play It: Australia*

---

21. Ibid., p. 162.

22. Ibid., p. 163.

23. *Shakespeare's Violated Bodies*, p. 17.

24. In 'Confessions of apprehensive performer', *Text and Performance Quarterly* 17:1 (1997), 25–32, Ronald J. Pelias uses a play-script structure to explore multiple perspectives on stage fright; in 'Performative Writing as Scholarship' (see note 1), he homages Marianne Moore's poem 'Poetry' as self-reflexive analysis.

25. *Shakespeare's Violated Bodies*, p. 18.

26. 'Performing Writing', pp. 85, 90, 94.

27. *Shakespeare's Violated Bodies*, p. 18.

Plays Shakespeare is perhaps even more extensive than Aebischer's. This range of evidence, in support of her main argument that Shakespearean theatrical meaning-making 'is negotiated as part of the creative, contractual work of culture',[28] includes: 'experiential awareness' (10); 'attending rehearsals' (11); 'interviewing actors' (11); 'archival research' (12); reviews (13); literary criticism (13); audience response (37); delivery of text (39); close description of staged action (43); stage lighting (58); vocal quality (61); stage mechanics (110); and stage design (119). Moreover, in an echo of Aebischer (who is not cited in this book), Flaherty concludes (where Aebischer introduced) that 'I have wrestled with the minutiae, the un-theorised and ephemeral, felt moments of performance and rehearsal' and that, further, the 'fractious life of such fleeting and subjective impressions – their simultaneous indelibility and resistance to theorising – has been, throughout, a spur to continue'.[29] *Writing Performative Shakespeares* is spurred to deploy such a theorising, chiefly via the conceptual complexity of performative writing, irrespective of initial, yet somewhat uncertain claims, that this project has been practice rather than theory-led. It also has something to say – the below is almost here, but will be deferred a little longer – about Flaherty's introductory claim, echoing Aebischer, echoing Rutter, that her book is 'conceived as a performance and as a collection of lived moments rather than a totalising and definitive critical edifice'.[30]

Before returning to the respective and shared claims by Rutter, Aebischer and Flaherty for provisionality, contingency, indefiniteness and indeterminacy in their representations of Shakespearean performance, the next section will summarise how each of their texts could be said to share characteristics with performative writing. These three, and the other Shakespeare in performance scholars mentioned above who underpin this study, arguably exemplify as many as five of Pollock's 'Six Excursions into Performative Writing'. The six excursions, in the order that Pollock discusses them, and each preceded by the phrase 'Performative writing is', are: evocative; metonymic; subjective; nervous; citational; and consequential. I have already considered how the authors above evoke Shakespearean theatrical performance, as well as occasional references to some of the other elements; I will now discuss in more detail the degree to which they fulfil each of these other elements as articulated by Pollock and further illustrate the various categories via methodological examples from the case study chapters of this book.[31] Then I will return to the issue of indeterminacy as a means of considering the ways their texts differ from performative writing, differences which are crucial to the articulation and definition of this project.

Performative writing: Shakespeares

When John Russell Brown argues in the introduction to *Shakespeare and the Theatrical Event* that 'Feelings, sensations, and physical presence will be taken into account'[32] in the effective writing of Shakespeare in performance criticism, he expresses a sympathy with strategies here discussed as exemplary of performative writing (which is not to say that this particular methodology has any sort of absolute claim on such strategies). The desire Brown expresses in the book's concluding chapter, however, that such criticism should 'consider a play's total

28. *Ours As We Play It*, p. 20.

29. Ibid., p. 236.

30. Ibid., p. 15.

31. The case studies chapters are intended as examples of what Liz Shafer called, in her plenary lecture for the 2012 Australian and New Zealand Shakespeare Association Conference, 'micro-histories with attitude'. Unlike a conventional introduction, I have referred to the chapters not in chronological order, but as they illuminate the following discussion.

32. Page 4; see also pp. 151–152.

33. *Theatrical Event*, p. 217.

34. Ibid., pp. 217–220.

35. 'Performing Writing', p. 82. On p. 12 of *Performance: An Alphabet of Performative Writing* (Walnut Creek: Left Coast Press, 2014), Ronald J. Pelias writes that 'performative writing is a highly selective camera, aimed carefully to capture the most arresting angles.'

36. *Enter the Body*, p. 145.

theatrical effect',[33] and his consequent glass-half-empty summary of a range of Shakespeare in performance studies,[34] is antipathetic to Pollock's second categorisation that 'Performative writing is *metonymic*'. Pollock explains that such writing offers 'a self-consciously partial or incomplete rendering',[35] seemingly an obvious inevitability with Shakespeare in performance criticism, although the degree of self-consciousness in the rendering of incompleteness probably represents the extent to which the writing is performative. Rutter deploys just this strategy in declaring that 'I want to re-read *Othello* through Wanamaker's performance, a performance that opened up Emilia's story to detailed scrutiny, putting in view what it invited spectators to read as the suppressed narrative of Shakespeare's play, a narrative whose subject is suppression.'[36] Though I am not entirely comfortable with the notion of reading performance – more of this below, too – Rutter here is demonstrably metonymic, opening up consideration not only of this particular production, but of the whole play, via a vital but not extensive role. Thus the chapter examines but one production, albeit crucially contextualised by discussion of various early modern discourses of misogyny, and of that production, only those moments when Emilia is on stage, parts of five scenes (2.1, 3.3, 3.4, 4.3, 5.2) throughout the play.

Such partial readings – though the degree of partiality or, its utopian opposite, comprehensiveness, differs – are unavoidable. Brown, for example, observes of Marvin Rosenberg, perhaps the most comprehensive of Shakespeare in performance critics, that 'he never had enough words for all the moments he wished to record'.[37] Aebischer and Flaherty, to offer two more respective examples of partiality, focus, in certain parts of their books, on Lavinia (across four theatrical productions) within, and as a metonymic revelation of, *Titus Andronicus*,[38] and on masculinity as represented by four Australian Hamlets.[39] The partiality of performative writing, though, refers not just to the inevitability of selection and deselection, the choices made in the evocation of the other-worldly, but also of the partial capacity of language to represent itself, experience, absence at all. Thus, it does not recognise Rutter's labelling of the 'provisional, contingent, never definitive' nature of her writing as 'limitations'.[40] Similarly, exponents of performative writing – perhaps, indeed, anyone theatrically minded – recoil at suggestions such as those proffered below by Jonathan W. Thacker. In the foreword to Susan L. Fischer's *Reading Performance: Spanish Golden-Age Theatre and Shakespeare on the Modern Stage*, having acknowledged that 'performance is viewed subjectively, and is unique, fundamentally unrepeatable, and subject to evolution over the course of a run', Thacker argues, as a commendation of Fischer's method, that 'the critic can reduce the effect of these inevitable handicaps by a number of steps'.[41]

Rather than view the representation of theatrical ephemerality as a handicap to be overcome, metonymic performative writing 'dramatizes the limits of language, sometimes as an endgame, sometimes as the pleasures of playing (*jouissance*) in an endlessly open field of representation'.[42] This description neatly encapsulates the intents of the Sudoku Shakespeare chapter of this book. The main body of the chapter, laid out in Sudoku form, consists of nine (plus three bonus) pages with nine boxes on each page. Each of the boxes contains

37. *Theatrical Event*, p. 215.

38. *Shakespeare's Violated Bodies*, pp. 31–46, 49–52.

39. *Ours As We Play It*, pp. 23–70.

40. *Enter the Body*, p. xiii.

41. Jonathan W. Thacker, 'Foreword', in Susan L. Fischer, *Reading Performance: Spanish Golden-Age Theatre and Shakespeare on the Modern Stage* (Rochester, NY: Tamesis, 2009), p. xiii.

42. Pollock, 'Performing Writing', p. 83.

not more than 150 words so that the particular evocation of a box – for example, on a page whose theme is sexuality and sub-theme is rehearsal narratives – is subject to a strict economy and is sometimes maddeningly partial. Moreover, many of the boxes make sense only via cross-reference with other boxes, but even an exhaustive cross-referencing of each of the boxes would still amount to only a partial account of the actual staging choices, especially by contrast with, for example, Manchester University Press's Shakespeare in Performance series, which requires considerable (and predominantly chronological) description of the productions its authors choose to document. Though 'endlessly open field of representation' might initially seem hyperbolic, the Sudoku Shakespeare chapter, which can be entered or exited at any of the 81 (+27) boxes, and in which any reading path between those boxes is possible, potentially represents such a field, especially given the expansion of meanings which each reader will bring via their own (perhaps endlessly) open fields of response.

Under Pollock's third heading, 'Performative writing is *subjective*', she further explains, distancing such practice from autobiographical writing which presents 'a coherent self across time', that 'Writing that embodies this kind of subjectivity tends to *subject* the reader to the writer's reflexivity, drawing their respective subject-selves reciprocally and simultaneously into "critical intimacy"'.[43] Such a critical position might elicit discomforted groans from more established and conventional position holders, but here is Aebischer conducting (with considerable, established and not altogether unconventional sophistication) just such an engagement: 'When I weep at the end of a performance of *King Lear*,' she writes, 'I am never quite certain whether it is in empathy for the infinite sorrow of the dying king or in rage at letting myself be manipulated into sharing his sorrow.'[44] Here, the reader of Aebischer's text is invited to consider the author's uncertain subject position, an uncertainty prompted by response to a performance moment; moreover, the reader will probably have seen a performance of this play and of its last scene, perhaps even the productions which Aebischer discusses, and may reflect on an identification with Aebischer's confusion. Just prior to Rutter's various reflections on this very scene (already mentioned above), she writes, more compactly, and probably with more certainty than Aebischer, that 'in writing performance I'm writing myself'.[45] Lastly on this theme, though examples are legion,[46] Roberta Barker's situating of her critical practice, that the 'politically engaged critic cannot indicate what whole audiences thought about a production', and that 'she can only trace her own interventions with those components of a performance and its reception that her temporal and ideological positions allow her to see'[47] invites an implicit engagement with that practice. Barker's description of herself in the third person here opens up potential alliances – or critical intimacies – with like-minded interventionists.

Chapter 5 of this book, 'Engaging Shakespeare', could not have been written if I had not been centrally present within the research that eventually generated it. Indeed, it is a defining feature of this book that I have been physically present and often critically intimate with each of the selected case studies. The specific form of that presentness for three of the chapters (2, 5 and 6) has been

43. Ibid., p. 86. The most recent and compelling examples of this type of (Shakespearean) criticism can be found in the Shakespeare Now! series. See, for example, Philippa Kelly's *The King and I* (London: Continuum, 2011) and, if with a more literary than theatrical focus, William McKenzie and Theodora Papadopoulou's collection, *Shakespeare and I* (London: Continuum, 2011), where the editors argue, on the very first page, for 'the value and importance of self-investment in any consideration of literary art' and 'the necessity of articulating personal investment in literature'.

44. *Shakespeare's Violated Bodies*, p. 155.

45. *Enter the Body*, p. xvii.

46. See, for example: Robert Shaughnessy, *Representing Shakespeare: England, History and the RSC* (Hemel Hempstead: Harvester Wheatsheaf, 1994), p. 33; Escolme, *Talking to the Audience*, p. 95; Coursen, *Reading Shakespeare on Stage*, p. 18; Gay McAuley, *Space in Performance: Making Meaning in the Theatre* (Ann Arbor: University of Michigan Press, 1999), pp. 137, 233.

47. *Early Modern Tragedy*, p. 24.

practice-led, practice-based or practice as research (the terminology is predictably multiple). This is not a book about practice as research (PaR), but given that *Writing Performative Shakespeares* attempts to re-entangle practice and theory, and creative and critical approaches, the emerging methodologies of PaR shape not just the three chapters in the brackets above, but the book as a whole. Estelle Barrett summarises the subject-driven analyses of my project, for example, through her description of the 'innovative and critical potential of practice-based research [which] lies in its capacity to generate personally situated knowledge and new ways of modelling and externalising such knowledge'.[48] Along the same lines, Robin Nelson's explication of practice as research looks for 'a *resonance* between complementary writing and ... praxis itself'.[49] In 'Engaging Shakespeare', I overlay initial experiential memories of a performance (praxis) I took part in as an actor with subsequent (complementary) rewritings by several members of the production's audience. The juxtaposed narratives create what Pollock identifies as 'double and multiple voices'[50] and draw the respondents into a critical encounter with the highly self-conscious and reflexive tenor of my performative account. This, I suggest, typifies Pollock's rendering of performative writing as subjective.

Pollock's fifth category – I am skipping the fourth, 'nervous', for now – is that 'Performative writing is *citational*'.[51] This conceptual arrangement, with its major debt to Judith Butler's queering of gender via J. L. Austin's speech-act theory, has become almost a commonplace of recent Shakespeare in performance criticism.[52] The most influential of such critics, the one who has helped to create that theoretical commonplace, has been W. B. Worthen, who, in *Shakespeare and the Force of Modern Performance*, before a lengthy discussion of Austin and Butler (and Derrida and others), defines dramatic performativity as 'the relationship between the verbal text and the conventions (or, to use Butler's term, "regimes") of behaviour that give it meaningful force as performed action'.[53] Worthen's text forms the basis of Flaherty's methodology, which likewise locates 'performative meaning' at 'intersections between the imaginative plenitude of the play-text and the conscious exigencies of the cultural moment in which it is performed'.[54] Other studies already mentioned above choose to be more attentive to the historical moment in which the play-text was first performed. Though each study, including this one, is interested in the present and in a present/past dialogue – how, for example, does a production represent its pastness in its engagement with the present? – some, like Flaherty, focus more on present citations, and others, like Rutter, Aebischer and Barker, demonstrate their investment in the present via rigorously historicist analyses.[55] Perhaps this represents a reflection of the respective contexts of the productions discussed: Flaherty's examination of Australian Shakespearean production is less interested in the text's originary contexts, whereas Rutter, Aebischer and Barker, all writing about transatlantic, mostly English productions, delve into, for example, the sermons, tracts, medical and legal documents constitutive of that discursive past; the continuity of place seemingly requires a more focused exploration of the dis/continuity of time. *Writing Performative Shakespeares*, which examines productions from Australia and the UK, expends citational energy in the service of its present/

48. 'Introduction', in Estelle Barrett and Barbara Bolt, eds., *Practice as Research: Approaches to Creative Arts Enquiry* (London: I. B. Tauris, 2010), p. 2.

49. *Practice as Research in the Arts: Principles, Protocols, Pedagogies, Resistances* (Basingstoke: Palgrave Macmillan, 2013), p. 11, italics original. On p. 20, Nelson defines praxis as 'the imbrications of theory within practice.'

50. 'Performing Writing', p. 88.

51. Ibid., p. 92.

52. See, for example, Escolme, *Talking to the Audience*, pp. 109–111 and Barker, *Early Modern Tragedy*, pp. 17–20.

53. Page 3.

54. *Ours As We Play It*, p. 4.

55. Kim Solga introduces *Violence Against Women* with the following statements on this theme: 'I shape my argument around the deliberate collision of the historical and the contemporary as I try to imagine what it might mean to represent early modern experiences of violence against women on the stage in an ethical way, a feminist way, today ... [her book] invests in both the "then" of the early moderns and the "now" of contemporary Western performance, but

past dialogue, perhaps in closest methodological alignment with Escolme, who more self-consciously focuses on the dialogue between then and now which contemporary Shakespearean performance conducts, especially as the explicit concentration of her book concerns conversation.[56]

Pollock's observation, via Butler, that 'Identity cannot escape its discursive construction in/as iteration but through performance, it may exert a counter-pressure'[57] is exemplary of Barker's project to offer dissident and de-naturalising interpretations of realist performances. Thus, opposing the critics who judged Paul Rhys' Hamlet naturalistically and psychologically consistent, and therefore, as part of a wider argument, a critical endorsement of essentialist and immutable views of identity, Barker supposes that 'Rhys' acting produced a vision of subjectivity as an unpredictable appropriation of multiple, sometimes contradictory social possibilities'.[58] Barker has to work hard, I think, to find here what Escolme, summarising cultural materialism, calls the 'cracks and fissures in dominant ideologies'.[59] In the last chapter of this book, 'Ghosting Shakespeare', I posit an Indigenised *Hamlet*, a socially contradictory possibility that cites histories radically other than those of Shakespeare's play. The ghost, which is raised by the citation of a contemporary Indigenous artwork, a mural with 'Remember Me' stencilled at the centre of the Australian Aboriginal flag, is ethereally able move through those ideological cracks and fissures and perhaps to invite closer scrutiny of them. The first chapter of the book, 'Materialising Shakespeare', 'stages its own citationality',[60] more of present, than past contexts, via the form of a pinboard. This is designed as a complementary writing to the praxis of theatre-making in a pedagogical context whereby the archive genealogies of those productions are juxtaposed with descriptions and analyses of that practice. All the chapters in this book are self-consciously citational – rare, of course, is the academic work without notes and/or bibliography – but they fulfil Pollock's last excursion into performative writing to varying degrees.

Sixth, and lastly, 'Performative writing is' – but has no special claims to being – 'consequential'.[61] It is motivated, Pollock continues, by 'its capacity for political, ethical agency' and 'enters into the arena of contest to which it appeals with the affective investment of one who has been there and will be there at the end' and 'who has a stake in the outcome of the exchange'.[62] Each of the authors who inspire this book – feminist, materialist, interventionist – present a variation of Rutter's, via Joseph Roach, concluding commitment:

Performing the ending, Wanamaker's Emilia invents that which requires me never to forget. Performing Wanamaker performing Emilia, I want her performance remembered, for as her Emilia, at the end, accounted 'for how we got here', so she likewise embodied 'alternatives to our present condition'. Remembering performance for me is not just history but prophecy. Accurately recalling the past, we can make shrewd guesses about what's to come.[63]

If with not quite the same conviction for accuracy, I similarly commit, throughout this book, to consequence. Ghosting Shakespeare offers the most deliberately consequential chapter, attempting, as it does, to intervene in oft-repeated

---

not in order to draw simplistic transhistorical links between the two. Rather, I challenge the urge towards transhistoricity reproduced in so much contemporary early modern performance, and I explore the ramifications – especially for women – of taking early modern wonders for late modern signs', pp. 1–2.

56. *Talking to the Audience*, pp. 5–6. In her latest book, *Emotional Excess on the Shakespearean Stage: Passion's Slaves* (London: Bloomsbury, 2013), Escolme's performance analyses are supported by interrogation of a range of early modern (not just play-) texts.

57. 'Performing Writing', p. 92.

58. *Early Modern Tragedy*, p. 195.

59. *Talking to the Audience*, p. 8.

60. 'Performing Writing', p. 94.

61. Ibid.

62. Ibid., pp. 95–96.

63. *Enter the Body*, p. 177. Solga, also via Roach, writes, 'Performance for me is a cultural doing, a historical doing, but it is also a means of cultural and historical intervention' and thus, 'I

am writing towards hope, towards the potential performance embeds to stage an encounter with the past that opens up a new view of the present and the future. *Violence Against Women*, pp. 3, 28.

discourses of remembering and then forgetting Australian Aborigines. Sudoku Shakespeare also nervously – more of these nerves anon – addresses representations of blackness via productions of *Othello*, and other chapters consider issues such as the broader politics of performance-making (Chapter 1), the frequent cultural overlap of sexuality and violence (Chapter 3), and the agency and efficacy of Shakespearean audiences (Chapters 4 and 5).

To sum up this section, studies of contemporary Shakespeare in performance from the last decade or so might be defined, according to Pollock's criteria, as types of, or as typifying certain aspects of, performative writing. The works discussed above by Rutter, Aebischer, Escolme, Barker, Solga and Flaherty, and, to perhaps a lesser extent, those by Worthen, Brown, Shaughnessy and Purcell, all bear the hallmarks of performative writing in that they, to varying degrees: one, offer evocative representations of the other-world of Shakespearean performance; two, offer partial and metonymic representations of that world; three, situate themselves in subjective relationship to the other-world they partially evoke; four, depend for this evocation upon a range of discursive citations, present and past, popular and elite, local and global; and, five, commit themselves to consequential, transformative ends. But, my structure now anxiously demands, in what ways are such texts not representative of performative writing (remembering that they have made no such claims), and, by extension, in what ways will *Writing Performative Shakespeares* depart from these, its inspiration?

Writing nervous S/Zhakespeares
A few thousand words ago I promised to return to Rutter, Aebischer and Flaherty's claims that their respective representations of Shakespearean theatre, as a metonymic reflection of the ephemeral nature of the theatrical event itself, are marked by indeterminacy: Rutter concedes that her writing is 'provisional, contingent, never definitive'; Aebischer offers representations and analyses which will 'preclude determinacy'; and Flaherty promises that her work will not become 'a totalising and definitive critical edifice'. My problem with these claims is that, as Roderigo complains to Iago of promises unfulfilled, 'It hath not appeared' (4.2.214). A Shakespeare in performance critic whose discussion is prefaced by the acknowledgement of the fundamental indeterminacy of theatrical representation and the writing thereupon is a bit like the Shakespearean character who promises brevity before speaking; they do not follow through. Another way for me to put this is to say that the studies I have discussed thus far, while they bear many of the hallmarks of performative writing, do not, despite protestations of indeterminacy, exhibit Pollock's fourth formulation – which, admittedly, is not straightforwardly synonymous – that 'Performative writing is *nervous*'.[64] Indeed, I was somewhat disingenuous earlier in describing Aebischer's writing as performative given my partial quotation of Pollock's first sentence from this section on nervousness. Earlier, I noted and quoted, accurately enough, that Aebischer's method 'crosses various stories, theories, texts, intertexts, and spheres of practice'; the full quotation, framed by a beginning and end which more accurately depicts the nervousness of performative writing, states:

64. 'Performing Writing', p. 90.

It anxiously crosses various stories, theories, texts, intertexts, and spheres of practice, unable to settle into a clear, linear course, neither willing nor able to stop moving, restless, transient and transitive, traversing spatial and temporal borders, linked as it is in what Michael Taussig calls 'a chain of narratives sensuously feeding back into reality thus (dis)enchained'.[65]

The studies I have discussed thus far do not – and the question of whether they should or could is open – demonstrate this anxious, restless and traversal approach. They are not nervous; they are secure and confident, definitive and determinate.

Pollock cites Roland Barthes's *S/Z* not in this section on nervousness but in the second excursion to metonymy,[65] but Barthes' playful criticism provides an apposite bipolar structure – such as Pollock also deploys, via Julia Kristeva's 'Stabat Mater', in her third section on performative writing and subjectivity[67] – for the following discussion of assured and assertive, as opposed to nervous and unsettled writing. Raman Selden and Peter Widdowson begin their brief analysis of *S/Z* by declaring it 'an impressive poststructuralist performance':[68] here is their explication of Barthes' two types of texts reformatted as *S/Z* might playfully endorse:

A realistic novel offers a 'closed' text with a limited meaning.	
	Other texts encourage the reader to produce meanings. The 'I' which reads is 'already itself a plurality of other texts' and is allowed by the avant-garde text the maximum liberty to produce meanings by putting what is read in touch with this plurality.
The first type of text allows the reader only to be a consumer of a fixed meaning,	
	while the second turns the reader into a producer.
The first type of text is called 'readerly' (*lisible*),	
	the second 'writerly' (*scriptible*).[69]

The politics of exhibiting nervousness, for female academics, in writing or in other discursive contexts, is, of course, loaded. The female scholar, especially the younger female scholar, as are most of those lauded here, arguably must resist the demonstration of nervousness, or, to list some synonymous positions such as Pollock's fourth category might require, of equivocation, uncertainty,

65. Ibid., pp. 90–91.

66. Ibid., p. 83.

67. Ibid., p. 87.

68. Raman Selden and Peter Widdowson, *A Reader's Guide to Contemporary Literary Theory*, 3rd edn (New York: Harvester Wheatsheaf, 1993), p. 133.

69. Ibid., p. 134.

temperance or qualification: such positioning does not secure book contracts, attract grant money, result in flattering teaching evaluations or result in colleagues attending departmental seminars. With this qualifying caveat, then, I will discuss in further detail, if with some uncertainty, the ways in which I believe the criticism that precedes and propels this work is seemingly nerveless and thus tending towards the definitive and determinate.

Further, I will continue to deploy the bipolar structure in the service of the following discussion of:

fixity, unity	multiplicity, fracture
the best-seat perspective of the majority of Shakespearean performance criticism	nervous shifting from various, contrasting and sometimes unfavourable audience positions
the authoritative single-mindedness of the majority of performance interpretation	the demonstrative representation of uncertainty and multiple, even competing, analyses
reading performance	writing performatively

Almost all writing about Shakespearean theatrical production and, in particular, the description of the stage action, has been written from the perspective – actual or figurative – of the most expensive seat in the theatre in which it was staged. That seat is usually either in the stalls or the lower gallery and is about four to eight rows from the stage. It is near enough to see beads of sweat on the actors' brows, far enough not to be spat on because of enthusiastic enunciation, but perhaps not always quite far enough to appreciate the entirety of a design that exploits the architectural limits of the particular theatre. Consider Bridget Escolme's description of Antony Sher's outward playing in the 1999 RSC Swan Theatre production of *Macbeth*: of the response to Macduff and Lennox's descriptions of the previous night's apocalyptic weather, Escolme records that 'Sher looks conspiratorially out at us from his upstage

I take the opposite strategy in Chapter 3 of this book, 'Red Button Shakespeare'. Nervous that my perception and interpretation of the 2008 Globe production of *King Lear* might be particularly (and, I must concede, partially) circumscribed by whichever vantage point I managed to secure – and I prefer standing in the yard adjacent to what would otherwise be called an upstage corner and looking back at the majority of the audience – I decided to apprehend the (partial) action of the blinding of Gloucester from a range of different viewpoints. Thus, across six different attendances at this production I placed myself: 'front and centre' in the yard; at either of the upstage corners, once to watch the action, as it were, from 'behind' (which had the unintended effect of sharpening an aural appreciation of the scene), and once to ignore the action and just watch spectators' reactions to it; and in the galleries, both at the balcony' to deliver the 'rough night' line (2.3.61), which prompts from the audience a 'laugh at the understatement.'[70] Sher is specifically situated on the upstage balcony; the 'us' of the three-sided and three-tiered audience is not. Perhaps Sher cranes his neck (or eyes!) right and left and up and down (the DVD recording of the production anticipates the end of the play in cutting off Macbeth's head, just out of frame), but a more precise location of Sher's gaze at this point and of the differentiated perspectives by which it could be viewed, might suggest who, in the audience, was being invited into the conspiracy and who was excluded. Similarly, when Escolme describes Mark Rylance's 2000 Globe Hamlet, she first observes that he spoke his opening lines in the play with his back to the audience, a repeat of his 1989 RSC blocking. Then, writes Escolme, 'he later turns to face us.'[71] The problem with this sentence is that it could have been written of the 1989 RST production, the audience perspective of which, in the end-on proscenium configuration, was far more uniform. To write of the audience at the new Globe as an 'us' to be faced is a surprising conflation in a book devoted to actor–audience conversation.

sides and in front. The structure of the chapter, designed to represent this multivalence of perspective,[72] is four parallel columns that can be read vertically and/or horizontally. Vertically, the four columns detail (from left to right):

the text of the scene, including deletions;

the actions, gestures and movements of the actors;

the aural score of the scene, including music, sound effects and delivery of text;

the response to and reception of the scene, both by individual audience members and subsequent press reviews.

To read horizontally is to compare at any given and simultaneous moment in the scene – and there are gaps – where the actors are, what they are doing, what sounds can be heard and how people are responding. The red button of the title of the chapter alludes to the interactive technology most associated with televised sports coverage; by pressing the red button you can access different perspectives on the action and so too here via the four, performative columns.

An even more frequent marker of representations of Shakespearean stage practice than the elision of the critic's physical position in the theatre in relation to the stage and the silent assumption of best-seat perspective is the figurative extension of this position into a kind of disembodied and idealised spectatorship. Compare Aebischer on two productions of *Titus Andronicus*, the 1987 RSC production staged in the Swan Theatre and Kaos' 2001/02 touring production:

Donald Sumpter's Marcus was unmistakably empathic in his stunned and pained reaction to the mutilated Lavinia, whom he approached like a traumatised animal before finally catching her in his comforting arms.[73]

Lavinia returned onto the white-tiled stage – with her clothes bloodied and torn and her back to the audience. She dragged herself along the backstage wall, her mouth leaving a long smear of blood on the gleaming tiles.[74]

70. Escolme, *Talking to the Audience*, p. 8.

71. Ibid., p. 63.

72. 'Performative writing, then, takes as its goal to dwell within multiple perspectives, to celebrate an interplay of voices, to privilege dialogue over monologue. It cherishes the fragmentary, the uncertain.' Pelias, 'Performative Writing', 419.

73. *Shakespeare's Violated Bodies*, p. 45.

74. Ibid., p. 51.

This first description, the style of which is repeatedly reinscribed by Shakespeare in performance criticism, dematerialises the theatre – ironic given Aebischer's focus on embodiment – as both actors and witnessing spectator are abstracted from either the stage sets or the auditoria seat with which they are in contact, never mind the spatial relationship between them; this (very evocative) approach sees into Sumpter's Marcus' thoughts.

The second description, more common in a new wave of academic theatre reviews in journals such as *Shakespeare* or *Shakespeare Bulletin*, rematerialises the theatre – and makes explicit the embodiment focus – as the tiles are situated and described, the costume, movement and special effects evocatively and graphically re-presenced.

These varying accounts of representational effect read to me as if Aebischer

watched the former on the video at the RSC archive

whilst the latter was etched into her memory via a live and especially collective, including pedagogic, experience of the production.

The use of video or DVD recordings of stage productions, to which this book has certainly had recourse, potentially reifies the ideal and abstracted spectator of theatrical performance. Aebischer distinguishes between

live 'performance'

and a 'performance text', such as 'the textualisation of an individual performance through the technical device of video'.[75]

75. Ibid., p. 17.

and Barker acknowledges that her 'interpretations of the performances in question generally depend on multiple encounters with video recordings of the productions' which results in 'a double remove from the playhouse encounter between theatrical actors and spectators'.[76] Both authors appear wholly conversant with Philip Auslander's deconstruction of the

76. *Early Modern Tragedy*, p. 23.

liveness /

mediatised binary,

but nevertheless, and quite rightly, in my opinion, register their concern with the altered modality that theatre recorded onto film creates;

what they do not do is reflect on the position of that camera (except inasmuch as it sometimes cuts off the edges of the stage action, such as with Antony Sher's head as Macbeth atop the balcony) which invariably suspends from the first gallery in rough approximation of the front and centre perspective.

'Red Button Shakespeare' also resists this fixity in reproducing, as a further visual correlative of its parallel structure, 'screen grabs' from all three camera positions – front, 'lozenge' and side on – which the Globe archivists have installed in order to reflect the theatre's own multivalent points of perspective.

An even more significant instance of

fixity

        versus

                multiplicity

and which represents,
I think, an extension of
best-seat perspective

        versus

          a consideration of the
          whole theatre and its
          variously spatialised
          and stratified vantage
          points,

        is, and this is the crux of the in /
determinacy issue,

the expression of interpretive certainty[77]

77. 'Authority is yet another problem in translating performance into print ... The very mindset of print must be disrupted to allow for a performance-centered ethnography, a performance-based way of experiencing the page.' Joni L. Jones, 'Performing Osun without Bodies: Documenting the Osun Festival in Print', *Text and Performance Quarterly* 17:1 (1997), 70–71.

Here is Carol Rutter, quite obviously front and centre at The Other Place and then sometime after closely studying the archive video of the production in the bowels of The Shakespeare Birthplace Trust.

She writes of the developing intimacy both between Desdemona and Emilia, and between these characters and the spectators in the audience, in 4.3 of Trevor Nunn's 1989 RSC production of *Othello*:

Thus, when Stubbs' Desdemona, guilt written on her face, found the key to her private drawer and moved to unlock it, spectators knew what was coming. The drawer would reveal what they didn't want to see, the secret that would discover the women to be the very hussies their fathers and 'honest' friends proclaimed them. So when that drawer produced nothing more dangerous than chocolates and suspense sagged into audible sighs of relief, spectators perhaps reflected that, like Othello, against all the evidence of sense, they had momentarily been Iago -ed; so imperative is the misogynistic presumption of women's deceit. Nunn's production had found a way of representing the radical self-contradiction written into the scene at the level of the actors' performances and spectators' responses.[78]

78. *Enter the Body*, p. 171.

What does Rutter do with performance in this passage? I think she approximates the novelistic voice of an omniscient narrator.[79] Rutter knows privileged things (her methodology is of 'serious gossip'[80]): she knows what Desdemona feels; she knows what the spectators know, what they don't want to see and what they feel; she is, however, a little more circumspect about what they might have 'reflected' on. The apostrophe outside the s in the penultimate word of this passage, however, characterises this reading – her precise word – as totalising and definitive.[81]

80. *Enter the Body*, p. xiii.

81. Perhaps unsurprisingly, my Shakespeare in performance heroines are most likely to be unnervously authoritative

I am not disavowing an authoritative position entirely;[82] I still require an hundred knights' worth of interpretive certainty.

79. It could be argued that Rutter's mode of writing here is ideally suited to an arch-realist production. Andrew James Hartley, in 'The Schrödinger Effect: Reading and Misreading Performance', in *Shakespeare Survey* 62 (Cambridge University Press, 2009), p. 232, makes the point I am attempting in his description of Patricia Tatspaugh's *Shakespeare Quarterly* review of the 2004 RSC *Hamlet*: 'It's a vivid, almost novelistic description, and is designed to convey the author's impression of the performance, though it is done so well that the reader has no room to question whether he or she would have focused on the same details, or whether others in the house found the ghost as scary as did the author.'

82. 'I do claim a certain authority as author of the book, and I claim as well to

in their critiques of sexist or misogynist representations or practices. Thus, Aebischer is positively disgusted by patrician actors who justify their eponymous centre-staged-ness via appeals to ostensible narrative or character-based claims which are transparently self-interested (see pp. 32–35 and 45–46 for trenchant dismissals of, respectively, Antony Sher and Brian Cox). And Flaherty, even though she confesses to 'swimming against the tide of popular opinion' (p. 184), diminishes, I think, the force of her valuable critique of Benedict Andrews' voyeuristic and neo-expressionist production of *A Midsummer Night's Dream* (2004), by only citing the minority voice who, swimming with her, was disgruntled by it.

83. I have been, of necessity, selective with these quotations. See pp. 50–57 of *Violence Against Women* for the force of Solga's overall argument.

85. 'Surveying *Survey*', *Cahiers Élisabéthains*, 40th anniversary special issue, '"Nothing if not Critical": International Perspectives on Shakespearean Theatre Reviewing' (2012), 37–44.

Here is Kim Solga, treading anew critical ground Aebischer (and others) have trod, Deborah Warner's production of *Titus Andronicus*. Solga concedes that her analysis proceeds 'from one recorded performance', but several of her concluding remarks about a production which she generally lauds for its political insight strike me as problematic for Shakespearean performance criticism:

Despite the tremendous critical potential of Lavinia's spectacular forgetting-in-plain-sight, Warner's ultimate message was not that Lavinia and her trauma had been missed and would continue to go missing ... Warner did a remarkable job of framing the experience of women's bodily and psychic suffering as an echoing loss within a clearly demarcated patriarchal territory, but her production ultimately failed to politicize its larger cultural elision in a way that might disorient audience expectations ... What Warner's production finally missed – even as it performed a woman's suffering as real, embodied, all-pervasive, and ultimately fogotten – was the opportunity to engage that suffering as a function of its representational history.[83]

Is Deborah Warner supposed to read this and say, 'D'oh, what was I thinking?' I'm not sure I fully understand Solga here, but theatre-making is not about presenting an 'ultimate message', nor a thesis to be measured against an academic 'reading' of the play, no matter how useful or sophisticated. Neither, in my opinion, should a production be evaluated in terms of what it 'failed' to do or 'finally missed'. Solga is a world away from the early *Shakespeare Survey* critics that I have labelled elsewhere as 'schoolmasters'[85] but this kind of performance criticism ghosts – a trope she returns to in this marvellous book – earlier modes which judge/grade a production against an idealised 'reading' of the play.

I certainly reserve the right, in imitation of Aebischer, to critique what I believe are unedifying demonstrations of power, either practised or represented.

Writing Performative Shakespeares attempts to provide counter-voices, both by quotation of contrary external sources and by representations of internal division and equivocation. Chapter 4, 'Graphic Shakespeare', presents a round-table discussion by academics who have watched Toneelgroep Amsterdam's internationally touring production, *Roman Tragedies*. Each identifies her or his individual viewing perspective. Red Button Shakespeare provides alternative interpretive responses to the blinding of Gloucester and, metonymically, to the play *King Lear* itself, relative to each of the vantage points from which I viewed the scene. Even more uncertainly and multivocally,[84] the Sudoku Shakespeare chapter's performative staging of the various discourses and practices which constituted *Othellophobia*'s conception, production and reception reveals theatrical meaning-making, at least in this particular instance, as radically unstable and hopelessly beyond directorial attempts at determinacy.

be able to convey a set of meanings launched into circulation by the meeting of *Hamlet* and a variety of actors and directors. But all meanings, as the play reminds us, are provisional and temporary, a result of negotiation and cultural struggle as well as individual effort and creativity. I am engaged in reconstructing the meanings generated by past performances of a text that makes the play of meaning one of its primary subjects. And "reconstructing" is itself a slippery process, since it depends on documentary sources, such as reviews and promptbooks, that are themselves culturally mediated. The result is an approximation that I want to make accurate, but which itself derives from a constraint associated with the responsibility of writing a book like this one – the need to produce a meaningful narrative, to offer more than just a lot of loose details to my readers.' Anthony Dawson, *Hamlet*, Shakespeare in Performance (Manchester University Press, 1995), p. 3.

84. 'A poststructural autoethnography might embrace multidimensionality, might aim to construct texts that are not easily ingested, that turn around and around so that we are encouraged (or forced or led) to a place of thinking differently and with more

I am nervous about 'reading performance': others are not, or not as much.[86]

I never thought about calling this book *Reading Performative Shakespeares*: others eponymously read (Shakespearean) theatre and performance.[87]

But, though Kim Solga's 'hope [that] my readings will be scrutinized and tested against other readers' and spectators' responses'[88] produces (for me) a critical uneasiness, it also invites circumspection. Perhaps my attempts at creating a heteroglot criticism are disingenuous. Yes, I have assembled a variety of critical voices and self-reflexively attended to the cracks in my own voice (literally in Chapter 5), but assembled (by me) they are. At least Rutter, Aebischer, Flaherty and Solga have authoritatively stuck their necks out such that the conversation can continue between their texts, each a respective contribution to polyvocality but not arrogant enough to presume to provide a voice other than their own.

On the one hand, the act of
reading performance

focuses

the subjective nature
of the analysis
this is my reading …
I want to read this moment …

On the other hand,
reading performance
textualises as an object

the eventness of
theatrical performance:

The appeal of close-reading in performance studies is partly the way it turns theatre back into text, stabilizing it, making it static and allowing us fundamentally … *literary* critics to do what we know we're good at … But to treat performance as text's ugly stepchild forces the construction of an aberration, something that was once alive but which has been cut up, flattened out and stitched together til it resembles a book.[89]

86. Rutter, *Enter the Body*, pp. xiii–xvii, 2–5, 24–26, 160–177. Aebischer, *Shakespeare's Violated Bodies*, pp. 16–17, 31, 43. Escolme, *Talking to the Audience*, pp. 24, 73, 95–96; contrast pp. 27, 29, 33, 101. Barker, *Early Modern Tragedy*, pp. 22, 75–76, 199; contrast pp. 65, 78, 164 . Solga, *Violence Against Women*, pp. 3, 24–25, 27–28, 44, 55.

87. H. R. Coursen, *Reading Shakespeare on Stage*. Susanne L. Fischer, *Reading Performance: Spanish Golden Age Theatre and Shakespeare on the Modern Stage*. James P. Lusardi and June Schlueter, *Reading Shakespeare in Performance: King Lear* (Rutherford: Fairleigh Dickinson University Press, 1990). Anne Ubersfeld, *Reading Theatre*, Trans. Frank Collins (University of Toronto Press, 1999). Ric Knowles, *Reading the Material Theatre* (Cambridge University Press, 2003).

complexity about the world and our places within it.' Susanne Gannon, 'The (Im)Possibilities of Writing the Self-Writing: French Poststructural Theory and Autoethnography', *Cultural Studies ⇔ Critical Methodologies* 6:4 (2006), 488.

88. *Violence Against Women*, p. 28.

89. Hartley, 'Schrödinger Effect', p. 235.

Writing perFORMative Shakespeares

The previous section split by readerly and writerly textualities cues the final section of this introduction, the notion that form is at the heart of *Writing Performative Shakespeares*. It is perhaps worth repeating at this stage that the experiments with form that constitute the chapters of this book were conducted before I had consciously engaged with the theory of performative writing. I did not read about, nor find examples of, formal innovation and decide to create my own. Just, for example, as I am about to complete this book, I find Ronald J. Pelias explaining me to myself, and not for the first (or last, more just below) time. The first page of *Performance: An Alphabet of Performative Writing* describes itself thus: 'This book moves playfully. It plays on the page in this performative act of writing about performance.'[90] The performances enacted here, the frequent turnings of the page into a stage, were called into play because I faced problems of written representation and couldn't solve them to my satisfaction without somehow post-structuring the conventional arrangements of the printed page. This last point (on my writing failure), with which I also began this chapter, should make clear that one thing I am not doing in this book is proselytising for performative writing. Pelias writes, speaking for others, it must be conceded, that

Performative writers do not believe that the world is one particular way. They do not believe that argument is an opportunity to win, to impose their logic upon others, to colonize. They do not believe that there should be only one house on the hill. They do not believe that they can speak without speaking themselves, without carrying their own vested interests, their own personal histories ...[91]

The forms that I have presented in this introduction and that follow in its six chapters are the best, vested solutions I could come up with in order to represent the performative dimension of Shakespearean production. As the writing I have already sampled in this chapter proves, even if I have taken minor issue with parts of it, conventional discursive writing about Shakespearean production is, can and will continue to be, powerfully evocative of its eventness.

This book, though, is about visual and spatial form, and in the same way that Della Pollock's seminal essay on 'Performing Writing' has offered a subsequent theorisation of the practice I perhaps naively – intuitively, Harry Feiner might argue[92] – undertook, the discovery of Johanna Drucker's marvellous *The Century of Artists' Books* illustrates (literally), and serves as an approximate template for, the formal creativity characteristic of the uniqueness of this project. Artists' books, like performative writing, are difficult to define because of the multiple ways in which they have been imagined and produced, but Drucker provides several indicatives of such a book. 'First of all', she writes, an artist's book 'interrogates the conceptual or material form of the book as part of its intention, thematic interests, or production activities' and therefore 'artist's [the apostrophe nervously shifts] books are almost always self-conscious about the structure and meaning of the book as a form.'[93] Drucker's chapter titles signal several of the distinguishing features of both artists' books and of *Writing Performative*

90. *Performance: An Alphabet*, p. 7.

91. Ibid., p. 13.

92. See 'Intuition in Practice: Emotion and Feeling in the Artistic Process', in Megan Alrutz, Julia Listengarten and M. Van Duyn Wood, eds., *Playing with Theory in Theatre Practice* (Basingstoke: Palgrave Macmillan, 2012), pp. 125–138.

93. Johanna Drucker, *The Century of Artists' Books*, Second Edition (New York: Granary Books, 2004), pp. 3–4.

Shakespeares. Thus, the chapter titles announce the potential properties of the artists' book as: democratically multiple; auratic; self-reflexive; visual; verbal; interested in sequence and its disruption; agent of social change; arena for performance; and document.

The chief sympathy between performative writing – perhaps especially as it is practised in this book, but I suspect in almost all such expressions – and artists' books is of the self-consciously explicit relationship between form and content. Thus, the formal arrangements of each of the chapters in this book seek doubly to express their respective arguments, both in the way the form facilitates the specific re-presencing of the performance in question and via a structural re-presenting of the overall argument. This is what I have attempted to do above: splitting the page – as in the famous first scene stage direction of the Quarto edition of *Titus Andronicus*, which demarcates the respective followers of Saturninus and Bassianus via separate columns – is designed, hardly originally, as this other example attests, to both facilitate and express the argument; thus, textually, via the words chosen, and spatially, given their page (dis)orientation, the form expresses – doubly, self-consciously – the content. Moreover, performative writing's negotiation of form and content not only facilitates and re-presents its argument, but also asks questions of that argument from within. Thus, with Phillip B. Zarrilli (and company), the chapters throughout this book consistently endorse the claims made for performative writing that its 'form and content invite a surplus of meanings'.[94] Or, to give another specific example, the formal disorientation of non-linearity and non-chronology in the Sudoku Shakespeare chapter makes its central argument, perhaps more convincingly than might be possible via conventional discursive writing, that the meanings generated by the production of *Othellophobia* were subversively in excess of my authorial and directorial desire to contain them.

In some respects this book sits more comfortably with artists' books than with performative writing. Certainly, I have been very much surprised by how almost exactly Della Pollock's formulation of performative writing describes the then unwitting project that has become *Writing Performative Shakespeares*, but the actual visual presentation of the various chapters, also conceived before I was alerted to the existence of artists' books, seems more akin to this latter form than to the former. Chapter 4, 'Graphic Shakespeare', is a collaboration with a comic book artist, Bernard Caleo. Thus, and I'm about to split the page again, where W. B. Worthen, via Hans-Theis Lehmann's conceptualisation of post-dramatic theatre, provides a brilliant summary of what I (think I) am attempting to get at here ... Bernard and I did it like this:

94. Phillip B. Zarrilli, Bruce A. McConachie, Carol Fisher Sorgenfrei and Gary Jay Williams, eds., *Theatre Histories: An Introduction* (London: Routledge, 2006), p. 365.

First, it [the post-dramatic shift from 'work to event'] implies a critical reconception of dramatic performance away from a notion of performance as *communicating* an *interpretation* of the text toward a notion of *affordance*: the text is one part of an ensemble of agents, objects and practices, whose perceived properties mutually interact in the

process of producing the signifying work, the poiesis of performance. Second, this shift entails the inscription of the spectator as one of the agents of the theatre, not the receiver of interpretations but a performer sustaining the signifying structure of the performance event, whose acts – however mute and motionless – frame, like the actor's, the event's significance.[95]

95. *Shakespeare Performance Studies*, p. 23.

Notwithstanding Bernard's contribution to Chapter 4 (and 6), this book does not claim to be an artist's book and does not exhibit – a resonant word – the virtuosic innovations not only with form, but with material, texture, colour, representation and imagination such as those in Drucker's collection. What types, then – perhaps as hybrids of performative writing and artists' books – of formal visual innovation make up this book? There are parallel columns, collections of boxes (some with comics in them), reoriented pages, frames-within-frames and text–image alignments. The forms are inspired by visual arrangements such as pinboards, number puzzles and interactive technologies. And what do the visual forms provide? Chiefly, they facilitate juxtaposition, juxtapositions such as:

1. theatre practice and its generated meanings (this is a feature of all six chapters)
2. rehearsal and production (Chapters 1, 2 and 6)
3. theory and practice (2, 5, 6)
4. citations and intertextualities (1–6)
5. my critical voice and other critical voices (1–6)
6. one production with other productions (1, 2, 4)
7. text with image (1–6)
8. affective with analytical modes of engagement (1–6)

This juxtaposition of the various spheres, materials, practices and discourses that are constitutive of Shakespearean theatrical meaning-making, is designed to emphasise the fact that such meanings are relative and constructed,[96] but just for a moment I will straighten out the respective chapters – their form and content – to offer a brief overview of the book's trajectory. Chapter 1, 'Materialising Shakespeare', is chiefly concerned with the training and rehearsal of Shakespearean actors, especially within the material context in which they work, a context represented via the visual form of a pinboard. The two productions discussed are of *Romeo and Juliet* and *Pericles*, which were staged at the Victorian College of the Arts by graduating students. The productions are especially interesting because of the progressive working methods of the respective director/pedagogues. Chapter 2, 'Sudoku Shakespeare', argues that the meanings made by a Shakespearean production occur at a nexus of text, theory, culture, rehearsal, production history, performance choices, reception and pedagogy: the form of the Sudoku puzzle attempts to facilitate scrutiny of this nexus and its interrelatedness. This chapter also considers two productions, both of

96. 'Performative writing', writes Pelias in 'Performative Writing as Scholarship', and hardly making an exclusive claim, 'rests on the belief that the world is not given but constructed, composed of multiple realities', 418.

Othello, both directed by me, both straddling university and professional contexts, but of widely divergent aesthetics: the first was a physical theatre adaptation intending to critique ideological (race and gender) faultlines of the play via grotesque exaggeration; the latter was an all-male, original practices production, though ideological critique was certainly, ten years later, still on my directorial agenda. Chapter 3, 'Red Button Shakespeare', considers the 2008 Globe *King Lear*, perhaps the most conventionally mainstream production discussed in the book. The chapter is concentrated on the blinding of Gloucester (3.7) in order to focus on audience response to (and potential interpetation of) a production, especially as it is apprehended from multiple vantage points. Chapter 4, 'Graphic Shakespeare', celebrates, via the celebrated production event of Toneelgroep Amsterdam's *Roman Tragedies*, the eventness of production, its atmosphere, its embodiment, its affect. The comic book form of the chapter is able to stage impossibilities, like an intertextual reminiscence of a previous production, or a round table conversation about *Roman Tragedies* (p. 103; actually taken from the published accounts of the production (at different times and locations) by those seated at the table). Chapter 5, 'Engaging Shakespeare', focuses on affect and audience engagement, especially in original(ish) practices productions. These observations on engagement are afforded by my specific involvement in this production (of *Henry IV, Part 1* in an approximate reconstruction of the Fortune Theatre), first as director and then secondly, and crucially, as (replacement, and untrained) actor. And Chapter 6, 'Ghosting Shakespeare', imagines, putting theory, for once, before practice, an Indigenised production of *Hamlet*.[97]

Across the entire book, therefore, the writing of performative Shakespeares entails elements such as: materiality, affect, rehearsal, production, atmosphere, audience response, multiple perspectives and more. Though I offer no proselytising call to performative writing, I do call for all Shakespeare in performance and production writing, performative or otherwise, to attend to elements like these. And, also across the entire book, the Shakespeares of *Writing Performative Shakespeares* include: internationally touring, large-cast, multimedia spectaculars; mainstream, conventionally rehearsed, professional revivals; professionally trained graduating productions; productions traversing the academy and theatre industry; and those more confined within the academy as practice-as-research projects. Thus, though this book emphasises its experiments with formal innovation in order to evocatively explicate the performative dimensions of Shakespearean production, the content, via varyingly representative case studies, is also, of course, significant: the chapters offer specific accounts and analyses of how, where and what Shakespeare means, or can be made to mean, at the start of the twenty-first century.

I will conclude this introduction via Johanna Drucker's articulation of the theatrical and theoretical properties of artists' books; she writes that:

The familiarity of the basic conventions of books tends to banalize them: the structures by which books present information, ideas or diversions, become habitual so that they erase, rather than foreground, their identity. One can, in other words, forget about a book even in the course of reading it … when a book calls attention to the conceits

97. The genres of the plays I discuss in this book are numerically imbalanced: one history (Chapter 5); one comedy, and even that is a late play (Chapter 1); and seven tragedies, though this number is skewed because of *Roman Tragedies* (Chapter 4). This book, like Worthen's *Shakespeare Performance Studies*, which has three chapters all devoted to tragedies, is not a book about performing Shakespearean tragedy. Three other chapters, two on comedies and one on a history play, ended on the cutting room floor.

and conventions by which it normally effaces its identity, then it performs a theoretical operation.[98]

98. *Century of Artists' Books*, p. 161.

Drucker's observations on artists' books, which might be unpacked according to the readerly–writerly split deployed above, apply to three levels of this book. Like artists' books, this book seeks to call attention to its various 'conceits and conventions' in order to confront habituated reading practices, such as the seduction into realist narratives of live performance which cannot but exacerbate the ontological distortion that the two-dimensional print representation of three-dimensional performance entails.[99] The reader of this book is continually reminded that they are reading and that this practice of reading is an active contribution to the evocation of performative Shakespeares. But Drucker's metaphor extends elsewhere. The argument above also analogously applies to performative understandings of identity construction, whereby the 'familiarity of the basic conventions' of a particular identity are habituated and erased such that they construct the appearance of an essence. Where a foregrounding of performative identity occurs, such as cross-dressed players, that which is normally effaced and forgotten becomes troubled and potentially questioned and reassessed. The reader of this book is, I hope, alerted to ways Shakespearean performance, via its staging of (iconic) identities and subjectivities, continues to contribute to the constitution of contemporary subjectivity.

99. 'What we lose in textualizing is performance.' Jones, 'Performing Osun without Bodies', 71.

A third reading of Drucker's observation on the defamiliarising properties of artists' books is the most apposite for *Writing Performative Shakespeares*. The ideas of erasure versus attention are also applicable, of course, to theatrical performance itself. Thus, this book expresses agreement with Bridget Escolme's critical assessment of 'Naturalistic theatre [as] that which attempts to erase its own theatricality' and with her championing of Shakespearean performance which, especially via explicit dialogue between actors and audiences, makes 'evident the work behind the illusion, its conditions and means of production'.[100] The case studies of this book, therefore, do not consider, as do many of the studies already discussed in this introduction, productions by the RSC, a significant proportion of which might be characterised as realist or (the sometimes, but not unproblematically interchangeable term) naturalist. Many of these productions, especially those discussed by Roberta Barker, who determines to find denaturalised moments within naturalised productions, have been produced within, to squeeze Drucker a little, structures of forgetting. Having said that, on the partial evidence of my limited visits to the recently remodelled and now thrust Royal Shakespeare Theatre, the RSC seems to be in something of a liminal phase of realist modes of production within a space not ostensibly designed for that purpose.

100. *Talking to the Audience*, pp. 13, 11.

If the very act of reading is naturalised, or, as Drucker puts it, 'banalized' by structures of habituated erasure, *Writing Performative Shakespeares* attempts the denaturalising of reading, such that the reader becomes a producer rather than consumer of meaning and interpretation. If identity itself is naturalised, or, as Barker puts it (via Butler), 'social discourses produce the illusions of agency and interiority',[101] *Writing Performative Shakespeares* affirms the denaturalising

101. *Early Modern Tragedy*, p. 19.

102. *Talking to the Audience,* p. 13.

103. 'Performative analysis exposes the contingent materiality of phenomena previously believed natural.' Craig Gingrich-Philbrook, 'The Unnatural Performative: Resisting Phenomenal Closure', *Text and Performance Quarterly* 17:1 (1997), 123.

of identity, exposing both the citational regimes by which a subject might be produced, and signalling through performance, like Barker (and Pollock), potential resistances to such subjection. And, if Shakespearean theatre has been predominantly (and anachronistically) naturalised, or, as Escolme puts it, has been produced according to 'an anti-theatrical set of assumptions about what theatre should be',[102] *Writing Performative Shakespeares* celebrates the denaturalising of Shakespearean performance, taking pleasure in its self-conscious demonstration of itself, especially in its demonstrably other-conscious relationship to its audience.[103] In this, *Writing Performative Shakespeares* argues not just for a new type of written, performative engagement with Shakespearean performance, but, indeed, for performative Shakespeares about which to write.[104]

CHAPTER 1
Materialising Shakespeare

Writing performative Shakespeares means writing material Shakespeares. Barbara Hodgdon, perhaps the original Shakespeare in performance material girl, describes *The Taming of the Shrew*, on the very first page of *The Shakespeare Trade*, as 'highly overinvested real estate, a property without boundary marks that attracts discussion about material histories, material texts, and theatrical as well as cinematic reproductions'. Moreover, these performative reproductions are 'where the play, re-textualized and re-textured by the actors' bodies and voices, appears in its most material form'.[1] The last chapter of *The Shakespeare Trade* catalogues the stuff Stratford-upon-Avon is made on – Shakespeare-related trinkets, monuments, souvenirs and relics – and the chapters in between deal with matter and matters such as: make-up (43); costumes (45); bodies (46); scrims (48); theatre programmes (83); production photographs (84); state documents (119); portraits (160); reviews (172); and mud (176). Carol Chillington Rutter, similarly willed towards materiality and performativity, is Hodgdon's heir (or one of them). Where Hodgdon considers 'a wedding dress that mattered', that worn by Alexandra Gilbreath in Gregory Doran's 2003 RSC *Shrew*, a dress she later re-viewed on an archive mannequin, Rutter, collaborating with Tom Cornford, writes about a practice-led research project to unpin and undress Desdemona (Hodgdon is also interested in undergarments, particularly an 'absent farthingale'). Hodgdon writes that 'When a costume performs, it becomes material for interpretation':[2] Rutter echoes, via Cornford, 'that a play operates as an archive of its own world, that it offers materials for its own interpretation.'[3] In *Enter the Body*, which like *The Shakespeare Trade*, has major chapters on both *Othello* and *Antony and Cleopatra*, Rutter is interested in, of course, bodies: the materiality of corpses (2), cadavers (9), decapitated heads (13), and the circumscriptions other materials perform on bodies corseted (22), wheelchair-bound (26) or blacked up (59). She focuses, too, on what these (actors') bodies wear,[4] and on the on-stage materials with which they interact (chapter 4, but especially 104–110, 115–120, 140–141).

Inspired by these studies and scholars, and by others like them,[5] this chapter poses three overarching questions (and a series of subsidiary questions) in order to explore the material dimension of performative Shakespeares. The overarching questions are: one, how does performance and production materialise through the processes and practices of rehearsal? Two, how is rehearsal (and, to a lesser extent, production) materially constituted? And three, how might the archive materials of rehearsal and production be deployed in order to evocatively reconstitute performance?

The first question, that concerning rehearsal process, is most searchingly

1. *The Shakespeare Trade: Performances and Appropriations* (Philadelphia: University of Pennsylvania Press, 1998), p. 1.

2. 'Bride-ing the Shrew: Costumes that Matter', in *Shakespeare Survey* 60 (Cambridge University Press, 2007), p. 82.

3. Carol Chillington Rutter, 'Unpinning Desdemona (Again) or "Who wold be toll'd with Wenches in a shew?"', *Shakespeare Bulletin* 28:1 (2010), 124.

4. Rutter writes (ibid., 107): 'In the theatre, costume is the most conspicuously charged material for writing a politics of the body, the boldest and at the same time the most nuanced, and for women's roles particularly, the most problematic, for costume determines the discursive space a role occupies and how the audience reads it.'

5. Ric Knowles is another theatre critic, often of Shakespeare, who attends to performance via materiality. In addition to what might be termed the micro-materialities of things such as props and prompt-books that Hodgdon and Rutter consider so carefully and productively, Knowles considers the macro-materiality of, for example: 'publicity/review discourse, front-of-house, auditorium, and audience amenities, neighbourhood, transportation, ticket prices, historical/cultural moment

of reception'. *Shakespeare and the Making of Theatre*, p. 19.

6. Laura Ginters, for example: "'And there may we rehearse most obscenely and courageously": 'Pushing Limits in Rehearsal', *About Performance* 6 (2006), 55–73.

7. Gay McAuley *Not Magic but Work: An Ethnographic Account of a Rehearsal Process* (Manchester University Press, 2012), p. 4.

8. Rutter, too, celebrates the revelatory capacity of gossip in *Enter the Body*, ch. 5.

9. http://vca.unimelb.edu.au/vca-about, accessed 1 May 2014.

10. The 2012 season of VCA Shakespeare included an open and light-filled *As You Like It* directed by Melanie Beddie and a claustrophobic 1930s New York *Merchant of Venice*, directed by Richard Murphett.

addressed by Gay McAuley, whose institution of Rehearsal Studies at the University of Sydney has produced a series of articles, both by her and those following her,[6] and which has culminated in *Not Magic but Work: An Ethnographic Account of a Rehearsal Process*. This book details the rehearsal and early production of a new Australian play by Michael Gow called *Toy Symphony*. McAuley offers preliminary observations about the practice of attending to rehearsals and then provides a close description and subsequent analysis of the entire rehearsal process, including production week. She aims to demystify theatrical process, especially the common ascription to the director of an 'authorial role' and rather 'make possible a more nuanced understanding of the real artistry involved in what it is that the director does and what the playwright contributes to the process', thus 'providing a deeper appreciation of the profoundly collaborative nature of theatrical creation'.[7] Obviously the role of the playwright is significantly different for a discussion of 'Materialising Shakespeare', given that Michael Gow is revealed coming and going from the rehearsal room and responding to suggestions by director Neil Armfield and his cast for rewrites throughout the process, but this chapter is similarly interested in the director's craft and in the 'collaborative nature of theatrical creation', and, even, in the rewriting of Shakespeare. Several other features of McAuley's ethnographic method will be emulated here, including: 'issues related to power relations between participants' (4); a self-reflexive problematising of the role of the observer (8); 'attempting to establish the nature of the social field within which the work is occurring' (9–10); an attentiveness to seemingly inconsequential discourse such as 'jokes, gossip, story telling'[8] (10); demarcating, but finding the interrelatedness, of the various phases of rehearsal (Part One, but see especially 188); the evocation of atmosphere (43, 144); crucially, the materiality of the rehearsal environment, the building and room in which the rehearsals take place and the objects therein (42, 65, 77, 99–100, 107); and interventions in the creative process made by the stage management team (64) or director (92, 120, 194).

Each of these features will be addressed in the following analysis, but in what ways does the work presented here differ from, and build upon, that of McAuley? First, and most obviously, this chapter will focus on the rehearsal of Shakespeare, whereas McAuley's published work on rehearsals has dealt with contemporary plays. The Shakespeare rehearsals that will be the subject of this chapter took place between late April and early June of 2013 at the Victorian College for the Arts (VCA) in Melbourne, Australia. The VCA, the Drama School of which opened in 1975, is Victoria's premier institution for the training of a broad range of performing artists.[9] In the recent past the graduating class of actors have performed in Shakespeare productions directed by VCA staff and invited guests,[10] although a pedagogical shift towards devised performance-making meant that no such season was planned for 2014. The 2013 season, under the somewhat indecorous title of 'Shakespeare Unsheathed', featured productions of *Romeo and Juliet*, *Pericles* and *The Tempest*, the first two of which will be discussed here. The fact that this chapter covers more than one production represents a further point of divergence from McAuley's recent monograph. In her preliminary observations and in previously published work

McAuley makes the case for the labour of attending to the entirety of a rehearsal process; I chose, instead, and was thus in an extremely unique and privileged (and hectic) position, to move between concurrent rehearsal rooms in order to directly compare the practices, each with the other. Though that often meant that there were gaps in my knowledge that McAuley's method seeks to avoid, the rewards of comparing the two processes, of attending to otherwise un-noted juxtapositions and resonances, as will be detailed below, were significant.

The work discussed here is different from that in *Not Magic but Work* in several other notable and useful respects. Firstly, the rehearsals discussed below arguably offer a more progressive type of theatrical endeavour. The rehearsal process described by McAuley is predominantly masculine, with male director, author, designer and star performer:[11] part of McAuley's reason for choosing this production seems to be that these practitioners are *masters* of their craft. Moreover, the process itself is quite conventional and orthodox, moving from textual discussion around a rehearsal table with pencils to the physical explor-ation of scenes on the rehearsal room floor to director's notes and refinement. By contrast, the work described here reflects the 'Shakespeare Unsheathed' pro-gramme note by VCA Head of Theatre, Alyson Campbell, that the 'history of theatre at the VCA is one of radicalism and experimentation'. The directors of *Romeo and Juliet* and *Pericles*, Bagryana Popov and Tanya Gerstle respectively, are formidable Australian female directors and theatre-makers whose rehear-sal methods challenge orthodoxy. In providing an account of these practition-ers and their methods I therefore continue the scholarship pioneered by Carol Rutter, Penny Gay and Elizabeth Schafer[12] of foregrounding the theatre craft of female Shakespeareans, and I address a gap identified by Christian M. Billing in his editorial introduction to 'Rehearsing Shakespeare: Alternative Strategies in Process and Performance':

To spec ourselves up in the rehearsal of Shakespeare, we need more in our rehearsal 'toolkits' than either psychology or cue scripts alone can provide. More pluralistic ap-proaches to the rehearsal of Shakespeare in contemporary contexts could (and should) in my opinion take account of (and therefore employ) many elements of the list of non-psychological, non-normative approaches ...[13]

Popov and Gerstle's approaches, which I can respectively encapsulate via the words 'play' and 'pulse', are definitively 'non-normative', though the phrase 'non-psychological' is more difficult to apply: though neither practitioner deploys a traditional Stanislavskian approach to character psychology, that decried by Billing above as normative, both approaches depend upon psycho-physical explorations designed to enable an imaginative inhabiting of character and narrative. This notion provides a final point of difference between this work and that serving as its inspiration: the actors that McAuley observes are, for the most part, trained, experienced and celebrated; the actors who are the subjects of this chapter were in the final year of their three-year training. This gap in experience, and the vocational and pedagogical dimension of the rehearsals here discussed, means that the analysis that follows is better able to

11. Neil Armfield (director), Michael Gow (author), Ralph Myers (set design), Damien Cooper (lighting), Richard Roxburgh (lead performer). That the costume designer was Tess Schofield seems to reinforce this argument. On the gendered nature of theatre companies, see Sarah Werner, *Shakespeare and Feminist Performance* (London: Routledge, 2001), pp. 46–47.

12. See Carol Rutter, *Clamorous Voices: Shakespeare's Women Today* (London: Women's Press, 1988); Penny Gay, *As She Likes It: Shakespeare's Unruly Women* (London: Routledge, 1994); Elizabeth Schafer, *MsDirecting Shakespeare: Women Direct Shakespeare* (London: Women's Press, 1988). The most recent (and compre-hensive) contribution to this area of study is Gordon McMullan, Lena Cowen Orlin and Virginia Mason Vaughan, eds., *Women Making Shakespeare: Text, Reception and Performance* (London: Bloomsbury, 2014).

13. 'Rehearsing Shakespeare: Embodiment, Collaboration, Risk and Play ...', *Shakespeare Bulletin* 30:4 (2012), 403.

delve into process, into how a moment of performance is created (or material-ised). To express this in mathematical terms, experienced actors can seemingly just provide the answer for a difficult formula: training actors are required to demonstrate their working out, to carefully plot, in conjunction with their di-rector-pedagogue, each step of the journey; this chapter will follow those steps closely, the footprints of which are perhaps more easily traced than those left by more experienced (and light-footed) actors. By such a focus, and especially within this specific vocational-pedagogical context, will I address the question of how Shakespeare production is materialised through processes of rehearsal.

The second overarching question of this chapter is: how is rehearsal (and, to a lesser extent, production) materially constituted? A series of subsidiary questions clarify, I hope, the value of posing this question: what is the size and shape of the rehearsal room, from what is it made, and how do these factors affect rehearsal practice? What kinds of physical objects are in the rehearsal room and what is their function? How are objects deployed in the development of character, story or theatrical image? In some ways this second overarching question also represents a subsidiary of the first: thus, addressing the materi-ality of rehearsal becomes part of the answer to the question of how rehearsal materialises into production. Hodgdon and Rutter, as I have already observed, contribute most of the discussion of the materiality of Shakespeare in perfor-mance, but their work is predominantly about finished production rather than rehearsal.[14] Therefore, in order to theorise this part of this chapter's analysis, I turn to two other, non-Shakespeare, though certainly performative, texts. The first is Daniel Miller's *Stuff*. This work of social anthropology explores a sim-ple premise via several discrete and wide-ranging case studies: humans don't make things, things make humanity; moreover, understanding the nature of things enables the further understanding of humanity. Miller's more specific observation regarding the 'unexpected capacity of objects to fade out of focus and remain peripheral to our vision, and yet determinant of our behaviour and identity',[15] recalls one of the foundational aims of this book, indebted to Judith Butler's account of gender performativity, to un-erase or defamiliarise the pro-cesses by which productions make meaning/s. Via Miller, I substitute the words 'rehearsal' and 'performance' for 'behaviour and identity' and seek to prioritise and reanimate those peripheral and faded objects which are determinant of rehearsal practices and final productions. Thus, in the same way that Miller demonstrates respective behaviours and identities constituted by the wearing of a sari, the inhabitation of a home or the use of a mobile phone, will I demon-strate the creation of performance through the use of objects such as different coloured ribbons, various items of costume and large, mobile metal boxes.[16]

My second reference point for a discussion of rehearsal materiality is an analysis of the role of objects in the enormously successful television show, *The Wire*. In 'Political Geographies of the Object', Katharine Meehan, Ian Shaw and Sallie Marston are intent on exploring 'the metaphysics of objects themselves' in order 'to argue that objects enable, disable, and transform state power', and 'need to be seen as political forces, precisely because of their ability to execute (as well as subvert) a certain, particular reality'.[17] The authors' foundational (and

14. With the exception of 'Unpinning Desdemona'.

15. *Stuff* (London: Polity, 2010), p. 51.

16. 'A study of clothing', writes Miller on p. 41, 'should not be *cold*; it has to invoke the tactile, emotional, intimate world of feelings empathetically.'

17. Katharine Meehan, Ian Graham Ronald Shaw and Sallie A. Marston, 'Political Geographies of the Object', *Political Geography* 33 (2013), 2–3.

italicised) notion that an 'object is *force*-full' recalls W. B. Worthen's (titular) use of that term in the context of Shakespearean performance: Worthen teases out, in a series of Shakespearean case studies, a definition – already cited in my introduction, but requiring recitation here – of '"dramatic performativity"' as 'the relationship between the verbal text and the conventions (or, to use Butler's term, "regimes") of behaviour that give it meaningful *force* as performed action'.[18] Via Worthen, then, I substitute the word 'performative' for 'state' or 'political' in order to apply these arguments about force-ful objects to an analysis of the materiality of rehearsal practice. Thus, in the same way that an object is force-full in the represented world of *The Wire* in that it produces state or political power – the objects scrutinised in the *Wire* analysis are technologies of surveillance – an object is potentially force-full in the rehearsal room in that it produces performative power – perhaps these might be labelled technologies of theatricality. I therefore ask the same questions of rehearsal room objects, albeit with a difference of emphasis, that Meehan and colleagues ask of the surveillance wiretap, the camera and the school test: 'What work does it do? How does the object generate and transform power?' Directing these questions at prop objects, objects that will end up in the final production, like bottles, scarves, knives or chalk, and, perhaps especially, at non-prop objects, those used during process but not for production, like a mattress, a basketball or sticks, enables analysis of the material constitution of rehearsal and, more broadly, of how rehearsal materialises into production.

The third and final overarching question posed by this chapter is: how might the archive materials of rehearsal and production be deployed in order to evocatively reconstitute performance? It is a question that has already been asked and answered, of course, by Barbara Hodgdon and Carol Chillington Rutter. Hodgdon turns archives 'into narrative – or performance'. She writes: 'Taking costume as an interface between theatre and archaeology, I ad-dress performances past through a material mnemonics' and she aims at 're-dreaming performance'.[19] In multiple publications Rutter uses 'the material traces of performance to remember, re-construct, and re-perform performance': she recognises that the 'archive is a site in tension with performance but a site, too, of its own performativity'.[20] Neither is it just Hodgdon and Rutter who have mined and re-presented the archive. Following Carolyn Steedman's *Dust: The Archive and Cultural History*, Maggie B. Gale and Ann Featherstone argue that 'the archive is a place of *creative* possibilities'[21] and Peter Holland, contributing to Rutter's special edition cited just above, gestures 'towards the archive as a site of, embodiment of performance'.[22] Harnessing all these ideas most fruitfully for the organisation of this chapter is Bridget Escolme, also writing in Rutter's special edition. Escolme offers a challenge to

Make dialogic archives ... Use archives dialogically …[in order to create] a conversation between actor testimony, scholarly voice and journalistic critical response that endeavours to acknowledge that each comes from a different perspective and set of discourses. Try to find ways of making archive usage dialogic by critiquing your own position alongside that of the actor; be transparent about the ideological underpinnings of your

18. See Introduction, note 50 above.

19. 'Shopping in the Archives: Material Memories', in Peter Holland, ed., *Shakespeare, Memory and Performance* (Cambridge University Press, 2006), p. 138.

20. 'Introduction', *Shakespeare Bulletin* 28:1 (2010), 2, 3.

21. 'The Imperative of the Archive: Creative Archive Research', in Baz Kershaw and Helen Nicholson, eds., *Research Methods in Theatre and Performance* (Edinburgh University Press, 2011), p. 18. Italics original.

22. 'The Lost Workers: Process, Performance, and the Archive', *Shakespeare Bulletin* 28:1 (2010), 15.

23. 'Being Good: Actors' Testimonies as Archive and the Cultural Construction of Success in Performance', *Shakespeare Bulletin* 28:1 (2010), 89.

own discourses in the analysis of those of others … Where full archives exist, use all their elements in dialog.[23]

This is a challenge that this chapter seeks to meet, a challenge made especially possible by the 'fullness' of the archives of the productions of *Romeo and Juliet* and *Pericles* (which are worked on not just by training actors but by an abundance of training production staff). The fullness of the archives from which I am drawing includes: rehearsal photographs; production photographs; immaculately kept prompt-books; 'house-keeping' reports; incident reports; prop lists; rehearsal reports; floor plots; rehearsal journals; annotated texts; programme notes; stage manager's reports; actor interviews; director interviews; costume bible; and my journal. Escolme does not, however, offer any advice about the form of such dialogue, about how such a multiplicity of items might be made to speak to one another,[24] and for this I take inspiration from John Law's creative analysis of responses to the UK's foot and mouth epidemic of 2001, an archive re-presentation in the form of a pinboard.

24. Adam J. Ledger's solution (with Simon K. Ellis and Fiona Wright) to the problem of representing – indeed, of performing – the archive, is to (digitally) reimagine the structure of Bertolt Brecht's *Modellbuchs* which, he argues, 'prefigure contemporary concepts of documentation.' The juxtaposition of photographs, play text, stage directions, explanations, commentary and discussion means, he continues, that the '*Modellbuchs* are remarkably effective in their multi-faceted approach' and that 'strategies such as the combination of text and other media, the interweaving of modes of writing and the manipulation of images to highlight moments of the live event continue to have implications for theatre and performance practices today.' 'The Question of Documentation: Creative Strategies in Performance Research', in *Research Methods in Theatre and Performance*, p. 162.

Law applies Helen Verran's description of interactive software designed, in his words, to help 'to choreograph a set of juxtapositionary practices', to the form of the pinboard, whereupon he assembles a wide range of archival documents. Law's explication of pinboarding – written before the advent of the social media tool, Pinterest – as a method of archival excavation and exploration echoes many of the concerns of this book, several of which are articulated in the introduction. His notion that pinboards potentially 'make surfaces of tense juxtaposition – and then give the imagination room to work', as well as (presumably) unconsciously invoking the opening Chorus from *Henry V*, describes the intention in *Writing Performative Shakespeares* of encouraging, even demanding, of the reader – you – a deliberate effort to complete the work via active reading. Law's suggestion that 'what I think the pinboard does, and does effectively, is to erode metaphysical singularity' and that it is 'a learning surface that re-enacts non-coherence and multiplicity' reinforces introductory observations made here via the form of split columns. And this observation, that the 'paradox is that a two-dimensional but otherwise unstructured surface is potentially quite permissive about the character of relations between the pieces arrayed upon it', and that its 'two dimensions produce not two dimensions but many' speaks to my earlier citation and discussion of Pascale Aebischer's argument that writing about performance inevitably entails a flattening of three dimensions into two. Finally, Law concedes, 'Since I can't take you to the pinboard and let you look at it carefully, I want to talk you through a handful of items that appear on it.'[25] He then quotes from several of the pinned items and discusses their significance. I make no such concession: writing performatively, and Law does this to a certain extent, means taking you to the pinboard. And that is what follows …

25. 'Pinboards and Books: Juxtaposing, Learning and Materiality', www. heterogeneities. net/publications/ Law2006PinboardsAndBooks.pdf, accessed 18 May 2014, pp. 4, 10, 18, 11.

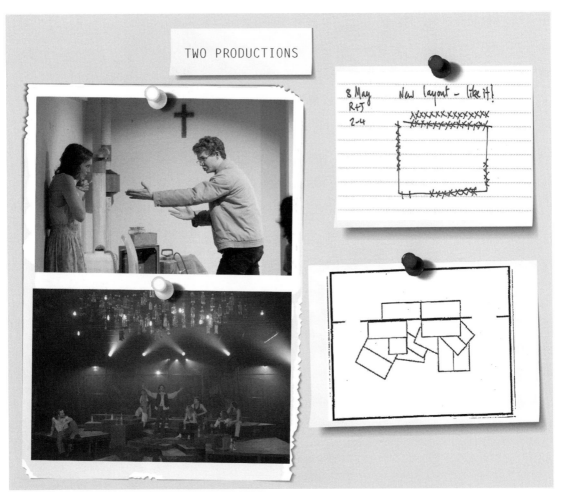

Two productions

On the last page of the first (64 A4 page) journal I recorded during the rehearsal periods of the two productions here discussed I have written, 'CHALK AND CHEESE.' The capitals, I suppose, are indicative of the excitement I was feeling that the two subjects of my comparative research should turn out to be so diametrically contrasting. Perhaps this should not be so surprising given that the respective texts of *Romeo and Juliet* and *Pericles* are themselves so obviously and severally different. Where the former is definitively canonical and the subject of constant and various reiteration, the latter is often regarded as a bastardised text, of uncertain or dubious provenance and rarely performed in Australia.[26] Moreover, the respective directors' treatment of their chosen texts confirmed and perpetuated these estimations. Bagryana Popov lamented in interview (with me) that she hadn't cut more of the text

of *Romeo and Juliet*, whereas Tanya Gerstle cut swathes of her chosen text away, such that she decided to rename it as an adaptation, *Pericles Punished*.

These differences in the choice of text, and in the respective dramaturgical shaping of those texts, were further manifested by the theatrical spaces in which the productions were placed and in the way those spaces were configured. *Romeo and Juliet* was staged in what is called PS2, a very large rectangular rehearsal room converted for this occasion, and others, into a performance space. *Pericles Punished*, by contrast, was staged in what is called Studio 45, a longer and more narrow space that doubles as a storeroom for scenery and props (Tanya confided to me that none of the other staff much like working in this space because it is dreary, dark and has a concrete floor, all material properties that were exemplary for her intended project). My journal excerpt above records Bagryana's

MAKING WORK - REHEARSAL PHASES

Interview - Tanya Gerstle

30.45

So there's **Intuitive Investigation**, which is getting on the same page cognitively, then there's **Immersion**, so that's where you're atmospherically building a shared language, sound is coming in, light is coming in, the space and the way they're using the space, the story is being read in so the progression of imagery is aligned with, you know, is being generated by "where are we in the story?" So they're imaginatively responding but they don't have to think about "what's my line, what do I say?" It's just about "who am I? And who am I playing with?" So you do that and that's quite quick. That's two to three days... So they already have built up in them a whole lot of shared understanding of how they use the space, the sound, the light, the style of how they're moving, how they're relating to each other, all that, so they've got that experience. Then you go back and you do it again. And that's the third phase and it's called **Mapping** and that's where they are actually having to speak the lines themselves... The feeding in is to allow them not to think what's my line, they just catch it, it's like a butterfly... Then there's the **Rendering**, which is the bringing it all together.

Interview - Bagyrana Popov

9.27 **Cycle 1** is **Meeting the Text** for the first time, so you go through the whole play and start to establish relationships. **Cycle 2**, you start to **Shape** and then **Cycle 3** is you really **Hone** in on the shape. It just didn't seem to be that clear... In my mind the key points were meeting with the actors — that was the first point of clarity, and then deciding what the space orientation was going to be, that was another point of clarity... There are other **sub-phases**, though. The metal objects coming in was a major one. That was really hard and the reason it was really hard was because I had just understood what we were doing and what we were doing was simple. It was about the relationships, the people and the space and I was starting to get a sense of what I think of as purity in the space. This is on a diagonal, this is close, this is there. And then the objects came in and they were great, but we hadn't worked with them and they came quite late to really integrate... the points at which the major elements stepped in and were confirmed. The actors, the casting, the space orientation and then all the objects in the room.

painstaking decision to settle on the spatial configuration of the *Romeo and Juliet* space. It is dated 8 May, which means that this arrangement of having the audience on all four sides – an in-the-square formation – of the playing area was made on the thirteenth day of rehearsals. My exclaimed approval – 'Like it!' – reflects my enjoyment of thrust staging and direct address. The *Pericles* staging was cheese to this chalk. The playing space was quite confined – half that of *Romeo* – and had a pre-established set, a series of oblique and multi-level blocks. Moreover, the audience would be placed in an end-on configuration. The twin photographs pinned (on p. 32) also testify to a general difference between the productions, where *Romeo* was predominantly brightly illuminated and *Pericles* was in gloomy darkness. These choices facilitated the alternative approaches of a continual deployment of direct address to the audience for the former production and the

complete erasure of metatheatricality – the textual cuts from *Pericles* included the entirety of Gower – for the latter. Finally, though there were certainly similarities in rehearsal approaches, particularly in the, as Bagryana terms it in interview below, 'primary method' of 'dropping in', here were further contrasts. The *Pericles* rehearsals were marked by very clear phases: research; improvisational exploration of the world of the play, first without speaking the text at all, and then improvising and speaking the text at the same time; and then closer choreographic refinement. The *Romeo* rehearsals, by contrast, were more a continuous spiral of playful exploration of the text and gradual discovery and shaping of the action. It was absolutely serendipitous, but these two productions could hardly have been more different in terms of textual decisions, spatial arrangement, stylistic choices, and, for the most part, rehearsal practice.

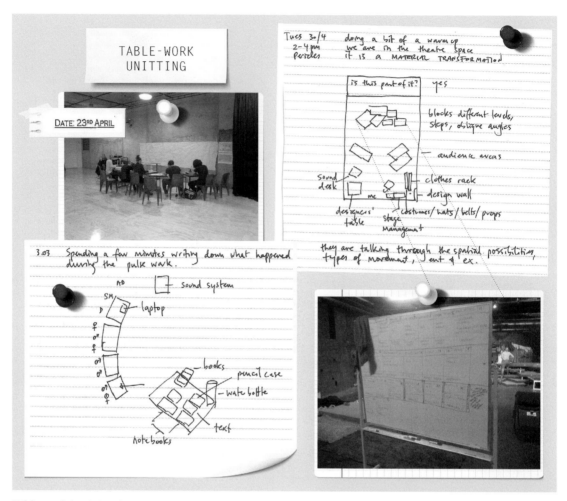

Table-work / unitting / transition to space

The first six days of *Pericles* rehearsals follow a similar pattern. After a Pulse (see below) warm up the actors sit at desks with their scripts, notebooks and pencils. In front of the desks they take turns to read the parts they are playing and, as a group, decide on units of action. Each unit – they end up dividing the play into 23 units – is labelled (for example, 'The Riddle', 'War Zone', 'Fight Club') and then further analysed for sub-divisions of 'Beats'. They also make notes about the main event and turning point of each unit and the who, what and (possible) where of the action, as well as any ideas that occur in the reading and discussions. The actors call this 'table-work': Tanya calls it 'Intuitive Investigation': Stanislavski calls it 'Affective Cognition'.[27] Rani, an articulate (they all are) and confident discussion leader, makes two very interesting suggestions: one, that Thaisa, whom she is playing, might

be the Fisherman who meets and tends to (and gently flirts with) the bedraggled Pericles; and two, that Simonides, who she's obviously not playing, might be a kind of Muslim cleric. The first idea is met with enthusiasm; the second, not so much. Later in the week each member of the cast shares some research with the group. Rachel and Chelsea present some very confronting material about sex trafficking in Europe and Asia, including newspaper articles and documentaries. Seb and Rani present dances and Oliver and Tristan show a documentary about Saddam Hussein's son. On the second Tuesday of rehearsal (30 April) they move into the performance space. The photograph above shows, in the foreground, a whiteboard upon which the units of the play have been transcribed (they are also typed up and circulated by the stage management team) and, in the background, the actors beginning to engage with their new playing space.

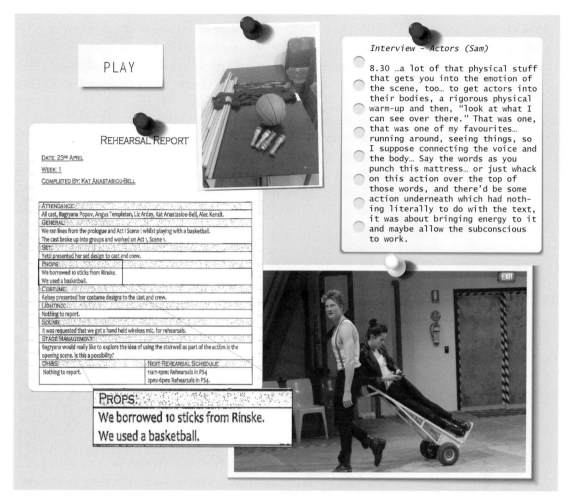

PLAY

REHEARSAL REPORT

DATE: 23ᴿᴰ APRIL
WEEK: 1
COMPLETED BY: KAT ANASTASIOU-BELL

| ATTENDANCE: |
| All cast, Bagryana Popov, Angus Templeton, Liz Arday, Kat Anastasiou-Bell, Alec Kensit. |
| GENERAL: |
| We ran lines from the prologue and Act I Scene I whilst playing with a basketball. |
| The cast broke up into groups and worked on Act 1, Scene 1. |
| SET: |
| Yetti presented her set design to cast and crew. |
| PROPS: |
| We borrowed 10 sticks from Rinske. |
| We used a basketball. |
| COSTUME: |
| Kelsey presented her costume designs to the cast and crew. |
| LIGHTING: |
| Nothing to report. |
| SOUND: |
| It was requested that we get a hand held wireless mic. for rehearsals. |
| STAGE MANAGEMENT: |
| Bagryana would really like to explore the idea of using the stairwell as part of the action in the opening scene. Is this a possibility? |

OH&S:	NEXT REHEARSAL SCHEDULE:
Nothing to report.	11am-1pm: Rehearsals in PS4.
	2pm-6pm: Rehearsals in PS4.

PROPS:
We borrowed 10 sticks from Rinske.
We used a basketball.

Interview - Actors (Sam)

8.30 …a lot of that physical stuff that gets you into the emotion of the scene, too… to get actors into their bodies, a rigorous physical warm-up and then, "look at what I can see over there." That was one, that was one of my favourites… running around, seeing things, so I suppose connecting the voice and the body… Say the words as you punch this mattress… or just whack on this action over the top of those words, and there'd be some action underneath which had nothing literally to do with the text, it was about bringing energy to it and maybe allow the subconscious to work.

Play

The defining (and differently emphasised) feature of the *Romeo* rehearsals is play and playfulness. This approach, I take it, is intended to harness the actors' creativity. Bagryana makes much use, for example, of the actors creating the physical environments of their playing spaces. Artemis' Nurse creates and then cleans Juliet's room whilst she speaks the text of 1.3, Shelli's Peter sets up the party that will become 1.5 and then invites people, including observers like me, to attend. Sam sets up the Friar's cell in one corner of the room and Emil and Jackson establish a meth lab for the Apothecary scene, citing *Breaking Bad* as an inspiration. They each speak the text whilst interacting with the various objects that now constitute their respective playing spaces: sometimes these material environments survive into the final production and sometimes they are just rehearsal exercises. A basketball is used early in rehearsals, again, I think, almost as a distraction from the perceived difficulty of the words. Tamara's Lady Capulet bounces the ball as a cover for her awkwardness whilst discussing marriage matters with Juliet. More playfully she puts it under Emma/Juliet's T-shirt on 'Are made already mothers' (1.3.72). Emma mischievously lets the ball fall and Tamara grabs it again, bounces and talks more confidently. Much later in rehearsals, Bagryana will use a basketball game to transition into the Capulet/Montague rivalry. And when a number of trolleys are brought to the rehearsal room the cast are, without needing invitation, endlessly inventive with them, much as described by Eli Simon in the clown training exercise, 'Object Transformation'.[28] Again, this playfulness comes into profitable use later in the rehearsal process when the road cases are introduced (in week 5) and are choreographed into 'The Ballet of Metal Objects' (see below).

What is Pulse?

Pulse is a shared language for the improvising ensemble. Like a group of jamming jazz musicians, the ensemble of improvising performers plays solo and together. United by a set of performance and compositional principles they respond to external sources and internal impulse, where the performer's entire instrument is available to create image and sound. It allows the ensemble to create structured, non-linear narrative improvisations. When they begin the Pulse, they have no idea what will emerge. They are attempting to allow the piece to evolve organically; to work from a place where the unconscious and conscious meet, to synthesise inspiration with technical understanding. The only structure that exists for them is a shared language.

Teaching Notes

Embedding the Principles

The shared language of Pulse is developed through repeated practical investigation. An ensemble begins from a still point in the empty space and the Performance Principles are introduced through the framework of four fundamental actions; running, walking, standing and falling. Side coaching during and debriefing after each Pulse connects these principles to the kinaesthetic experience. Using the four actions, each individual

Interview Tanya Gerstle

13.30 for the actor to experience, to physically, kinaes-
thetically, imaginatively experience the language so it
sticks, it marks them in some
way that's not just intellectual...

43.50 the space is an imaginative playground so I knew that
things would get solved. You
put actors in a room with a
whole lot of objects and go,
"Go", give them some genera-
tive ideas and stuff happens.

PULSE

Abstracting

Build the world together.

ACTION. DO. Just DO. ANYTHING GOES.

When in doubt, run, walk, stand.

One person reads / feeds the text → (an actor)
as one element   who respects
                                        and reads
                                        text clearly

MUSIC as an offer

PHYSICAL offer

OBJECT as an offer

Try the opposite. (e.g. if offers have become
                          similar in colour)

Externalise The emotion, as the actor.

Pulse

The pinboard cuts short page 1 of Tanya Gerstle's Master's Thesis, 'Pulse: A Physical Approach to Staging Text'. She goes on to write, '... each individual becomes aware of, begins to recognise, and eventually applies the Performance Principles: sustaining action, development, climax, Jo Ha Kyu, repetition, contrast, patterns and clusters.' I can perhaps best elucidate this text by describing the very first work I observed in the *Pericles* rehearsal room. Tanya hadn't yet arrived but the actors were, as I thought, warming up. My journal records: 'Running, stopping, lying down, improvising.' Tanya arrives at 2.08 (as a full time member of the VCA staff she has to balance artistic and administrative demands) and starts to offer instructions: 'work the geometry of the space; not only horizontal, vertical and diagonal ... Be drawn towards duos, trios and chorus; join in rather than observe'. The images that the actors

are creating are, at times, breathtaking. They concentrate with every sinew. I note Tanya saying 'end of a yoha cue (?)' which I read in her thesis is actually 'Jo Ha Kyu', and later discover is a concept of movement articulated by the medieval Japanese aesthete, Zeami. Pulse has many variations in the rehearsal process. On this second day Tanya instructs the actors to 'drop in a character' and they improvise various situations, which they discuss and 'retrieve' in journals immediately afterwards. In week 2 the action of the scene or the text of the play will be 'fed' to them from outside as they improvise, always starting with walking, running, standing and falling. In the fourth week the actors will repeat the text (still fed from outside) as they go through the Pulse improvisations. All this work is done with theatrical lighting (or lack of it). The photo above shows Tanya watching intently, choosing the images she wants to use. I write notes using a head-torch.

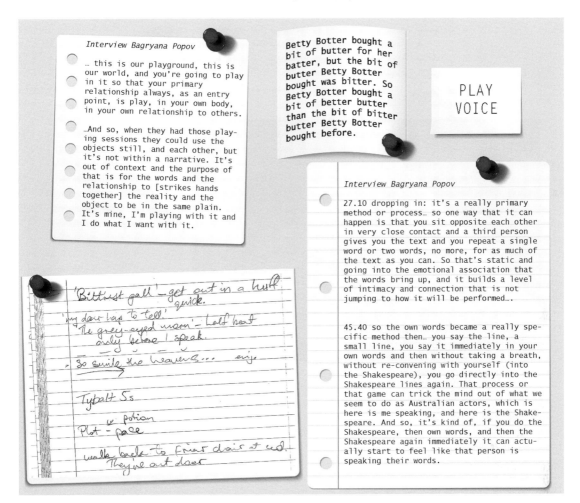

Interview Bagryana Popov

… this is our playground, this is our world, and you're going to play in it so that your primary relationship always, as an entry point, is play, in your own body, in your own relationship to others.

…And so, when they had those playing sessions they could use the objects still, and each other, but it's not within a narrative. It's out of context and the purpose of that is for the words and the relationship to [strikes hands together] the reality and the object to be in the same plain. It's mine, I'm playing with it and I do what I want with it.

Betty Botter bought a bit of butter for her batter, but the bit of butter Betty Botter bought was bitter. So Betty Botter bought a bit of better butter than the bit of bitter butter Betty Botter bought before.

PLAY VOICE

Interview Bagryana Popov

27.10 dropping in: it's a really primary method or process… so one way that it can happen is that you sit opposite each other in very close contact and a third person gives you the text and you repeat a single word or two words, no more, for as much of the text as you can. So that's static and going into the emotional association that the words bring up, and it builds a level of intimacy and connection that is not jumping to how it will be performed….

45.40 so the own words became a really specific method then… you say the line, a small line, you say it immediately in your own words and then without taking a breath, without re-convening with yourself (into the Shakespeare), you go directly into the Shakespeare lines again. That process or that game can trick the mind out of what we seem to do as Australian actors, which is here is me speaking, and here is the Shakespeare. And so, it's kind of, if you do the Shakespeare, then own words, and then the Shakespeare again immediately it can actually start to feel like that person is speaking their words.

'Bitterest gall' – get out in a huff quick.
my don't have to tell.
The grey-eyed morn – held heart only before I speak.
So smile the heavens… enjoy
Tybalt 5s
v potion
Plot – pace
walk back to Friar Lawr at end.
They're out doors

Playing with voice and text

Tanya cites the seminal VCA educator, Lindy Davies, as an important influence for the development of Pulse and Bagryana also adheres, herself a graduate of the VCA, to Davies' method, specifically via June Jago,[29] of 'dropping in'. With Shelli's Benvolio sitting opposite Dan's Romeo, Bagryana repeats the seemingly (to me, at least, at first) inconsequential 'Tut, man' (1.2.44) over and over until she feels Shelli has playfully exhausted, and therefore, inhabited, the phrase (the whole process won't afford this kind of detail and will speed up). Bagryana also has a deep and variously filled bag of Cicely Berry-like[30] textual tricks (and she does refer to trickery in interview), though. Guiding Artemis through the Nurse's first long speech (1.3.17–49), her instructions include: 'say it [phrases, not the whole thing] in Greek'; 'now speak to her in Greek – what do you want to say to her? Now go back to the text.' ''Tis since the earthquake now eleven years', continues Artemis: 'how long since the GFC?' asks Bagryana. 'Now go back to the text': here is the directorial nurturing of 'emotional association'. Jackson receives similar assistance with the Queen Mab speech. 'Repeat what you can remember in your own words', instructs Bagryana, 'and whenever you feel like it, add your hottest dance move.' The paraphrase is expletive-ridden but I note in my journal, 'that was cool'. Jackson is then required to go back to the Mab text, which is fed in – 'but you're going to insert Dan's name into the speech, beginning, middle and end of lines.' I note that the dropping in process, at least in this instance, tends to produce a surfeit of gestures. Bagryana works with these as part of the developing physical score of the work,[31] but I wonder if they will be whittled away. Working on Mab much later she instructs Jackson: 'Drop it. Drop it more. Drop it even more. Even more.'

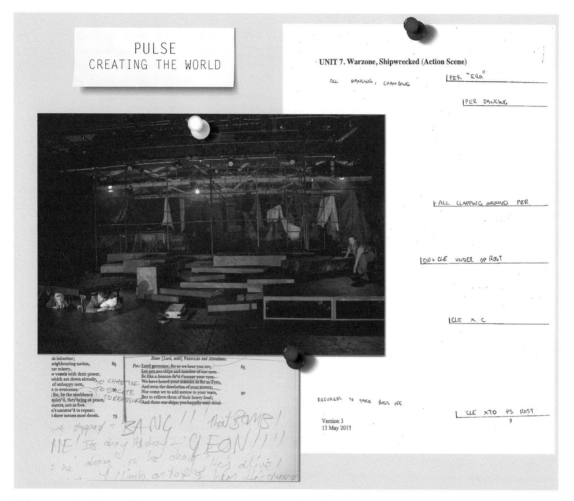

Pulse – creating the world

On the 30th of April I witnessed a remarkable session. This was the first day the *Pericles* actors had in the transformed space (see the photo and journal entry above). I arrived in the afternoon so they must have worked on the first three units in the morning (1.1–1.2). From 2.40 to 3.58 p.m. the actors improvised (pulsed) units 4–7 (1.3–1.4). This was the beginning of creating two interpolated scenes, the 'border crossing' and the 'war zone'. I will attempt to evoke this session by interspersing my description and analysis with *quotations* from my scribbled journal notes. *2.40 Pulse in the new space, a bit circumspect to begin with, gaining confidence ... TG calls out Unit 4, calls out the action ... the actors start improvising the scene, one of the actors reads in some of P's lines ... sound comes up, it's in stage light, the production team have head torches ...* Rani's journal entry (on p. 36) notes

that offers can be made in a number of ways, including via music, which affirms Tanya's thesis description of the work where 'collaborative practice meets a production process'. Further, she writes, 'It is non-hierarchical in the sense that all ensemble members, actors, director, light and sound artists contribute during the process and all offers are equally valid.'[32] The rehearsals taking place in front of me also confirm these lofty ideals. *P. physicalises – off he goes, climbs the wall, creeps/crawls under the rostra ... they've got him [P] lying down and covered in costumes, music up – it's beautiful. Chelsea and TG on stage feeding text in. TG intervenes with Ollie [Antiochus]. O ties up Pericles. Half literal/half metaphorical ...* How does the Pulse work? The starting points – walking, running, standing, falling – seem to be designed to, in that oft-repeated practitioner's phrase, 'get the actors out of their heads and into their bodies'. But it's more than this.

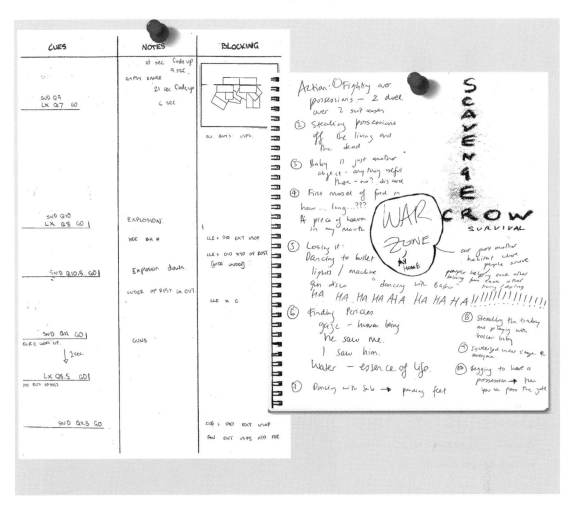

There's a commitment to the body and to the ensemble and to the world they are creating that is intense; there's a giving over to something like a pre-rational abandon. It's never planned, but the actors cross from what Tanya calls the 'four fundamental actions' into the world of the production and bring a kind of dangerous psychophysicality with them. Is it a gateway to something liminal? It's very serious play. *TG: 'Pericles leaves Tyre – by land. Everyone to leave Tyre for their own reasons. Find your own journey/costumes, the border crossings'. They improvise leaving/escaping, they play, they make alliances/they fight ... explosions on soundtrack, gunshots, they're wounded. Lights faded, the whole thing is improvised. Baby crying, war machine, literally climbing the walls, crazy. All the men are up on the wall, the women are on the floor. Seb makes baby crying noise, it's still war machine on SFX. Playing a game with the baby, taken it. Chase – she's*

SCREAMING. It's football. Per. helps – she's got it back. Fuck. Silence, spaced around. 3.28 p.m. TG reads again, 'My Dionyza, shall we rest us here?'... 3.45 p.m. CAN THEY MAKE THE PRODUCTION AS THRILLING AS THIS? Now learning dance from P. Explosion.. run, hide. Planes, sirens. And they're racing, sound design & TG laugh. Full on war ... Silence, out they come from under. Another bomb. Does no-one die? CPR. Is the baby dead? Yes. Wailing. Dragged away, checked by a scavenger, discarded ... After 78 minutes of improvising, and throwing themselves into very physical work, the actors huddle with Tanya, who whispers some observations to them and then asks them to 'retrieve' their discoveries in their journals. Over the coming weeks these 78 minutes will be pared back to the specific phrases and images that Tanya will select but much of the finished production, its aesthetic and feel, was created in this Pulse session.

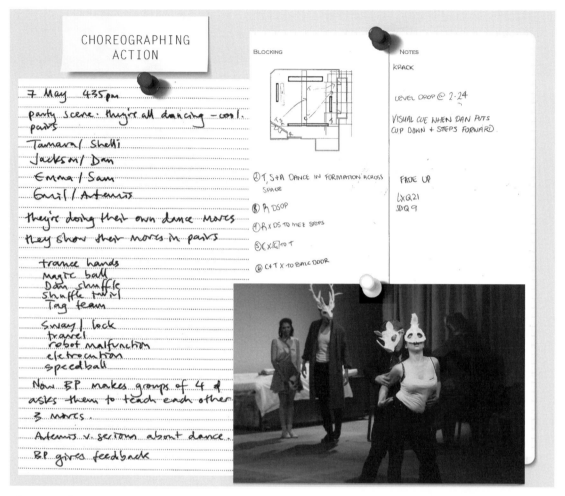

The handwritten prompt-book notes read:

CHOREOGRAPHING ACTION

7 May   4.35pm
party scene: they're all dancing – cool
parts
Tamara / Shelli
Jackson / Dan
Emma / Sam
Emil / Artemis
they're doing their own dance moves
they show their moves in pairs
    trance hands
    Magic ball
    Dan shuffle
    shuffle turn
    Tag team
    Sway / lock
    travel
    robot malfunction
    electrocution
    speedball
Now B.P. makes groups of 4 &
asks them to teach each other
3 moves.
Artemis v. serious about dance.
B.P. gives feedback

BLOCKING

①T, S + A DANCE IN FORMATION ACROSS
    SPACE
② R DSOP
③ R X DS TO mez STEPS
④ C X ⬚ to T
⑤ C + T X TO BALC DOOR

NOTES

KRACK

LEVEL DROP @ 2·24

VISUAL CUE WHEN DAN PUTS
CUP DOWN + STEPS FORWARD.

FADE UP
LXQ 21
SDQ 9

Choreographing action

Bagryana seems very rarely to preconceive the way a scene, let along the entire production, will play out. Like Tanya, she works with what the actors bring to rehearsals: in different ways, they both set up the rehearsal room as a playground and then incorporate aspects of that play into the production. Bagryana, though, is prepared to defer fixing elements of the production until what seems the latest possible moment, a potentially anxiety-producing process for training actors wanting to shine in their graduating show. The dance that begins the party scene grows out of initial pairs creating dance moves and then demonstrating them to each other and shaping more developed sequences. The prompt-book (above) records how the initial creative work translated into the finished production. The eighth sound cue (SDQ8) is 'Krack' by the Belgian electronic group, Soulwax, and is prompted,

of course, by 'Come, music, play' (1.5.24). After one more line, the three most proficient dancers in the company, 'T, S + A DANCE IN FORMATION ACROSS SPACE.' Character is fluid in this scene. T is Tamara/Lady Capulet, S is Shelli/Peter and A is Artemis/Nurse (dancing above). 2.24 into the song the music changes, Dan/Romeo puts down his cup and the sound level is decreased to facilitate the spoken text. In an echo of the Quarto of *Romeo and Juliet*, T, S and A are the initials of the actors' names, whereas the third blocking note – 'R DSOP' refers to Romeo crossing downstage opposite prompt (in the plot of the space on the prompt-book above the downstage is low, opposite prompt to the left and prompt to the right: Kat, the Stage Manager, was stationed at a desk in the little alcove in the bottom right corner). C and T also refers to Capulet and Tybalt: this is also the difference, of course, between named characters and ensemble dancers.

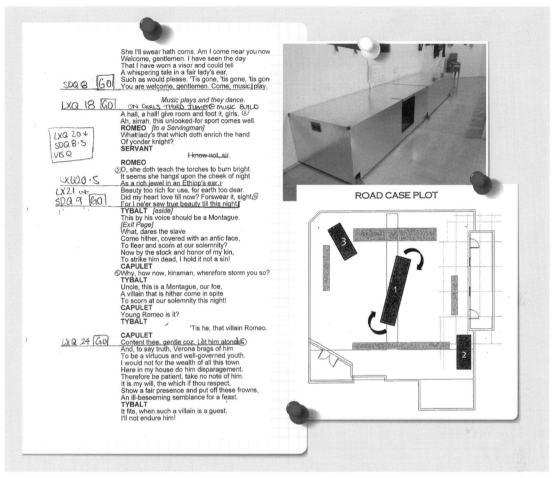

The Road Case Plot details where these large metal cases on castor wheels were moved at various stages in the production. Though I noted that Bagryana seemed relaxed about deferring final decisions about the production until late in the process, the arrival of the road cases towards the end of week 4 meant that creating 'the ballet of metal objects' was pressured and not able to be integrated into the production quite as organically as she might have wished. Indicative of Bagryana's openness is her question to the actors as they began experimenting with cases for the pre-show and opening scene:

BP: What are we doing with this?

Sam: We're ferrying illicit goods or dead bodies.

Emil: They're like opening credits. Who's doing what is inconsequential.

A few days later:

Jackson: Who are we when we're moving objects?

BP: On my agenda.

The road cases are used, at various stages in the production, as: Capulet's boardroom-like table; a barrier and somewhere for Mercutio and Tybalt to fight; and Juliet's bed and monument. Most stunning was the transition from Juliet drinking the potion (4.3) to her being entombed. Sam's recently slain Tybalt had already started moving her bed from the centre prompt side back to position 2 (above). She saw him – 'O look! Methinks I see my cousin's ghost' (55) – drank the potion and lay down to sleep. When she was discovered by her distraught family, most of the woeful exclamations were cut; instead, she was slowly transported behind the 'downstage' audience as a beautiful dirge was sung by her parents. Romeo entered upstage prompt-side, buoyantly hoping 'My dreams presage some joyful news at hand' (5.1.2). As he continued his 'cheerful thoughts' (5), Juliet was mournfully wheeled, right in front of him, to her tragic fate.

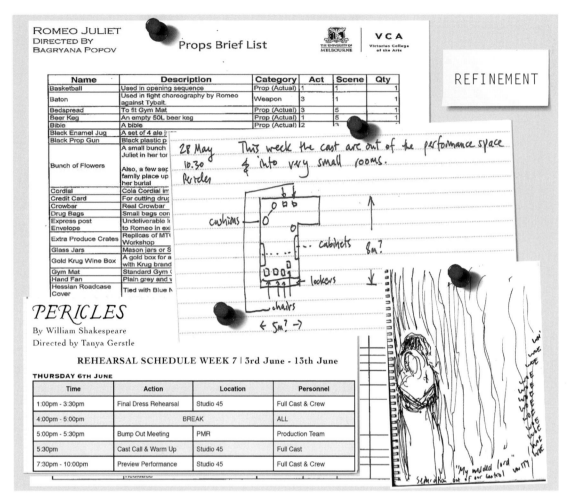

ROMEO JULIET
DIRECTED BY
BAGRYANA POPOV

Props Brief List

VCA
THE UNIVERSITY OF
MELBOURNE
Victorian College
of the Arts

REFINEMENT

Name	Description	Category	Act	Scene	Qty
Basketball	Used in opening sequence	Prop (Actual)	1	1	1
Baton	Used in fight choreography by Romeo against Tybalt.	Weapon	3	1	1
Bedspread	To fit Gym Mat	Prop (Actual)	3	5	
Beer Keg	An empty 50L beer keg	Prop (Actual)	1	5	1
Bible	A bible	Prop (Actual)	2		
Black Enamel Jug	A set of 4 ale j				
Black Prop Gun	Black plastic p				
Bunch of Flowers	A small bunch Juliet in her tor Also, a few ser family place up her burial				
Cordial	Cola Cordial in				
Credit Card	For cutting drug				
Crowbar	Real Crowbar				
Drug Bags	Small bags con				
Express post Envelope	Undeliverable l to Romeo in ex				
Extra Produce Crates	Replicas of MT Workshop				
Glass Jars	Mason jars or S				
Gold Krug Wine Box	A gold box for a with Krug brand				
Gym Mat	Standard Gym				
Hand Fan	Plain grey and v				
Hessian Roadcase Cover	Tied with Blue N				

28 May 10.30 Reroles

This week the cast are out of the performance space & into very small rooms.

cushions

cabinets 8m?

lockers

chairs

← 5m? →

PERICLES

By William Shakespeare
Directed by Tanya Gerstle

REHEARSAL SCHEDULE WEEK 7 | 3rd June – 13th June

THURSDAY 6TH JUNE

Time	Action	Location	Personnel
1:00pm - 3:30pm	Final Dress Rehearsal	Studio 45	Full Cast & Crew
4:00pm - 5:00pm	BREAK		ALL
5:00pm - 5:30pm	Bump Out Meeting	PMR	Production Team
5:30pm	Cast Call & Warm Up	Studio 45	Full Cast
7:30pm - 10:00pm	Preview Performance	Studio 45	Full Cast & Crew

"My melded lord" ss??

Refinement and the actor's process

Part of the difficulty of creating the ballet of metal objects was that soon after the objects arrived, both casts had to vacate their respective performance spaces whilst the production teams made them ready for final production. The (postgraduate discussion) rooms that most of the sixth week of rehearsals took place in were not actually big enough to have accommodated the largest of the metal road cases. This meant, though, that there was a fascinating new phase of work that was, understandably, more focused on text, delivery and meaning. My observations were further enriched by another serendipitous comparison. I had never before made a connection between Friar Laurence and Cerimon, but hearing the latter speak, ''Tis known, I ever / Have studied physic', study that revealed 'the blest infusions / That dwells in vegetives, in metals, stones' (3.2.33–34, 37–38), it was impossible not to hear

an echo of the Friar's famous utterance. Tristan's Cerimon had a very difficult task: gone were the Gentlemen to whom his speech is addressed so that, like the Friar, his speech was solus. Sam's Friar, though, had the advantage (to my mind) of speaking directly to his audience and of carefully explaining to ready eyes and ears of 'poison', 'medicine power', and 'canker death' (2.3.24, 30). His work was to concentrate on clarity of image and of speaking long lines as one thought and in one breath. Tristan, by contrast, went through a very long process of trying to motivate his speech to himself. Various solutions were proposed: talking to the dead bodies on the shore, talking to himself, sunbathing and luxuriating in his medical knowledge. Tanya kept enjoining him to find the given circumstances[33] of the scene and the place from which to speak. At the time I thought the problem was having to internalise the monologue but I later reflected that the

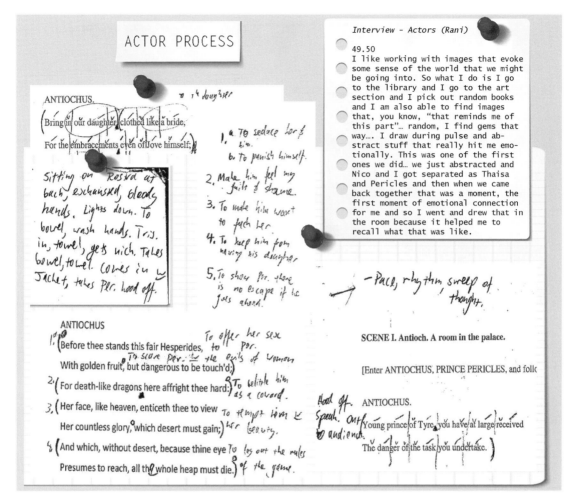

scene just wasn't quite making sense and that variations of motivation couldn't solve its problems. This is particularly ironic because I had assumed that one of the real values of Pulse work is in creating a deeply felt engagement with given circumstances, but my response to this particular scene was that the decision made in the Pulse improvisation, that Cerimon was a kind of ego-centric peace-keeping medic, wasn't helpful and created more problems than it solved. Rather than start again, though, with a different interpretation, actor and director ploughed through with considerable frustration.

Romeo, I don't think, was ever better than when it was in the little room. It was here that Bagryana tightened up the cues of the production. She had been trying to get the cast into a more energised state in the large rehearsal /performance space, demanding that they not drag their feet or amble in the space and that they should focus on main-

taining presence. That was a difficult ask in the near cavernous expanse of PS2, but in the little room – which, the first time I entered, was full of sweaty, fighting bodies and was quite pungent – the energy really zipped. Bagryana spent much time on cues and watching and listening to 2.4 in that small space. With Shelli's inspired clowning as Peter and the young men very much enjoying their ribald teasing of the Nurse, this was as pleasurable a version of that scene as I can recall. Bagryana commented, somewhat ironically, that it 'was really starting to breathe': and she was right. I didn't think it had quite the same effect in the production space but there was a great reckoning with the play in this little room.

A very significant part of the professionalisation of the actors was indicated by the amount of work they did on their parts on their own. Ollie's annotated scripts detail his very disciplined, if scratchily handwritten, prepar-

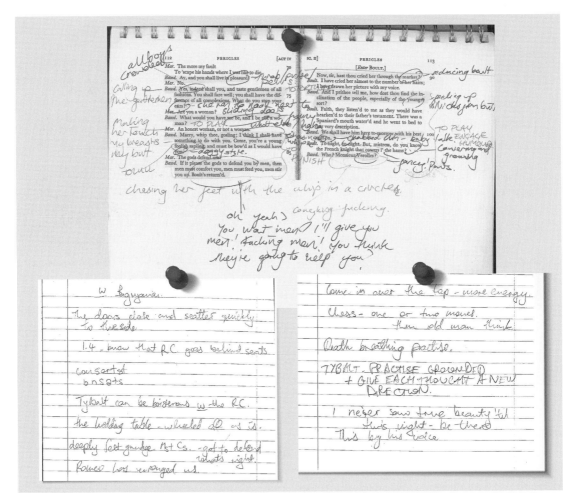

ation. The two excerpts on the previous page record three separate kinds of preparation: one, the recording of the action that is required, here including the opening of the production, which echoed YouTube clips of terrorist activities; two, metrical analysis of each line, including long and short beats and the positions of caesura; and three, close analysis of individual objectives and intentions, such as 'to tempt him with her beauty', designed to find modulation and differentiation within speeches. Rani's journal featured similar metrical and objective-based annotations but hers was also much more visual. She shied away, in interview, from describing herself as much of an artist, but noted that either found or created images (also on the previous page) facilitated a visceral engagement with the narrative. Rachel's annotation of her script (above) records the action of the scene – 'chasing her feet with the whip in a circle' – the intentions that she is attempt-

ing to communicate – ' TO PLAY/ENGAGE/HUMOUR' – and paraphrases that provide a subtextual colouring to her delivery – '"Oh yeah? You want men? I'll give you men! Fucking men! You think they're going to help you?"' Finally, Sam's notes from the director (just above) demonstrate his careful attention to Bagryana's instructions and his determination to improve. These notes focus on his portrayal of Tybalt (a nice double with the Friar). The notes cover the following areas: the physical mechanics of the scene, such as wheeling off the wedding table; the creation or sustaining of mental or emotional states, such as 'Got to defend what's right' or 'Romeo has wronged us'; technical matters like the intriguing 'Death breathing practise' or the advice to 'GIVE EACH THOUGHT A NEW DIRECTION'. Sam spoke in interview about returning to these notes prior to rehearsing the scene and before each night of the final production.

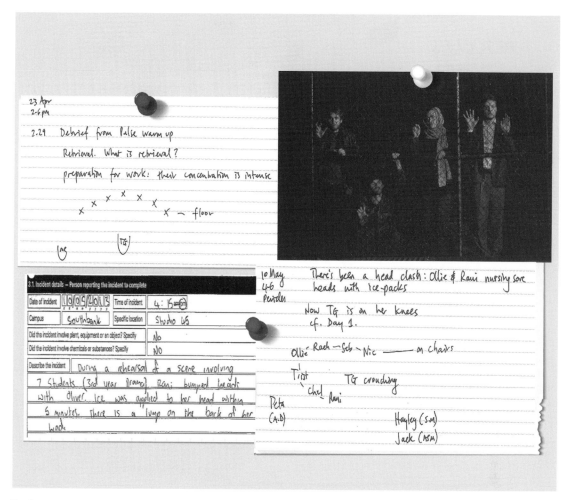

Body count

Seven weeks of intense physical and emotional work results in tired and sometimes vulnerable bodies. Part of the materiality of making Shakespeare, perhaps even more so with training actors, is the toll it takes on the body. One of the Incident Reports generated by the two productions features, above, the head-clash between Rani and Ollie. I've reproduced my journal entry from this incident, partly because it juxtaposes so compellingly with an entry from the very beginning of the process. On April 23, my first day in the room, I sit awkwardly off to one side (I've brought biscuits to celebrate Shakespeare's birthday, which proves a winner). Tanya sits in a chair and the actors crowd around their guru as she expostulates her method. Seventeen days, and part of a quite amazing journey, later, these positions are reversed. Tanya crouches whilst the actors are on the chairs. She's still speaking about method, but perhaps less as teacher and more as collaborator. At the end of this session she gives each of the wounded actors a gentle pat on the head. The injury/illness roll-call includes:

> Seb sick / Artemis chest strain
> Ollie and Rani's head clash
> Chelsea turned her ankle / Nick hurt his hand
> Jackson (former boxer) kicked in the head
> Dan bruised heel / Jackson tonsillitis
> Seb bad back / Dan bruised hand
> Rachel bruised knees from crawling
> Tristan hurt his ankle / Ollie knocked his knee

I should point out that the directors and stage management teams were scrupulous with attention to matters of health and safety: putting on Shakespeare, though, especially in war zones and battle grounds, can be quite hazardous and occasionally punishing to the body.

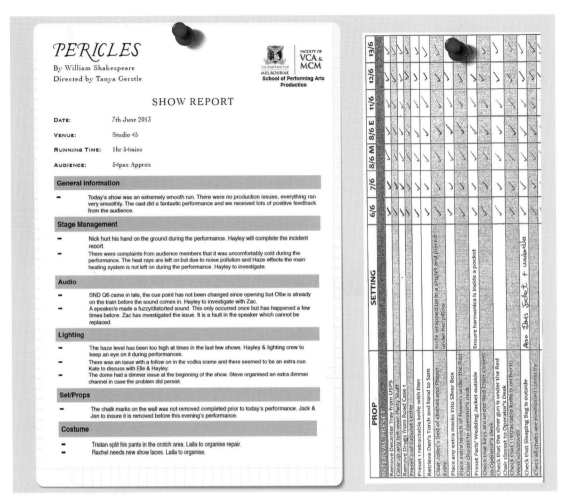

Conclusion: materialising Shakespeare

Here is an insight into backstage material Shakespeare. On the left I have created a composite Show Report for *Pericles Punished*. What I mean by this is that I have collated parts from several reports to give an overview of the sorts of material issues that occur during the run of the play. I have, in most cases, noted where problems have arisen and will require solutions. The reports provide a picture of a material production as a living, changing entity: it is temporal, atmospheric, embodied, acoustic, mutable and perishable, and it requires more personnel to maintain these materials than there are in the cast. The Stage Manager Hayley has an extensive team, all of whom are at various stages of their production, design or management training, and as the material supporters and co-creators of the production, are also highly invested in its success. On the right is just a fraction of the Prop Checklist that Assistant Stage Manager Alec would laboriously tick off before each show. These props have been sourced from other theatre property departments (if difficult to find), from local stores and second-hand shops and from other miscellaneous places (the prop assembler and handler has to be an extremely resourceful individual). Again, this list of props needs to be checked, repaired, refilled and reset during the course of the production. These documents, and the items and practices they detail, tell an important, if often neglected dimension of the material story of Shakespearean production.

I conclude this chapter (and offer the beginnings of answers to my original research questions of how rehearsal and performance materialises, how rehearsals are materially constituted and how archives might be deployed in the service of evoking performance) by returning to my board and the materials pinned to it. First, what do the

46

prompt-book excerpts (on pages 38–41) reveal about the rehearsals and productions I have discussed? The beginning of Unit 7 of *Pericles Punished* is chosen partly because it demonstrates that significant parts of this Shakespeare production were non-textual: every prompt on this page of the book concerns sound (SND), lighting (LX), action and movement cues. On sound, the two excerpts record (silently) music for a 'gypsy dance', explosions and gunfire for *Pericles* and the music for the party dancing in *Romeo and Juliet*. You can search 'Krack' (by Soulwax) on YouTube and play it until 2.24 on the track, at which point the music is faded to allow Romeo to speak his desire. The lighting cues make more sense in juxtaposition with the photographs, of which more below. Action and blocking such as the ensemble clapping in a circle around Pericles as he dances and then of Cleon and Dionyza hiding under the rostra, and of the various paths the characters take during the Capulet party also help to performatively reconstruct the performance archivally. What I haven't been able to replicate on the page with the prompt-book excerpts is their palimpsest-like qualities. The markings of cues (by stage managers and perhaps occasionally their assistants) are inevitably, at least until the very last minute, done in pencil. These prompt-books and others like them therefore bear the material traces of the production in flux as various experiments with staging are altered or refined during the course of rehearsals.

The photographs, especially in juxtaposition with the prompt-books (and other materials), also tell a material story. They corroborate, for example, and add an affective layer, to the hiding under the rostra to escape an explosion, and they give a fuller indication of the way the space was lit. The dance photograph (p. 40) embodies, or suggests the (sensual) embodiment of that dance. In the shadow to the right of the dancers sits stage manager Kat closely observing the prompt-book cues and behind Juliet is the road case which functions variously as her bed and tomb. The opposite page photograph of this item (actually, it's a different road case, somewhat longer) gives a sense of its materiality, of the considerable weight of the objects and of the also considerable difficulty of moving them, especially as a 'ballet'. The shiny surface of this object perhaps reflects off the collection of glass bottles suspended from the *Pericles* ceiling (p. 32). Other photographs show plastics, wood, fabric and metals, hard surfaces and soft, objects sought for their utility and effect.

The interviews and journal entries address issues of process, of focusing interiority and physicality, of synthesising the body and mind. This is where the directors make comments like 'emotional association' (p. 37) and 'they're imaginatively responding' (p. 33) and the actors

likewise speak of 'connecting the voice and the body' (p. 35) and of finding 'emotional connection' (p. 43). I'm especially interested in Tanya Gerstle's observation that the Pulse experience 'marks them in some way' (p. 36). There are physical marks, such as the annotations on scripts that detail objectives, actions or metrical arrangements or drawings in journals but each of these marks is designed to support the psycho-physical marking Gerstle speaks of, the body (mind) being inscribed by the repetition of materially constituted action. Sam's remembering of saying 'the words as you punch this mattress' (p. 35) might produce both these external marks – on the mattress, momentarily, on his knuckles, perhaps – and an internal connection. I didn't actually see him perform this exercise, but I watched Emil's Capulet do it in order to try to summon the rage of a disobeyed father (I actually felt at the time that a counter action, like tickling, might have produced a more variegated tone, but the anger certainly erupted). Another of Bagryana's psycho-physical techniques, which did not emerge through the archive materials, was to observe the actors' body language and gestures when they were not actually working. On one occasion she noticed Shelli playfully sitting on one of the other actors towards the end of a break. She seized on a specific (unconscious and un-self conscious) gesture, some kind of mocking with her hands, asked her to repeat it out of context and then apply it to some of Peter's text in 2.4. Bagryana regarded the whole text as a score, the lines constantly cueing physical action and gesture: where Tanya marked the actors through the improvisations of Pulse, Bagryana *played* through and with the text so that it marked the actors' embodiment and, when it really worked, interiority, too.

These differences of emphasis were reflected by those moments when I thought each production soared via its respective material constitution. With *Romeo*, it was differently materialised, or rematerialised, almost dematerialised, in the four days in the discussion room. No road cases (which I loved), nor trolleys, nor costume, nor design, this was when the actors played with the text most freely and materialised as characters, relationships and narrative (perhaps this great reckoning was made possible by their previous material adventures). With *Pericles*, the production most soared (for me) in that initial Pulse session, almost text-less. Read in from outside but not spoken by the actors, the materials of set, costume, light and sound, of bodies running, crawling and jumping in the space, of high emotional stakes produced a thrilling theatrical vision. That neither production perhaps scaled quite these heights again proves just how valuable attending to the material practices of the rehearsal room can be.

PERFORMATIVE NOTES

Pinboard (page 32) Dress rehearsal photographs by Jeff Busby: Emma Smith (Juliet) and Samuel Duncan (Friar Laurence); *Pericles* ensemble. Excerpt from my rehearsal journal. Detail from *Pericles* floor plan.

26. Ausstage, the online database of Australian performance, records seven professional productions since 1974. www.ausstage.edu.au/pages/search/event/results/, accessed 27 November 2014.

Pinboard (page 33) Interview excerpt (Tanya Gerstle). Interview excerpt (Bagryana Popov).

Pinboard (page 34) Excerpts from my rehearsal journal (2). My rehearsal photographs (2).

27. Sharon Marie Carnicke, 'Stanislavsky's System: Pathways for the actor', in Alison Hodge, ed., *Twentieth-Century Actor Training* (London: Routledge, 2000), p. 23.

Pinboard (page 35) Rehearsal Report (plus detail). Dress rehearsal photograph by Jeff Busby: Tamara Natt (Benvolio) and Jackson Trickett (Mercutio). Interview excerpt (Samuel Duncan). My rehearsal photograph.

28. Eli Simon, *The Art of Clowning* (New York: Palgrave Macmillan, 2009), pp. 27–29.

Pinboard (page 36)
Excerpt from Tanya Gerstle's M.A. Dissertation, 'Pulse: A Physical Approach to Staging Text' (held at the Lenton Parr Library, VCA). Interview excerpt (Tanya Gerstle). My rehearsal photograph. Excerpt from actor's journal.

Pinboard (page 37) Interview excerpts (2) (Bagryana Popov). Tongue-twister. Excerpt from actor's journal.

29. June Jago's extensive career is documented on the Ausstage website; she is described as 'Actor, Stage Director, Vocal Arranger'. www.ausstage.edu.au/pages/contributor/9923, accessed 27 November 2014.

30. These sorts of exercises run throughout Cicely Berry's *The Actor and the Text* (London: Virgin Books, 2000).

31. See Carnicke, 'Stanislavsky's System', pp. 24–27.

Pinboard (page 38) *Pericles* Prompt-book (verso). Dress rehearsal photograph by Jeff Busby: *Pericles* ensemble. Excerpt from actor's annotated script.

32. 'Pulse: A Physical Approach to Staging Text', p. 9.

Pinboard (page 39) *Pericles* Prompt-book (recto). Excerpt from actor's journal.

Pinboard (page 40) *Romeo and Juliet* Prompt-book (verso). Dress rehearsal photograph by Jeff Busby: Artemis Ioannides and Emil Freund dancing, Jackson Trickett and Emma Smith observing. Excerpt from my rehearsal journal.

Pinboard (page 41) *Romeo and Juliet* Prompt-book (recto). My rehearsal photograph. Road Case Plot.

Pinboard (page 42) *Romeo and Juliet* Props Brief List. *Pericles* Production Week Schedule. Excerpt from my rehearsal journal. Excerpt from actor's journal.

33. See Jean Benedetti, *Stanislavski and the Actor* (London: Methuen, 1998), p. 6.

Pinboard (page 43) Excerpts from actor's annotated script (2). Interview excerpt (Rani Pramesti).

Pinboard (page 44) Excerpts from actor's journal (2). Excerpt from actor's annotated script.

Pinboard (page 45) Dress rehearsal photograph by Jeff Busby: *Pericles* ensemble. Excerpts from my rehearsal journal (2). Excerpt from Incident Report.

Pinboard (page 46) *Romeo and Juliet* Props Checklist. *Pericles* Show Reports (conflated from the entire production run).

APPENDIX 1

Pericles Punished – **Cast and Production team:**
Antiochus/Leonine/Lysimachus – Oliver Coleman
Pericles – Nicholas Kato
Cerimon/Cleon – Tristan Barr
Boult/Helicanus/Simonides – Sebastian Robinson
Thaisa – Rani Pramesti
Escanes/Marina – Chelsea Zeller
Bawd/Dionyza – Rachel Perks

Director – Tanya Gerstle
Assistant Director – Peta Hanrahan
Stage Manager – Hayley Sward
Assistant Stage Managers – Jackson Harper, Jennifer Knight
Set Designer – Shane Thompson
Costume Designer – Jaz Tweeddale
Costume Makers – Laila Shouha
Lighting Designer – Kate Kelly
Sound Designer – Zachary Barraclough

Production details:
Studio 45, Victorian College of the Arts, Melbourne.
7–13 June, 2013.

Romeo and Juliet – **Cast and Production team:**
Juliet – Emma Smith
Romeo – Daniel Last
Nurse – Artemis Ioannides
Capulet – Emil Freund
Tybalt/Friar Laurence – Samuel Duncan
Lady Capulet/Benvolio/Friar John – Tamara Natt
Montague/Balthasar/Benvolio/Servant – Shelli Grant
Mercutio/Apothecary – Jackson Trickett

Director – Bagryana Popov
Assistant Directors – Liz Arday, Angus Templeton
Stage Manager – Kat Anastasiou-Bell
Assistant Stage Managers – Alec Kensit, Elise Mercurio
Set Designer – Yvette Turnbull
Costume Designer – Kelsey Henderson
Costume Maker – Hannah Murphy
Lighting Designer – Christopher Payne
Sound Designer – Rowan Fairbrother

Production details:
PS2, Victorian College of the Arts, Melbourne. 6–13 June, 2013.

CHAPTER 2
Sudoku Shakespeare

If you're an adventurous reader I invite you to skip this introduction and go straight to the puzzle (you can always come back). What follows is a very brief (and mostly spoiler-free) introduction to the productions discussed in this chapter – both directed by me and both of *Othello*, the first, a ninety-minute adaptation of Shakespeare's called *Othellophobia* and the second, almost a decade later, an all-male, original practices production – and an orientation into the main, performative body of the chapter, the Sudoku puzzle. One of the initial driving ideas behind the *Othellophobia* production was to have a *Matrix*-style fight as figuratively expressive of the struggle between Othello (played by a master of t'ai chi ch'uan and capoeira) and Iago (a black belt in karate) in the temptation scene (3.3), though given Iago's clear superiority as a covert strategist, such a fight might have resembled a rope-a-dope, but without its famous *punch*-line. This production was conceived as a research project at University College Winchester (UCW), where I was a Lecturer in Drama, and the cast was made up of professional and student actors. Both of the two versions of the production were framed by the idea of the action as Brabantio's monster and beast-filled nightmare: the first version (2003) moved seamlessly between a real and fantasy world, whereas the second version (2004) began in a real, recognisably modern world and then shifted into the timeless, if historically rooted, nightmare. It was a production which took a heavy emotional toll on me and which I felt was in some respects not just a failure, but the antithesis of what I had set out to achieve, but it was these and other difficulties which made the writing up of the experience, at least for me, so compelling: these writings make up the majority of this chapter (pp. 54–62). I swore I wouldn't return to the play, but in 2013 I did just that, albeit with a completely different kind of production. This original practices production, a staged reading put together in a week, was a joy to work on. Reflections on this production of *Othello* (pp. 63–65) are offered as an intertextual coda to the material on *Othellophobia*.

I must, I suppose, defend, or at least explain, the form of this chapter, the Sudoku puzzle. With Joni L. Jones, 'My goal here is to change a reader's expectations of the page without being glib or gimmicky.'[1] Glib or gimmicky the form of this chapter might initially appear, but it became the only way I could find to explicate the 'performative force', to cite a phrase to which I will return below, of *Othellophobia*. Because my role in the making of the production was as much facilitator as director, I was determined, when required to later theorise the practice, to not only document the various contributions of the co-creators (see Appendix 2 for a full list of the production team), but also to analyse the ways these practices intersected and interacted. And the meanings generated

1. Jones, 'Performing Osun without Bodies', 72.

UNIVERSITY OF WINCHESTER LIBRARY

by *Othellophobia* were not, of course, restricted to this multiplicity of creative production, but also and equally to the ideas, texts and theories that fuelled its conception, and to the myriad interpretive responses of its reception. In Chapter 1 I considered how rehearsal constructed performance; here, as an extension of this theme, I broaden the scope to consider a nexus of text and image, theory and pedagogy, culture and history, rehearsal and performance and, crucially, reception as the sites where meaning is made.

Here follows an example of the process I am describing, illustrated by the moment in the production when Othello defended his elopement with Desdemona to Brabantio and the Senators (1.2): described in box 3.6 (by which I mean the box with the ghosted number six on page 3) in the puzzle below, this action was staged as a bear-baiting. The performative thrust of this chapter is that such a scene made meaning/s via an intersection of, for example: Terence Hawkes' description of early modern bear-baiting; the capoeira and *Matrix*-inspired choreography; the soundtrack of dogs barking; and the various intertextualities that individual audience members brought to their reception of the scene. I tried all sorts of forms and structures, different rows, columns, fonts and textual interweavings, not to capture, which is the wrong metaphor, but to articulate, however faintly, this cross-referencing constitutive of theatrical meaning-making. None of the initial solutions were at all satisfying until I hit upon the idea of the Sudoku puzzle with its discrete but juxtaposed and linked boxes. The puzzle resolved my desire for a kind of hard-copy hypertext, whereby, to some extent, the freedom to cross-link, as on the internet, would be available to the reader of the following pages. George Landow defines hypertext as 'text composed of blocks of words (or images) linked electronically by multiple paths, chains or trails in an open-ended, perpetually unfinished textuality'.[2] Though not linked electronically, the blocks of words, what Barthes calls 'lexia',[3] enable such paths through the juxtaposition and interplay of, as in the example above, theoretical underpinning with aspects of the rehearsal process with the way the production was received in the press (incidentally, it has been suggested to me on numerous occasions that this chapter might be better in actual (or virtual) hypertextual form on the internet. That might be so, but hypertextual links fix the cross-linked paths they create: here you can potentially link any box without being to led to such a connection). Hard copy or electronic, this sense of whether the open-endedness actually produces a 'perpetually unfinished textuality' is another matter; you can obviously read all of the boxes, although perhaps you could continue to find new resonances between them and to other external texts. Moreover, since I first employed the puzzle form to facilitate juxtaposition and cross-referencing, I have now added a further three pages on the subsequent production of *Othello* (and related observations), and other performative writing strategies via a performance installation version of this form: these later developments evidence a degree of unfinished textuality.

The form of the puzzle attempts to fill the latent absence identified by Marvin Carlson's observation that 'Performance by its nature resists conclusions, just as it resists the sort of definitions, boundaries, and limits so useful to traditional academic writing and academic structures'.[4] The academic writing practised

2. Cited in Gabriella Giannachi, *Virtual Theatres: An Introduction* (London: Routledge, 2004), p. 13.

3. Roland Barthes, *S/Z: An Essay*, trans. Richard Miller (New York: Farrar, Straus & Giroux, 1975), pp. 13–14.

4. Marvin Carlson, *Performance: A Critical Introduction* (London: Routledge, 1996), p. 189.

here evokes, via form and content, the anti-definitiveness and boundary-crossing of both performance events and subsequent attempts to write about them; though the box in the top left corner of the first page and the box in the bottom right corner of the last page ostensibly appear as starting and finishing points, entry to, exit from and movement within the puzzle is not bound by conventional linearity. Also helpful for this project is Mike Pearson and Michael Shanks' provocation that 'Rather than pretending to be a final and complete account of things, a closure, the performance document, an equivalent of the dramatic text, might be in itself equally fragmentary, partial and encouraging of interpretation.'[5] Their text is exemplary of my method: in fact, in attempting to demystify those processes, practical and theoretical, which co-created the meaning of *Othello* as it was staged as *Othellophobia*, less of the actual production is revealed than might have been by a more traditional theatre 'review'; instead, this space is ceded to other priorities and the performance document becomes increasingly fragmentary and partial and, hopefully, more 'encouraging of interpretation'. It is this notion of the reader being what Barthes calls 'a producer of the text',[6] of choosing how to read it and how to make meaning of it (or, Hawkes-like, mean through it)[7] which constitutes the writing/reading as performative. For just as J. L. Austin characterises performative speech acts as those utterances which also enact, which say and do something,[8] this chapter (and, indeed, the whole book) offers writing which actively encourages, perhaps demands, interpretation.

Two further and (almost) final critical interventions, published at about the time the first production was being staged, further situate the puzzle as the writing of performative Shakespeare. Ric Knowles and W. B. Worthen offer strikingly similar, though seemingly independent – neither cites the other, though each is in the other's acknowledgements – explications of the way theatre means, theories that this book attempts to practise:

'Meaning' in a given performance situation – the social and cultural work done by the performance, its performativity, and its force – is the effect of all these systems and each pole of the interpretative triangle [of performance text, conditions of production and conditions of reception] working dynamically and relationally together.[9]

… the work of scripted drama and its performance, what we might call 'dramatic performativity' – the relationship between the verbal text and the conventions (or, to use Butler's term, 'regimes') of behaviour that give it meaningful force as performed action.[10]

Both texts are concerned with performativity, with interrelationships, meaning and force but there are differences between them: the first, by Knowles, measures performativity via, as the book's title promises, materiality; the performance, through the conjunction of a series of material factors – including, for example, script, design, the actors, working conditions, auditorium, audience amenities, ticket prices, cultural moment of reception – produces a performative force, its meaning. Especially illuminative of the intentions of this chapter is Knowles' characterisation of performative meaning working 'dynamically and

5. Mike Pearson and Michael Shanks, *Theatre / Archaeology* (London: Routledge, 2001), p. 13.

6. *S/Z*, p. 4.

7. Terence Hawkes, *Meaning by Shakespeare* (London: Routledge, 1992).
8. See Jonathan Culler, *Literary Theory: A Very Short Introduction* (Oxford University Press, 1997), chapter 7.

9. *Reading the Material Theatre*, p. 19.

10. *Shakespeare and the Force of Modern Performance*, p. 3.

relationally'; the puzzle offers a creative space on which this relational dynamism might be (re)staged. The second quotation, by W. B. Worthen, expresses performativity more as a process or discourse, whereby a series of citations – to 'regimes' such as modes of performing identity or subjectivity, historical reconstruction and authenticity, or globalisation – situate, authorise and produce the meaning/s of performance. Thus, I am concerned with the way both *Othello* and *Othellophobia* (and the original practices *Othello*) generate/d meanings as a result of their material construction and with how their citation of various discourses, historical and contemporary, enabled this meaning. In summary, this chapter documents two productions of Shakespeare's *Othello* that is hypertextual in the way it weaves together the different narratives and discourses that shaped its production and reception. The hypertextuality facilitates the chapter as performative in that it: one, reveals a thickish description of the production/s in action; two, explores the effects (and affects) of that action, how the play means; and three, demonstrates how that meaning is contingent upon a series of citations, the examination of which might otherwise be elided or occluded.

The puzzle of Sudoku requires that every row, every column, and every 3×3 box contains the numbers 1–9. As I have adapted the puzzle for this chapter, the nine boxes concern different aspects of the production, some of which inevitably overlap, and given that every row, column and box (in this case, a single page of the puzzle) must contain each of the numbers 1 through 9 only once, the form of the puzzle affirms the notion that each of these spheres, narratives, discourses and practices is equally (or near equally) as important as any of the others in (in)determining the meaning of the play.[11] The boxes have ghosted numbers and the numbers decode as follows (these refer specifically to the first nine pages about *Othellophobia*):

1. **textual** – the text of the production was heavily filleted in order to play through 90 minutes without an interval and to leave space for the physical dimension of the production; these boxes provide an edited selection of those parts of the text most relevant to the conceptualisation of the production.

2. **theoretical** – much of the theoretical underpinning of the production was drawn from literary or theatre studies; the practice of the production – including martial arts, dance and clowning – was far more interdisciplinary.

3. **anecdotal/personal/cultural** – this is a testimony of how personally invested I (and others) was/were in the work and how the play shaped the participants' personal lives throughout the production.

4. **rehearsal processes** – this process, as noted above, was extremely collaborative: the other creative authors included; the designer (of costumes, set and lighting)/producer, choreographer, fight director, bouffon director, composer, voice/text coach, assistant director and, of course, the actors.

5. **production history** – this was predominantly the recent stage history of the play (and there were many to choose from) in 2003/04 in the UK as post-colonial Britain continued to wrestle with its own phobias.

6. **finished production** – there were two versions of *Othellophobia*.

7. **critical reception** – the production was reviewed by the *Bath Chronicle*, *Times Educational Supplement*, *The Stage* and *Time Out*, and by colleagues.

11. 'In this ideal [writerly] text, the networks are many and interact, without any one of them being able to surpass the rest; this test is a galaxy of signifiers, not a structure of signifieds; it has no beginning; it is reversible; we gain access to it by several entrances, none of which can be authoritatively declared to be the main one; the codes it mobilizes extend *as far as the eye can reach*, they are indeterminable (meaning here is never subject to a principle of determination, unless by throwing dice); the systems of meaning can take over this absolutely plural text, but their number is never closed, based as it is on the infinity of language.' *S/Z*, pp. 5–6.

8. **pedagogical** – this mainly concerned a second year class at UCW called Shakespeare and Ideology, which ran concurrently with the production.

9. **visual/photographic** – these are images taken from the DVD recording of the production and contemporary and historical paintings and photographs which inspired or influenced the work.

The nine pages are arranged, in no particular order, according to themes: 1. sexuality; 2. emotion; 3. history; 4. stereotypes/binaries; 5. animals; 6. nightmare/monsters; 7. race/blackness; 8. stupidity; 9. Desdemona.

Though it can be read perfectly acceptably one page after another, to see the puzzle as conceived, the pages should be laid out thus:

1	2	3
4	5	6
7	8	9

This pattern, on the wall or on the floor, will allow the reader to make connections along lines, vertical or horizontal, or from page to page. Here are some ways, according to degree of difficulty, the puzzle might be read:[12]

1. *Easy: thematically* – a whole page at a time, perhaps according to the reader's interest, for example, the Desdemona and then the Sexuality page.

2. *Moderate: follow a number* – again by interest, you might prioritise the production history (5) and develop an overall sense of those production moments that most impacted upon the production of *Othellophobia*.

3. *Difficult: chronologically (roughly)* – you might want to attempt to reconstruct an approximate chronology of the production's conception, creation and reception; this would mean reading (perhaps) the text boxes (1), followed by the theoretical (2) or production history (5), then onto the anecdotal, rehearsal, pedagogical and visual (3, 4, 8, 9), followed by the finished production (6) and then critical reception (7).

4. *Fiendish: resonances* – there are deliberate connections between boxes, sometimes on the same page and sometimes across pages: you might attune your reading to discovering such connections; for example, boxes 2.6 (page 2, box 6), 8.9 and 9.5 are linked by the trope of smudged make-up and also, less obviously, connect to 1.3 and 3.2.

The addition of the three extra pages

10	11	12

creates further resonances, both within these pages themselves and back to the main, initial puzzle. They are not organised with quite the same precision as those that precede them. They don't, for example, contain each number, 1–9, on each page. For these pages, I have simply written about aspects of the production that most interested me, rather than dividing equal space to each sphere.

All that remains is to plot (or not) a reading path; please, try the puzzle.

12. Joni L. Jones also provides reading assistance for her performative writing: 'The next four pages may require performative reading, in which the reader finds a point of interest on the page, and lingers or moves on to another ... Readers will engage with the text in whatever ways suit them. The pages are necessary physical divisions that should not imply sequential relationships; the reader is encouraged to move between these four pages following whatever seems satisfying, puzzling, or interesting.' 'Performing Osun without Bodies', 72.

I was teaching a Shakespeare and race class in parallel with the production of *Othellophobia*. After several weeks of theoretical discussions, we split the class into two groups who worked on edited productions of the play, one as a tragedy and the other as a comedy, and with the shared brief of foregrounding the ideological implications of staging the text. The comedy group was largely devoid of sexuality, excepting Iago's homoerotic/phobic desire for Othello; the tragedy group started with the murder – and with the young black actor topless – and then constructed a sexually assertive and promiscuous Desdemona.

This is a text saturated by sex, and nasty sex at that. Iago warns Brabantio that 'an old black ram / Is tupping your white ewe' (1.1.89–90), and that 'you'll have your daughter covered with a Barbary horse' (111–12), images which prefigure the tupping/covering/ smothering of the final bedroom act. Emilia complains that 'when they are full, / They belch us' (3.4.99–100) but advises reciprocal treatment: 'The ills we do, their ills instruct us so' (4.3.99). This threat, however, is idle; the women have no means by which to return the violence enacted on them, let alone to resist it.

I met up with one of the actresses in the show to discuss elements of the production. It was a fine hot day so we sat outside at a local pub. The outdoor furniture meant that she had to sit, perfectly demurely, with her legs either side of a slightly obtrusive pole. When I returned with drinks she reported the comments of a nearby male drinker: 'Stay out here much longer and you'll turn dark, love. Still, you've got a mighty shaft between your legs there.' Is it merely fanciful to connect this kind of comment to *Othello* in a manner similar to that of Harold Bloom's connection of *The Merchant of Venice* to the Holocaust?

I saw Ricky (brother of Ray) Fearon's Othello for Concentric Circles at the Haymarket in Basingstoke with a large group of women. Their chief topic of conversation was of waiting to see Othello naked. The production's publicity did not disappoint; at the beginning of 3.3 Fearon started stripping to his fetishised white boxer shorts and muscular body and then took a shower as Iago began to reel him in: more exemplary Othellophilia I have not seen. Making not quite the same point a local review decided, 'His vulnerability was highlighted in a highly original shower scene, when he stripped down to his underpants.'

My first idea for Desdemona's murder, according to the strategy of exploding and exposing the play's stereotypes through grotesque exaggeration, was to have Othello beat her to death with a six foot phallus; the cast didn't go for it ... What evolved through rehearsals, in collaboration with the designer, was that the tie around Othello's waist, and which could be read as phallic, was used to strangle her. The Brabantio figure was on stage throughout this, and later made a noose from the tie with which to hang Othello – obviously a horrible historical image – and prevent him taking his own life.

Adi Bloom, reviewing *Othellophobia* for the *Times Educational Supplement*, focused on the production's use of the death/desire dynamic as outlined by Jonathan Dollimore. Bloom picked up that the murder was troublingly bestialised and eroticised and, as in the play, inextricably linked to her father: 'When Brabantio discovers the betrayal of his daughter, Desdemona, he glares like a wildcat about to pounce ... [her] murder is a culmination of animal baseness. Declaring "I would kill you and love you", Othello pulls her to him, her writhing death throes a reflection of his lust.'

Othello and Desdemona's sexual union in Cyprus was represented far more poetically; this was the one moment in the production where the sexuality was healthily unpolluted. The consummation took the form of an improvised dance which happened upstage throughout the drinking scene; thus the apparent health was physically juxtaposed with the ensuing sickness. Brabantio watched both scenes, impotently unable to interrupt the love-making, but enabled to oversee and endorse Iago's machinations with Cassio's drinking – and soon the dance was halted by a screaming, Artaudian siren.

Celia Daileader coins the term 'Othellophilia' to describe overt, if sometimes unconscious, sexualisation of the black classical actor; this cultural process approaches 'biracial porn [and] functions to exploit both white women and black men'. It is defined by dramaturgies which foreground 'violence, physicality, sexuality, the demonic; black leather, leopard skin, black nudity against white dishabille'. Though she lauds the casting of black actors in non-black Shakespearean roles she laments the all-too-common 'pageant of black fantasy flesh, the fruits of allegedly colour-blind casting'.

Marvin Rosenberg begins his exhaustive chronicling of *Othello*'s various social, literary and theatrical histories with a biblical echo; 'From the beginning, men wept at Othello.' Emotional responses form the spiritual core of this history, which Michael Bristol argues 'signals a chronic unwillingness amounting at times to outright refusal to participate in the performance of a play as the ritual or quasi-ritual affirmation of certain social practices'. I think this is perhaps an optimistic, carnivalesque reading: as often as not, such responses might express (latent) sympathy with Brabantio, if not Iago.

Like *Shakespeare in Love* (1999), *Stage Beauty* (2004) trebles the emotional impact of the play (*Othello*) it stages: the tragic ending of the play itself is played; so is the audience's intense involvement in, and euphoric/cathartic response to, the tragedy; and, the characters playing the parts are romantically involved and their parts reveal their characters. Billy Crudup playing Kynaston playing Desdemona (and Othello) seeks the emotional truth of the death scene. This can be read as an attempt to kill his 'feminine side', which the film suggests is the result of abuse, and once achieved allows him to embrace heterosexual love.

At a Sunday afternoon rehearsal, with opening night fast approaching and much still to be worked on, Oni turns up. Oni is Olu's very beautiful baby daughter. She is here an hour before the scheduled close of rehearsal, I suspect, because her mum quite rightly wants to make clear her prior claim to her overworked husband. Olu tries to focus on his performance, but Oni, for this afternoon his wayward daughter, walks in and out of scenes, a haunting presence disrupting all around her by her beguiling smile and curls – chaos is come again – and I feel powerless as a controlling figure of the production's meaning.

Perhaps *Othello* is the Shakespeare play which has elicited the most involved (and recorded) emotional responses from both readers and spectators. Iago says 'I will wear my heart upon my sleeve' (1.1.65) but it is Othello who, Tom Cruise-like, speaks of his 'soul's joy', such that he 'cannot speak enough of this content' (2.1.176, 188). His young bride continues to be the locus of the emotional 'rack' Iago ties him to, and, having murdered her, he describes himself as 'one whose subdued eyes, / Albeit unused to the melting mood, / Drop tears as fast as the Arabian trees / Their medicinable gum' (5.2.344–48).

My emotional reactions to this play have changed over time. Reading it for the first time at 20, I was shattered by the destruction of what appeared to be an ideal romance; on the page Othello's blackness did not register with my yet-to-be-politicised eyes and my response was of an essentialised despair at love destroyed. Maybe ten years later I noticed the first signs of Othellophobia: unease reading the play; a focus on the sexualised/bestialised construction of Othello; further unease sitting in naturalistic (white audience) theatres; a nauseous inability to watch any contemporary adaptation of the play. Is it just me?

At the end of the production Brabantio was very much involved in Desdemona's death. At different moments he held them, ambiguously either trying to prevent the murder or facilitate it. Othello struck Desdemona and then pulled her up onto him using his waist-tie. Her strangulation as she sat astride him was disturbingly sexual and at the end he invariably had her white makeup smudging his face. Then, farce; Brabantio breathed life back into Desdemona so that Othello had to keep cartoonishly killing her. All the reviews singled out the murder as harrowing; several were upset about the too immediate comedy.

When I went to the cinema to see *Far From Heaven* (2002), a story of prohibited love between a white woman and a black man, there was a poster for the Australian film, *Rabbit-Proof Fence* (2002). Its warning about the narrative of Aboriginal assimilation, in this case the removal of 'half-caste' children from their families for institutional instruction, read 'mild emotional content'. It made me so mad I went back with a permanent marker and scrawled next to it, 'white English perspective'. The poster for *R-PF* eerily re-images Parker's *Othello* poster, with an oversized Branagh looming over the three girls/Fishburne plus Jacob.

Of the two student productions, the tragedy group sought to provoke emotional responses to the play by turning Othello into a victim of domestic abuse (and cuckolding). This was tied to universalised notions of character which largely attempted to erase race as a central consideration of the production. The comedy group totally resisted any sort of emotional engagement with the narrative. The characters were represented as very broad stereotypes and even the serious actions of the play – Iago still tricked Othello into murdering Desdemona – were mocked as not worthy of serious attention.

Olu's agenda was recuperative; like many black actors he wanted fiercely, and entirely justifiably, to resist a white-constructed Othello and to affirm a black identity which was powerful and autonomous. His chief means for this were historical and cultural: for the former he did extensive research into Moorish history and used this to inform his characterisation; for the latter he developed a British/Nigerian accent as a way of focusing otherness. My agenda, contrarily, was 'explosive': I wanted to expose what I saw as pernicious (transhistorical) white constructions of the part; we were on a collision course ...

Karen Newman outlines some of the early modern explanations for blackness, in particular George Best's late sixteenth-century theory, extrapolated from the birth of a black baby to a black father and white mother, that 'it seemeth this blacknes proceedeth rather [as opposed to the previous notion of exposure to the sun] of some natural infection of that man'. This infection is given a scriptural aetiology which confirms, according to Newman, 'the link between blackness and the devil, the myth of black sexuality, [and] the problem of black subjection to authority'.

One of the actors who was later cast in Max Stafford-Clark's enormously successful 'African' *Macbeth* (2005) came to see the first version of the production. He was extremely generous about the show and was especially complimentary about Olu's citation of Africa – specifically Yoruban Nigeria – through accent and gesture, and saw this as a means of taking ownership of the role and moving it away from white authority. A colleague of mine – white, European, female – took an opposite view, supposing that it 'felt too much like "cultural tourism" rather than subverting or asking questions of the content'.

Here is Ben Kingsley historicising his appearance via the Moorish Ambassador to Elizabeth I, and yet offering a contentious, nay offensive, universalism: 'Thus from the beginning of rehearsal a being emerged who, if provoked at a primal level, would react with the violence of a psychopath.'

We aim, in the Shakespeare class, to develop a cultural materialist theatre practice. Part of this process is attempting to historicise any text which we study – in this case with particular reference to Newman and Virginia Mason Vaughan – and analysing its relationship to a present context. The students are often quite reluctant to let slip the security blanket of universalism, preferring to connect themselves to the play's themes of love, jealousy and honour. We steer them towards a specific contextualisation of the universal theme: what are the material factors which produce Othello's, as opposed to OJ's, jealousy?

Sello Maake ka-Ncube, the black South African actor who played Othello for the RSC in 2004, revealed to the *Times*' Robert Gore-Langton that 'basing the whole thing on race is a bit ridiculous … It's the emotional/psychological landscape that interests me.' His descent into madness, however, was a journey from civilised poise to African barbarism. As Patrick Carnegy's review lamented, 'his fall is all too swift. As he works himself up into a paroxysm, [pre-epilepsy] he grotesquely reverts to the stamping war dance of some tribal beast within'. Sher's Iago did a monkey-dance, but that, at least, was on the surface.

The Senate's questions to Othello about his elopement was played as a bear-baiting, which, as described by Terence Hawkes, involved 'the chaining to a stake and the whipping of a blinded bear ... The use of specially trained dogs [here, the Senators] to tear the bear's flesh … guaranteed violent mutilation'. More often connected to Macbeth's end, Othello defines himself when referring to Desdemona's powers of musical placation; 'O, she would sing the savageness out of a bear!' (4.1.186). His statement is a kind of performative fortification against such an appeasement, a renewed commitment to savagery.

Two historical and anecdotal accounts of the play's emotional impact:

… Desdemona killed before us by her husband, although she always acted her whole part extremely well, yet when she was killed she was even more moving, for when she fell back upon the bed she implored the pity of the spectators by her very face.

During a performance in Baltimore in 1822, a soldier on guard duty, seeing Othello about to strangle Desdemona, drew his gun and fired at the stage, breaking the arm of the actor playing the Moor.

Just as Olu's characterisation of Othello was informed by Moorish history, so, Othello's character is similarly defined by his/story. His (perhaps unintended) courting of Desdemona involves recounting his 'disastrous chances', of being 'sold to slavery' and 'all my travels' history' (1.3.133, 137–38). That relationship is symbolically sealed (and later undermined) by the handkerchief, which has 'magic in the web of it' (3.4.65). Dying, Othello recalls an incident in Aleppo where he, in an act of Christian and Venetian alliance, and in appropriating an alternative history, smote a traducing and turbaned Turk (5.2.349).

In rehearsal we started with the following stereotypes as a way of developing distinct and non-naturalistic ways of moving and of breaking down traditional modes of characterisation:

Othello – monster
Iago – devil
Desdemona – doll/whore
Emilia – nagging wife
Bianca – hysteric
Cassio – ladies'man
Brabantio – dotard
Roderigo – fool
Montano – soldier
Lodovico – messenger

Ernst Honigmann's optimistic reading – 'Shakespeare's determination to question "the normal" emerges from the large number of stereotypes that he sets up only to knock them down … each one fails to conform to our expectations' – is countered almost directly by Ania Loomba's – 'But the play goes on to show us that, despite his seeming different from other Moors, Othello ultimately embodies the stereotype of Moorish lust and violence – a jealous, murderous husband of a Christian lady'. My position is that Shakespearean stereotypes carry such weight (and threat) because they seem (and are sooft portrayed) as real people.

If I were to stage the play again (God forbid), I would take on board Ray Proctor's vehement defence of the poetic Othello. I would have two actors playing the part, one playing the 'noble Moor', those incredibly progressive characteristics Shakespeare creates, and one playing the stereotype, the fool, the buffoon. My fantasy casting for this production would be Hugh Quarshie – a very serious Shakespearean – and Lenny Henry – a genius with comic racial stereotypes. The production would be a struggle between the two for priority with perhaps one (alternately) killing the other.

There were two incarnations of *Othellophobia*. In the first the real and the nightmare worlds were mixed, the natural and animal physicalities interwoven. I came away from the first night of this show thinking I had perpetuated/confirmed a racist nightmare. In version two the scenes up until the end of the Senate were a real, modern world, with much of Iago's animal images filleted out. The remainder of the play was Brabantio's nightmare, when these images were reinserted, and during which he roamed as spectator: he occasionally influenced the action and he unleashed the uncontrollably destructive Iago.

One day during a break in rehearsals (for some reason) the conversation turned to Viagra (for some reason). One of the actresses turns to Olu and says 'Well, you wouldn't need that.' At a staff meeting the topic of sexual discrimination is raised; 'I vote Olu to be the rep' smirks an older Marxist colleague. Both remarks were intended as compliments, endorsements of Olu's physical beauty, but tied, I would suggest, to the stereotypical problems of:

Othellophobia
Othellophilia
negrobilia
Brabantioddities.

Iago is in charge of the stereotypes which drive the play – 'these Moors are changeable in their wills' (1.3.336) and 'I know our country disposition well: / In Venice they do let God see the pranks / They dare not show their husbands' (3.3.202–04) – and Othello internalises them (in the seduction/ temptation/capitulation scene, 3.3) – 'And yet how nature erring from itself-' (229) and 'O curse of marriage, / That we can call these delicate creatures ours / And not their appetites!' (270–72). Question: to what extent are these stereotypes 'internalised' by the text itself, as opposed to the characters it represents?

I gave a lecture to our Theatre and Society class entitled 'Monsters and Black Cool', in which I traced the 'coalescence' of early modern and postmodern stereotypes of blackness. I argued that modern Othellos, who begin according to black cool – e.g. gangsta rap or Samuel L. Jackson – and then, as their script demands, turn into monsters, further consolidate (and even exacerbate) the nasty binary which sustains the role. Leo Wringer (Nottingham Playhouse) and Ron Cephas Jones (Greenwich Playhouse) were especial agents/victims of this with their initially unflappable demeanours and subsequent monstrosities.

It is, though, a fine performance by Wringer – a fluent and accomplished Shakespearean actor whose soft and honeyed tones lapse into a raw, almost primitive utterance as he descends into madness.

The manner in which Jones allows his cool two-star general to become a caged animal pacing in ever smaller orbits to something crouched, reptilian [and] cowering …

The first, eclectic and contemporary, jarred because Othello went from Zen contentment to monster in a flash; the second, a US general in WWII, made Othello's investment in magic seem ridiculous.

The latter (1997) National Theatre Othello defined himself by reference to the former (1964). Of Olivier, David Harewood says, 'You can see the technique: the relaxed hands, hung low, the open mouth and the tongue stuck out', and yet as he gives into Iago he falls to his knees, rolls his bass Rs and beats his chest – Harewood, not Olivier. Then, the murderer, he grunts (16 times) like an animal.

John Ray Proctor – black American actor, scholar and martial artist – and I explored the possibility of staging *Othellophobia* in the US. His response to version 1: 'Your production makes Othello an animal, on so many levels, but it is not clear that Othello's animalism is caused by ... the white society in which he exists ... Your production repeats a cycle of ideology which posits that black men are thick tongued, aggressive and bestial ... making Othello an animal; I think I understand the impetus but I am absolutely positive that I cannot participate in this tradition.' He was right, about version 1 at least.

Perhaps surprisingly, the RSC's Education website is intent on demonstrating the historically constructed nature of discourses which underpin their universal author's works. The resources for teachers of *Othello* include this assistant director journal entry: '*Othello* is teeming with images of animals and beasts. Day Two: Text work, language, imagery. We discussed [Iago's] use of beasts and animal imagery to describe people and his consistent desire to reduce men and their actions to that of beasts'. Following this is an extensive list of the play's animal imagery and connections made to sexuality and jealousy.

Olu comes out of the rehearsal room at the Janacek Academy of Music and Performing Arts, Brno, Czech Republic. Suddenly he is surrounded by a group of skinheads. They menacingly start mimicking monkeys, the gestures and the all-too-familiar 'ooh-ooh' sounds an obscene parody of the choreographic work he has just been doing on an intercultural production of *The Wizard of Oz*. Some people watching from the outside laugh at the spectacle. He wants to tear them apart, all of them, and he is physically capable of it, but he just waits until the 'performance' ends.

Michael Neill writes that 'Iago locates their marriage in that zoo of adulterate couplings whose bastard issue ... are the recurrent "monsters" of the play's imagery'. Joyce Green MacDonald locates the transference of the monstrous to (include) the women in the play: they are 'racialized as black, assigned a set of negative sexual characteristics associated with Africa'. Bianca is described as a fitchew, which, along with monkeys, 'were thought to have particularly strong sex drives. Indeed, many early modern travellers gave credence to the notion that black Africans were the product of cross-species breeding between humans and apes'.

The teen adaptation *O* (2001) follows Shakespeare's structure with one very disturbing interpolated scene; in the grip of Hugo's lies, Odin, who is linked to a predatory hawk, begins his first sexual encounter with Desi tenderly but then, having imagined Michael in his place, brutishly thrusts into her until orgasm though she repeatedly shouts 'no'. Like the 2001 TV adaptation, Iago's temptations begin a third of the way into the film, but this 'spreading' of 3.3, though an acknowledgment that the capitulation is unjustifiably quick, at least in a contemporary version, fails, in both cases, to rationalise Othello's monstrosity.

Kenneth Muir's New Penguin introduction to the play lists, like a perverse rendition of Old McDonald's Farm, some of the text's animal references

'ass, daws, flies, ram, jennet, guinea-hen, baboon, wild-cat, snipe, goats, monkeys, monster and wolves'

spoken especially by Iago in the first three acts and then, almost as if accepting the baton, by Othello in Acts 3 and 4. To this list can be added, of course, the particularly sexualised and racialised references to the 'old black ram' and the 'Barbary horse' (1.1.89, 111).

In version 2 of the show we introduced more animals and more animal-like movements in order to better distinguish the 'real' world from the nightmare world. So not only did Othello move, at various times, like a bear, a tiger, and even the apelike creature, but there was also a snake, meercat, peacock, barracuda (actors!), cat and owl. On the soundtrack for the show were dogs barking and various other roars and screeches (directors!). However, whilst these additions added to the Goya-like disturbance of the staging, they muddied the notion that the text's obsession with animals is most expressly tied to Othello.

Olu and I had a big argument in rehearsal. I was pushing, in accordance with what we had talked about, or so I thought, about doing a literal monkey for the scene where Lodovico arrives (4.1.230ff.). 'I can't do it. I won't do it', he said. 'We've got to find a compromise.' I pushed further. He stormed out. After a while I went out and apologised. Then we did some work on the tiger and he was brilliant. The monkey eventually evolved into a movement he had learned from Australian Aborigines, an unnerving and performative glare at the audience, a very brave and confronting compromise.

This painting by Henry Fuseli perfectly encapsulated my idea for the production (a nightmare): the devil (Iago) sits atop the damsel (Desdemona), drawing her life from her; complicit and menacing, the Barbary horse (Othello) awaits his turn.

Brabantio has the nightmare – 'This accident is not unlike my dream' (1.1.141) – and Iago is the (unconscious, if you like) instrument through which the nightmarish devils and monsters are conjured. He says, 'Hell and night / Must bring this monstrous birth to the world's light' (1.3.385–86). Othello is right in supposing of Iago that there is 'some monster in his thought / Too hideous to be shown' (3.3.107–08), a thought which turns him, Hulk-like, into 'the green-eyed monster which doth mock / The meat it feeds on' (3.3.168–69), 'Begot upon itself, born on itself' (3.4.156).

One of the key themes of the nightmare was of being out of control: Iago goes out of control and wreaks havoc; the production itself was a monster that got away from me; the meanings I sought to generate mocked me and took on grotesque shapes. I explained this to a class, that I had attempted to do something with the play and that it had turned into a monster, a nightmare. A few years ago a group of boys had played the ending as a riotous comedy; a 17-stone hairy man played Desdemona, who, when attacked by Othello, retaliated with a series of devastating world wrestling moves – the play gave me the pile-driver.

My best friend at high school was an Aboriginal kid – black mum (a legend), white dad (not quite so impressive) – called Jeff. One day, coming home on the bus, I casually called him a 'black cunt'. He spat in my face and I wept for the entire trip (and never spoke of it). It was 'forgotten' but I had a recurring nightmare that I had gotten into heaven and that he had not (because he scored 7/10 on a test). During the rehearsals, whilst I was having dreams about Olu and I reconciling our friendship after the extreme tensions of the production, I received news that, back in Australia, Jeff had committed suicide.

Proctor's response to version 1 of the production was astute, and what I was hoping for, but in general white audiences did not respond this way. One of the problems was that Othello's animalism was, ironically enough, presented in a too naturalistic, and not sufficiently performative, manner. Thus, it was nightmarishly racist, to a certain viewer, but not enough for less (or differently) politicised viewers to be disturbed by an animal-like black man. One of my colleagues wrote; 'I thought [it] was going to be more exploratory than it was … I'm not sure what it was about the story that you found exciting or controversial.'

Iago was the instrument of the nightmare, Brabantio's unconscious unleashed. When the old man's nightmare began he simultaneously spoke some of Iago's words to Roderigo: 'An erring barbarian … she will find the error of her choice … I hate the Moor; let us be conjunctive in our revenge against him' (1.3.339ff.). From this point, Brabantio watched Iago carry out his demonic charivari. The problem, for Brabantio, was that Iago's menace could not be contained and thus not only was the marriage destroyed but everyone else with it. In version 2, Brabantio awoke, shocked, lights down.

IAGO

Awake! What, ho, Brabantio!

Brabantio sits bolt upright, as if waking from a nightmare, eyes staring.

INT. CASTLE – FLASHBACK FANTASY – NIGHT

Desdemona's arm is stretched over the bed, fingers splayed as in their earlier love-scene. Groans of pleasure. A hand reaches out to grasp her (as Othello did). This hand is white.

INT. BEDROOM – NIGHT

Othello's eyes flash open and he drops her hand in shock. He gets up.

Artaud's manifesto on cruelty was a key text for our shaping of the nightmare. In version 2 we had a blind man figure, mostly made up from Lodovico, who trampled all over both Cassio's wounding and Emilia's discovery of the murder. This expressed Quarshie's notion that 'Shakespeare's attempts to tie up the loose plot threads at the end of the play invite derision'. The blind man (and everyone else) kept accidentally bumping into Cassio's wound and then he looked in completely the opposite direction when Emilia pointed to the lamentable evidence. Perhaps needless to say, the actors with hitherto big moments were a bit miffed.

In the documents Newman uses to contextualise *Othello*, she finds 'always… the link between blackness and the monstrous, and particularly a monstrous sexuality'. Critiquing a 1983 *Cheers* episode, Marguerite Rippy observes the *Othello* myth perpetuated in the representation of an occasional character: 'a widening of the eyes, opening of the mouth, and general depiction of the stereotype of mental instability that recalls racial stereotypes from minstrel performance'. This reading puts the US on the psychoanalytic couch and unpacks a nightmare of 'the black sexualized beast threatening a white female victim'.

Othellophobia

i. A dread of watching Othello's stupidity and savagery.

ii. A series of fears related to stereotypical racist representation.

The production exploits the text's obsession with beastliness and the demonic by exposing these images through grotesque physical caricature.

I first noticed this fear/discomfort watching contemporary adaptations of the play; the teen film *O* and a TV film set in the London police department. When it got to the temptation scene (3.3), and Othello's impending credulity, I just couldn't watch any more.

'I hope it's not so unbearable on screen that people want to switch it off! ... I actually went to the filming on the day they were doing that scene [the murder], and it was really distressing to watch ... When they'd finished, Eamonn was in floods of tears, and poor Keeley was a physical wreck.' Andrew Davies' reflection on adapting a contemporary *Othello* (2001) reveals elements of othellophobia, but the uneasiness I am describing is more explicitly tied to the speed of 3.3, in particular, to Othello's too immediate capitulation – which is spread out in the film from the 40th minute – rather than the (consequent) violence of 5.2.

Can you identify the odd one out?

Quarshie argues that *Othello* endorses 'a racist convention'; he invents the word 'negrobilia' to 'describe the representations of black people commonly made by white people' which depict 'grinning "darkies" with woolly hair, thick lips and cavernous nostrils' and he suggests that *Othello* might be just such a representation. Thus he asks, 'if a black actor plays Othello does he not risk making racial stereotypes seem legitimate and even true?' and concludes that such an actor further risks 'personifying a caricature of a black man, giving it credence.' I agree with him but I still cast a black man as Othello.

Sometimes provincial reviewers comment most acutely. A local critic sardonically observed of the Concentric production that 'the decision to have Othello strip down and take a shower offered more beef to his cake than anyone expected.' For *Othellophobia* the city reviewers offered universalised praise, but found little offence in what was intended to be an offensive production; it was a scathing local critic who indirectly found me out: 'Olu Taiwo cuts a dash as the noble Moor, until he lapses into barely credible Black-and-White Minstrel parody.' Here, as a colleague observed to me, is a black man blacked up.

The students who had opted to turn *Othello* into a comedy explained to me that they didn't want their piece to be about race; it was to be about comic misunderstandings in relationships. On the spur of the moment I clutched at an analogy, not knowing where it would lead. *Titanic* (which I'd not seen) is a film, I said desperately, about love, jealousy and betrayal but it's all about the iceberg. *Othello* is also about all of those things but race is its iceberg: not just because of the racism in the world of the play, but because race shapes who the people are and how they act; it's the fucking iceberg!

Michael Ray Charles' artwork, controversial and negrobiliac, also influenced the production. He writes: 'a lot of blacks have accused me of perpetuating stereotypes, and I think there's a fine line between perpetuating something and questioning something. I like to get as close to it as possible in order ... to create that tension ... to have people question how they deal with these images.' He discusses an anxiety about responses to his art which label the subjects of his paintings as real people, not as images or representations. This problem is doubly resonant for the stage where the image is embodied by a real person.

Iago speaks (of) the 'blackest sins' (2.3.318), Emilia calls Othello a 'blacker devil' (5.2.132) and Othello himself internalises these ideas, supposing Desdemona's name as 'begrimed and black/As mine own face' and summoning 'black vengeance' to destroy her (3.3.388–89, 448). But worse than references such as 'thicklips' is Desdemona's description of Othello in the last scene. The text invites/invokes centuries of grotesque minstrelsy:

> ... I fear you, for you're fatal then
> When your eyes roll so ...
> ... why gnaw you so your nether lip?
> Some bloody passion shakes your very
> frame (5.2.37–38, 43–44)

Start neologising and it's difficult to stop. How about this? Brabantioddities: old white men misjudging the cultural climate (with reference to *Othello*). Example 1: After Quarshie had delivered his 'second thoughts' for the Shakespeare Centre (1998) an elderly gent apologised for the way *Othello* had been ruined by racism. Example 2: Ernst Honigmann's lecture at the Bath Shakespeare Festival (2003), in which he spelt out Desdemona's injudicious and corrective-inviting behaviour: Juliet Dusinberre followed this lecture with the remark, 'If your husband smothers you, don't forget it's your fault.'

'Ulrich Wildgruber,' writes Kennedy, 'his face obviously blackened in Negro Minstrel fashion, wearing a parody of an Emperor Jones Jacket, deliberately played Othello on the surface, underscoring the cliché and therefore deconstructing it... Ridiculously, and yet most movingly, as Wildgruber kissed and hugged her dead body, his black make-up smeared more and more on his cheeks, rubbing off onto Desdemona's white face.'

Olu's Othello was the fool at the end of the play described by Emilia. The aftermath of the murder was a clown trio with Desdemona playing 'straight', Othello the inept, and Emilia the reprimanding boss. First he had wearily (and in exasperation) to keep re-finishing the murder. Then, as Emilia entered he stood in front of the body, went this way and that to prevent its discovery, and when discovered, feigned shock that there she was (shoulder shrug, 'gosh'). When Emilia could not register that Iago was the villain, Othello almost throttled her – 'He, woman ... Dost understand the word?' (5.2.151). It's all there.

Honigmann notices that perhaps Othello is short-sighted, but it might be more accurate to say that he is an idiot; described by Iago whilst in the trance as a 'credulous fool' (4.1.43), his credulity, trancelike throughout, is capacious. After first calling him a devil and then realising he has been duped, Emilia chastises Othello for his stupidity:

'O gull! O dolt! / As ignorant as dirt ... O thou dull Moor ... O murderous coxcomb, what should such a fool / Do with so good a wife?'
Othello agrees: 'O fool, fool, fool!'
(5.2.162–63, 223, 231–32, 319)

Two commonplace observations about *Othello*'s double-time scheme: 1. It's brilliantly conceived. 2. You don't notice the inconsistencies watching it on stage. But 'To my mind, it happens too quickly', writes Quarshie of Othello's speedy capitulation to Iago's lies, which is the reason Oliver Parker's film splits 3.3 to different locations to imply the passing of time. This scene deserves the same ironic *Guardian* scorn offered to the hit TV show *24*: '10.0 **24** Kim continues her most-kidnapped girl world record bid.' This show's real-time scheme requires a day's action packed into every hour: farcical, but mostly overlooked.

The comedy *Othello* was a master-stroke. Originally, a black student had been cast to play the part but he had to decline for reasons outside the class. The group's first response to having to have a white actor play Othello was to erase race but then they conceived of a wigga Othello, something like an Ali G character. He had convinced himself that he was black, his simple bride had believed him, and the regiment went along with the fiction because of his prowess as a soldier. Othello constantly said 'innit', did some of the world's worst rap dancing to prove himself to the Senate and generally behaved like a total dolt.

One of the rehearsal techniques we used was of the *bouffon* as practised by Richard Cuming (who played Brabantio in version 1) via Philippe Gaulier via Jacques Lecoq. Lecoq writes that the *bouffon* made fun 'not only of what the person did, but also of his deepest convictions ... when *bouffons* appear on stage, it is always to depict society.' We applied this to the epileptic fit, where all of the other players came on stage as various grotesque and lewd beasts and mocked the enthralled general. Othello is just such a *bouffon* in the last scene as described by Desdemona; uncontrollably rolling, quivering and gnawing.

This review (of version 1) from a colleague casts me as the Roderigo-like fool – this was *Othello* for idiots:

'It was very simplistic – it reminded me of a 4-hander version of *Macbeth* that I did many years ago, for 5 to 11 year olds ... There seemed to be nothing new about this production – no new angles, explorations, takes, etc. – but almost the opposite. The black/white issue was so blatant and stereotypical, that the complexities were not even touched upon. I find this rather worrying in this complex multi-racial world that we live in.'

Michael Bristol, like Peter Zadek, is interested in the play's surface as an expression of its cultural depths: 'To think of Othello as a kind of black-faced clown is perhaps distasteful, although the role must have been written not for a black actor ... To present Othello with a black face, as opposed to presenting him as a black man, would confront the audience with a comic spectacle of abjection rather than with the grand opera of misdirected passion.' Part of my problem in turning this theory into practice was in casting a black man; I thought it could be negotiated but the various depths kept breaking the surfaces.

Zadek's *Othello* (1976) was a key influence on *Othellophobia*:
'The method, intended to affront and shock, also proved a supple means of connecting the audience to the "hidden" play, going beyond traditional psychology into the realm of cultural myth and cultural fear ... The director was most outrageous at the end, treating the last scenes in an overtly sexual manner ... The murder became a parody of a sex crime. When the audience laughed and shouted at him, Wildgruber shouted back, then recovered enough to continue the scene – five minutes or so of pandemonium, a pandemonium of comic terror.'

Desdemonas have been dubbed and risked being daubed: Lois Potter describes the 'fate of Suzanne Cloutier, [in Welles' film] who was cast as Desdemona entirely on the basis of her looks and sometimes literally deprived of voice and identity by being dubbed and doubled by other women actors'. Perhaps the distinct possibility of daubing, such as in the 1964 Laurence Olivier/Maggie Smith pairing, prompts Honigmann's editorial note on the lovers' encounter in Cyprus; 'two gestural kisses, perhaps without physical contact, as Othello's make-up might blacken Desdemona's face'. Historical, if not hysterical.

In *White Girls Are Easy* Dotun Adebayo finds a black man who 'has capitalised on the notions that eternally surround black masculinity'. In *Forbidden Fruit*, David Dabydeen connects 'plantation and slavery' ideas about the size of a black penis with a prevailing attitude that 'with a black male you [can] have vigorous, passionate, brutish sex'. Both documentaries interview women intent on pursuing the black cock fantasy, and Reginald D. Hunter's comedy show 'White Women' tells the story of 'two stereotypes fucking each other': he, giving in to being constructed as a predator; she, capturing/subduing a black man.

Desdemona first appeared from out of an on-stage box like a doll, complete with white face and rosy red cheeks. Her movements were similarly marionette-like, sometimes dependent on others for motion. In 3.4, when Othello, duped by Iago, demanded to see the handkerchief, Desdemona changed from being the doll into a vixen. She moved sensuously, produced the wrong handkerchief from a garter belt, and turned his inquisition into a sex game. Enraged he picked her up and placed her on a spot; she turned back into the doll and flopped forward, inanimate until Emilia came and straightened her.

Brabantio fashions his daughter as perfectly virginal and dutiful: 'A maiden never bold; / Of spirit so still and quiet' (1.3.94–95). From such an elevated position is her virtue inevitably turned to 'pitch' (2.3.327), inscribed as she is as 'whore', 'subtle' and 'cunning' (4.2.20, 70–71, 88). The latent readiness of this transition is signalled by the juxtaposition of the two ideas within Othello's wailing, 'be sure thou prove my love a whore' (3.3.360). She may have trouble saying the word but Desdemona must hear it repeatedly, first from her husband and then from Emilia, who incredulously, and in our production, comically, repeats it.

We explored patriarchal constructions of femaleness: 'Underneath the dichotomization of women into virgins or whores, *Othello* implies, lies the belief that women may simultaneously appear as virginal and yet be promiscuous.' I can accept an argument that Desdemona makes sense, that her change from active to passive is justifiable, but I cannot reconcile her response to being struck – 'I have not deserved this' – with her response to being called a whore – ''Tis meet I should be used so' (4.1.231, 4.2.106). This discontinuity emerges from the virgin–whore binary which is unable to sustain consistency.

Building on Belsey and Sinfield's exploration of female character discontinuity as represented by early modern play-texts, Werner shows how rehearsal methods perpetuate, but occlude such discontinuities: 'By reading a play's language as revelatory of a character's feelings ... voice work ignores the representational and dramaturgical strategies of the text and withholds from actors the tools to deconstruct patriarchal character readings. It focuses on character at the expense of the play.' Our tools to disrupt character were a juxtaposition of contrary subject positions; how the actor clings to consistency ...

The comedy group's Desdemona was played as broadly as possible and in total defiance of unified characterisation. Her entrance to the Senate meeting was bottom-first through the curtain and with her skirt tucked into her pants. She had uneven pigtails, boots, pink and purple tights and she spoke in a slow, uncomprehending drawl. She was so parodied, so thick, that she believed her deranged husband when he said that he was black. The tragedy Desdemona offered an opposite representation; here was a consistent character, but instead of the naivety being overly amplified, her supposed sexual duplicity was taken seriously.

Desdemona pops out of her box

'child-like in her innocence'

'He called her whore'

'O monstrous act'

One colleague wrote, 'I realised what a dismal part Desdemona is, but by Jo playing it as this luminous archetypal character it worked as a perfect foil to Iago.' The reviews focused on her being 'child-like in her innocence and naivety', 'movingly innocent' and having 'simple trust'. This was another characterisation which 'got away' from me; we had not intended to create an idealised and passive victim, but the way we attempted to sexualise Desdemona, at least in the nightmare, was ignored. Another colleague did notice, however: 'her change to temptress in the handkerchief scene made so much sense.'

The first iteration of Sudoku Shake-speare evolved into a pedagogical performance installation. I enlarge all 81 pages onto A4 pages and then lay them out in a studio space. After an introductory orientation, the participants are invited to walk around the space, pausing to read pages as they go. Then, after about 10 minutes, I ask one person to read a page they find especially interesting and see if someone else can read another page which relates to the first one. And so on. The exercise has improved, I think, after adding a final section where the participants turn the pages over and contribute their own thoughts on the play and performance.

Was the production (or play) destroyed or marred by the kiss and its aftermath, this moment of unintended hilarity? Not as far as I could tell. My feeling in the room at the time was that the audience was swept up in the joy of the Othello–Desdemona union and that their laughter became a celebratory confirmation of this. And soon after came one of the most powerful moments of the production: Desdemona smoothed the smudge on Othello's face. It was, at one and the same time, the actor Andre taking care of the actor Tom, but also, quite beautifully, a young bride taking care of her new husband.

The production featured several moments that might have been anticipated, but weren't, and could have derailed the momentum, but, in each case, somehow didn't. The Herald was a clown: he seemed to lend further gravity to what came before and after. Emilia forgot her dress, couldn't get Desdemona's corset off quickly enough. It didn't matter. It helped. Best of all, after Othello was reunited with and kissed Desdemona, they left very visible make-up smudges, each upon the other. And not only this, but Othello, with one especially marked smudge right on his nose, looked like a clown. The audience laughed a lot.

This is from the programme notes:

We are playing a game with 'Original Practices.' Rules of the Game:

1. all-male cast
2. all actors are in make-up
3. thrust stage, audience on three sides
4. shared light for actors and audience
5. actors directly address the audience
6. actors double parts
7. the text is cut to 'two hours' traffic'
8. no interval
9. there are two entrance/exits
10. recycled, period costumes
11. minimal rehearsal (24 hours)

'After all the ink I have spilt on *Othello*,' writes major authority, Virgina Mason Vaughan, 'I currently find myself in agreement with Quarshie. If the play is performed as written, I am not sure Othello's part should be portrayed by a black actor at all, and it should not be seen as the pinnacle of a black actor's career as it so often is.' Her curious, apparently unwitting opening metaphor of ink-spilling, suggests a paraphrasing of famous lines from the play that might describe recent academic calls, by Mason herself and by Steigerwalt, for productions deploying, such as I have, blackface: was this most ungoodly role made to write Moor upon?

Idea: Hip-hop concept album based on Othello. Themes of racial discrimination and loss of social mobility translate well into modern culture.

In the unpinning scene (4.3), it took Bob a long time to unlace the corset. It not only didn't matter, but enhanced the scene and production considerably. Desdemona was very definitely the centre of this all-male production and this wasn't just because of Andre's beautifully controlled performance. As Bob laboured with the untying, Andre just kept singing 'Willow, willow'. Still untying, still singing. It highlighted Desdemona's serenity (against all odds) and strength. And it perfectly demonstrated the dramaturgical ingenuity of this scene as everything slowed down and took a deep breath for what was about to unfold.

The following text was also included in the programme notes, but more as a justification for the controversial experiment, rather than a prescient anticipation of what would transpire: 'A black Othello is an obscenity. The element of the grotesque is best achieved when a white man plays the role. As the play wears on, and under the heat of lights and action, the make-up begins to wear off, Othello becomes a monstrosity of colours: the wine-red lips and snow white eyes against a background of messy blackness.' And yet, Tom's Othello also transcended grotesquerie: I found the ending deeply affecting; the play won again.

The unconventional doubles for the production included: Desdemona/Bianca (interesting in terms of the virgin/whore binary); Roderigo/Emilia (both stabbed in the back by Iago). Both of these doubles required dramaturgical/theatrical sleights of hand.

There was another beautiful moment during the undressing scene, and this one was only possible because it was a staged reading, rather than a full production. As Bob untied, Andre held both of their scripts and held Bob's so that he could see it to speak Emilia's lines. More likely in an unpolished, perhaps original practices production, the help one actor offers another after a mistake or accident – dealing with what Jeremy Lopez calls the innate 'ridiculous or inefficient or incompetent' element of early modern theatre – draws, this production suggested, the audience further into the event. Without a stumble, no help is required.

Carol Chillington Rutter wants (and succeeds, I think) to dismantle an argument that the reduced 4.3 in the Quarto text of *Othello* represents authorial or actor-driven editing (and improvement). She writes that 'The unpinning is a "big fuss," and its complicated physical business, written so that it must be conducted in front of spectators' eyes, constitutes both the significant labor and the theatrical meaning of the scene.' Given Rutter's powerful feminist commitment, the practice-led experiments, via which she discredits her targets, describe women playing the roles, but I think she knows this particular task requires male actors.

Tiring House

Dear Rob,
just a reflection on the *Othello* experience. I was struck by the experience of being in the tiring house. The fact that it was directly behind the stage gave you a feeling of being connected to the energy of the playing space, unlike the experience of being in the wings. All the screens and flats (and the bed) as well as the light gave a sort of domestic feeling and the two doors provided interesting traffic, a kind of negative image of what was happening on stage.
Cheers Tom

This is the tiring house calm before the storm. Bob, doubling Roderigo/Emilia, described the playing as by the seat of his pants. After being dragged off as the stabbed dupe, he couldn't find his dress quickly enough, and came out carrying it (wig askew): cue big laughs.

Lebron James, black basketball superstar, mimics King Kong, perhaps unwittingly, for the April 2008 *Vogue* magazine cover. He bares his teeth and holds supermodel Gisele Bundchen under one arm. When he leaves the Cleveland Cavaliers in 2010 as a 'free agent' he generates an Iago-like hatred. Team owner, Dan Gilbert, sends an open letter to the club's fans, declaring, 'You simply don't deserve this kind of cowardly betrayal.' A 2013 YouTube tribute to James, before he re-defects back to Cleveland, is soundtracked by DeStorm's 'King Kong,' the original music video of which is replete with risible (race-themed) fantasy.

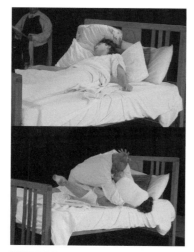

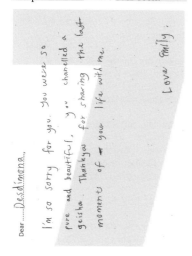

Dear......Desdimana...

I'm so sorry for you. You were so pure and beautiful, you channelled a geisha. Thankyu for sharing the last moments of my your life with me.

Love Emily.

I don't remember everything about Djanet Sears' lecture/performance for the 2011 World Shakespeare Congress in Prague but I should. Note at the top of my pad: 'Othello comes to Washington.' Next question from the playwright who offered, with *Harlem Duet*, such a brilliant transhistorical adaptation of / departure from *Othello*: 'who would Othello be if he were alive today?' But then: Olivier's Othello played on the big screen. And then the sound turned down. How ridiculous he looks. And then overlayed with Al Jolson, one of the funniest and most lethal deconstructions of both the play and production I have ever seen.

On 25 May, 2013, Adam Goodes, champion Indigenous Australian footballer, was called an 'ape' by a 13-year-old girl during a match against Collingwood. Collingwood's president, media personality Eddie McGuire, made a point of seeking Goodes out after the game and apologising on behalf of his club. On McGuire's morning radio programme four days later:

Co-presenter: ... the hand coming out of the Eureka tower. What a great promo that is for *King Kong*.

McGuire: Get Adam Goodes down for it, you reckon?

Co-presenter: No, I wouldn't have thought so.

The initial drive of this research project/production was to test, with all the limitations we were bringing to it – all-male cast, hastily-produced make-up, holding scripts on stage, etc. – whether an audience could still be caught up in the narrative, the tragedy, Iago's web. I wanted to measure this against the audience's tearful response recorded in Henry Jackson's letter: 'when she [Desdemona] fell back upon the bed she implored the pity of the spectators by her very face'. My collaborator on the project, Penelope Woods, came up with the inspired suggestion of soliciting our audience's feedback in the form of a letter.

Robert Shaughnessy subtitles the first section of a chapter on *Othello*, 'Othellophobia', a term used to denote troubled or hostile responses to the play, such as I intended with my production of the same name and the first iteration of this chapter as a journal article. He describes several seminal essays, most of them cited here (and elsewhere), 'which debated the possibility that Shakespeare's text might itself be complexly complicit with, or actively productive of, the sexual and racial stereotyping which older generations of critics had indulged, and more liberal modern critics had attempted to explain away, ignore or ameliorate'.

Two recent productions: in the pre-show to the NTLive screening of his production of *Othello*, Nick Hytner opines that the play could have been written yesterday. Well, the scene where senators questioned the leader of the armed forces about whether he had used 'indirect and forced courses [to] Subdue and poison this young maid's affections?' (1.3.112–13) just didn't, in my view, make sense. I do not believe that those (illegal) comments, would be made, at least in front of the man at whom they are directed. Much more brilliant is Ian Whitmore's *Othello: A Bestiary*, 46 concertina pages of images of the play's fauna (and flora).

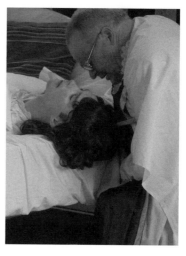

PERFORMATIVE NOTES

Page 54

Box 1.2. Celia R. Daileader, 'Casting Black Actors: Beyond Othellophilia', in Catherine M. S. Alexander and Stanley Wells, eds., *Shakespeare and Race* (Cambridge University Press, 2000), pp. 179, 185, 196.

1.3. Harold Bloom, *Shakespeare and the Invention of the Human* (London: Fourth Estate, 1999), p. 190.

1.5. Jane Meredith, 'Deadly Game of Consequences', www.newburytheatre.co.uk/archive/200302d.htm, accessed 9 June 2003.

1.7. See Jonathan Dollimore, 'Desire is Death', in Margreta De Grazia, Maureen Quilligan and Peter Stallybrass, eds., *Subject and Object in Renaissance Culture* (Cambridge University Press, 1996), pp. 369–386.

1.7. 'Othello takes a fearless turn', *Times Educational Supplement*, 12 March 2004.

1.9. Ray Fearon (Othello) and Richard McCabe (Iago), Royal Shakespeare Company, 1999, photograph by Donald Cooper, courtesy of the Royal Shakespeare Company Collection; David Harewood (Othello) and Claire Skinner (Desdemona), Royal National Theatre, 1997, photograph by Mark Douet, courtesy of ArenaPAL.

Page 55

2.2. Marvin Rosenberg, *The Masks of Othello: The Search for the Identity of Othello, Iago, and Desdemona by Three Centuries of Actors and Critics* (Newark: University of Delaware Press, 1961), p. 5.

2.2. Michael Bristol, 'Race and the Comedy of Abjection in *Othello*', in Robert Shaughnessy, ed., *Shakespeare in Performance* (Basingstoke: Macmillan, 2000), p. 165.

2.9. Screen captures from DVD recording of version 1 of *Othellophobia* (5.1, Desdemona's murder).

Page 56

3.2. Karen Newman, '"And wash the Ethiop white": Femininity and the Monstrous in *Othello*', in Jean E. Howard and Marion F. O'Connor, eds., *Shakespeare Reproduced: The Text in History and Ideology* (New York: Methuen, 1987), pp. 146, 147.

3.3. See Gāmini Salgādo, *Eyewitnesses of Shakespeare: First Hand Accounts of Performances 1590–1890* (London: Chatto & Windus, 1975), p. 30.

3.3. Kyle Brenton, 'Three Faces of Othello', www.amrep.org/othello/threefaces.html, accessed 23 May 2003.

3.5. Robert Gore-Langton, 'Black and White Moor show', *Times*, 19 February 2004.

3.5. Patrick Carnegy, *Theatre Record*, 12–25 February 2004, p. 243.

3.6. Terence Hawkes, *Shakespeare in the Present* (London: Routledge, 2002), p. 85.

3.8. See Virginia Mason Vaughan, *Othello: A Contextual History* (Cambridge University Press, 1994).

3.9. Abd el-Ouahed ben Messaoud ben Mohammed Anoun, Moorish Ambassador to Queen Elizabeth I, 1600, image courtesy of the University of Birmingham Collections; Ben Kingsley (Othello), Royal Shakespeare Company, 1985, photograph by Reg Wilson, courtesy of the RSC Collection.

3.9. Ben Kingsley, 'Othello', in Russell Jackson and Robert Smallwood, eds., *Players of Shakespeare 2* (Cambridge University Press, 1988), p. 173.

Page 57

4.1. Shannon Jackson writes in *Professing Performance: Theatre in the Academy from Philology to Performativity* (Cambridge University Press, 2004), p. 183, that 'Performativity names the iterative processes that do the "institutionalizing" in institutional racism and that do the "internalizing" in internalized oppression. Racism is thus the ultimate performative.' Though I've not the space to argue it here, perhaps the category of 'Shakespeare' could be substituted for racism in this sentence; thus Shakespeare becomes an 'ultimate performative', for example, in the way various iterations of Romeo and Juliet – pedagogical, theatrical, cultural, quoted and misquoted – construct romantic subjectivities.

4.2. William Shakespeare, *Othello*, Arden 3, ed. E. A. J. Honigmann (London: Arden Shakespeare, 2001), p. 61.

4.2. Ania Loomba, *Shakespeare, Race and Colonialism* (Oxford University Press, 2002), p. 95.

4.5. *The Stage*, 13 November 2003.

4.5. Posting on BBC e-feedback: www.bbc.co.uk/northamptonshire/stage/2003/othello/othello_review.shtml, accessed 10 July 2004.

4.8. Bruce R. Smith, *Shakespeare and Masculinity* (Oxford University Press, 2000), pp. 131–161.

4.9. See Kyle Lawson, 'That's Moor like it; Royal National Theatre does right by Othello', *The Arizona Republic*, 25 September 1997. Screen capture from *Othello* (1965), directed by Stuart Burge (original stage production directed by John Dexter) – Laurence Olivier (Othello) and Frank Finlay (Iago). David Harewood (Othello) and Simon Russell Beale (Iago), Royal National Theatre, 1997, photograph by Mark Douet, courtesy of ArenaPAL.

Page 58

5.1. William Shakespeare, *Othello*, New Penguin, ed. Kenneth Muir (Harmondsworth: Penguin, 1968), p. 22.

5.2. Michael Neill, 'Unproper Beds: Race, Adultery, and the Hideous in *Othello*', *Shakespeare Quarterly* 40 (1989), 410.

5.2. Joyce Green MacDonald, 'Black Ram, White Ewe: Shakespeare, Race, and Women', in Dympna Callaghan, ed., *A Feminist Companion to Shakespeare* (Oxford University Press, 2000), p. 196.

5.8. See www.rsc.org.uk/othello/current/home.html, accessed 26 August 2005.

5.9. This composite image was created by the production's designer, Alexandra Hoare: the base image is Francisco Goya's *The Sleep of Reason Produces Monsters* (1797–98); Photo: akg-images, London.

Page 59

6.2. '"And wash the Ethiop white"', p. 148.

6.2. Marguerite Hailey Rippy, 'All our Othellos: Black Monsters and White Masks on the American Screen', in Courtney Lehmann and Lisa S. Starks, eds., *Spectacular Shakespeare: Critical Theory and Popular Cinema* (Teaneck: Associated University Presses, 2002), pp. 39, 27.

6.4. Hugh Quarshie, 'Second Thoughts About Othello', International Shakespeare Association Occasional Paper No. 7 (Chipping Campden, 1999), p. 19.

6.5. Screenplay for *Othello*, dir. Oliver Parker (Columbia Pictures, 1995) obtained from www.geocities.com/thelunalounge/ site/sections/screenplays/screenplays.html.

6.9. Henry Fuseli, *The Nightmare* (1781); Photo: akg-images, London.

Page 60

7.2. 'Second Thoughts', pp. 3, 5, 18.

7.4. See 'Art:21', www.pbs.org/art21/artists/charles/clip1.html, accessed 27 November 2005.

7.5. 'An Interview with Andrew Davies', www.pbs.org/wgbh/ masterpiece/othello/ei_davies.html, accessed 27 January 2003.

7.7. Charles Hutchinson, accessed from www.mandanajones .net/othelloreview14.html, 9 June 2003.

7.7. Peter Patston, 'Tragedy lies in the treatment of Shakespeare', *Bath Chronicle*, 9 March 2004.

7.9. Michael Ray Charles, courtesy and copyright Cotthem Gallery, Brussels-Barcelona; Screen capture from *Othello* (1965); Laurence Olivier as Othello.

Page 61

8.1. *Othello*, Arden 3, pp. 17–19.

8.2. 'Race and the Comedy of Abjection in *Othello*', pp. 151–152.

8.3. 'Second Thoughts', p. 8.

8.4. Jacques Lecoq, *The Moving Body: Teaching Creative Theatre* (London: A&C Black, 2002), pp. 117–125.

8.5. Dennis Kennedy, *Looking at Shakespeare: A Visual History of Twentieth-Century Performance* (Cambridge University Press, 1996), p. 269

8.9. Ibid.

8.9. Ulrich Wildgruber (Othello), Hamburg, 1976, detail of photograph by Roswitha Hecke, courtesy of Deutsches Theatermuseum München, Archiv Roswitha Hecke; for the full image see *Looking at Shakespeare*, p. 269.

Page 62

9.2. Catherine Belsey, *The Subject of Tragedy: Identity and Difference in Renaissance Drama* (London: Methuen, 1985), pp. 149–221.

9.2. Alan Sinfield, *Faultlines: Cultural Materialism and the Politics of Dissident Reading* (Oxford University Press, 1992), pp. 52–79.

9.2. Werner, *Shakespeare and Feminist Performance*, p. 34.

9.3. Screened on Channel 4 (UK) on 30 May 2003.

9.3. Screened on Channel 4 (UK) on 4 December 2003; see www.bfi.org.uk/filmtvinfo/ftvdb/ for details on both documentaries.

9.3. See Fiachra Gibbons, 'Sexist and racist but certainly not surreal', *Guardian*, 14 August 2003.

9.4. Valerie Traub, *Desire and Anxiety: Circulations of Sexuality*

in Shakespearean Drama (London: Routledge, 1992), p. 34.

9.5. Lois Potter, *Othello*, Shakespeare in Performance (Manchester University Press, 2002), p. 142.

9.5. *Othello*, Arden 3, p. 175.

9.9. Screen captures from DVD recording of version 1 of *Othellophobia* (1.3, Desdemona's entrance; 3.3, the napkin; 4.2, false comfort; 5.1, murdered).

Page 63

10.2. Virginia Mason Vaughan, *Performing Blackness on English Stages, 1500–1800* (Cambridge University Press, 2005), pp. 105–106.

10.2. Jenna Steigerwalt, 'Performing Race on the Original -Practices Stage: A Call to Action', *Shakespeare Bulletin* 27:3 (2009), 425–435.

10.4. For the use of only two entrance/exits, which proved revelatory for rehearsal room decision making, we drew on Tim Fitzpatrick, *Playwright, Space and Place in Early Modern Performance: Shakespeare and Company* (Farnham: Ashgate, 2011).

10.9. Production photographs of the original practices *Othello* were taken by Olivia-Kate Glynn and are reprinted by her kind permission.

Page 64

11.2. 'Unpinning Desdemona (Again)', 114 (see Chapter 1, note 3 above). In the conclusion to this marvellous essay Rutter provides URL links to fascinating video recordings of her experiment being conducted with male actors.

11.3. This magazine cover was photographed by Annie Leibovitz and is easily accessible via Google images.

11.3. Dan Gilbert's letter accessed at www.webcitation .org/5r6UbJyWJ, 15 November 2014.

Page 65

12.2. Robert Shaughnessy, *The Routledge Guide to William Shakespeare* (London: Routledge, 2011), pp. 226–230.

12.3. Stathi Paxinos provides one of many newspaper articles on this local furore, 'McGuire apologises for Goodes King Kong gaffe'. www.theage.com.au/afl/afl-news/mcguire-apologises-for-goodes-king-kong-gaffe-20130529-2na8h.html, accessed 30 May 2013.

12.5. Borbonesa, *Othello: A Bestiary (with Floral Additions)*, illustrations by Ian Whitmore (Baskerville: Borbonesa, 2011).

12.8. Partially re-cited, see note for Box 3.3.

APPENDIX 2

***Othellophobia* Cast and Production team:**
Othello – Olu Taiwo
Desdemona – Jo Blake
Emilia – Sian Radinger
Bianca – Karen Tween / Anna Bosworth
Brabantio – Richard Cuming/ Marcia Carr
Roderigo – Chris Foulser
Montano – Nick Edwards / Danny Frost
Cassio – Kevin Matthews / Mark Young
Lodovico – Rebecca Scrivens
Iago – Olaf Mathar

Director – Rob Conkie
Designer – Alex Hoare
Composer – Guy Marshall
Movement Director – Olu Taiwo
Voice Work – Sian Radinger
Bouffon – Richard Cuming
Assistant Director – Adanna Oji
Stage Manager – Martin Hutchinson

***Othellophobia* Production details:**
The Arts Centre, University College Winchester: 27 November–
2 December 2003; 19–20 February 2004
Southhill Park Arts Centre, Bracknell: 26 February 2004
The Point, Eastleigh: 2 March 2004
The Bath Shakespeare Festival, Ustinov Studios, Bath: 8–9
March 2004
Central Studio, Basingstoke: 12 March 2004
The Old Fire Station Theatre, Oxford: 15–16 March 2004
The Blue Elephant Theatre, Camberwell, London: 24 March–
10 April 2004

***Othello* Cast and Production team:**
Othello – Tom Considine
Desdemona / Bianca – Andre Jewson
Roderigo / Emilia – Bob Pavlich
Brabantio / Montano / Lodovico – Chris White
Cassio / Senator – Tom Davies
Iago – Trent Baker
Duke / Herald / Soldier / Gratiano – Damien Millar

Director – Rob Conkie
Dramaturg – Penelope Woods
Designer – Ella Rowe
Production – Geoffrey Weber

***Othello* Production details:**
The Playroom, La Trobe University: 4 October 2013

CHAPTER 3

Red Button Shakespeare

The theme of interpretive variability in the previous chapter, Sudoku Shake-speare, is focused here, in Red Button Shakespeare, on the materiality and ephemerality of spectatorship, the notion that, as Andrew James Hartley puts it,

1. 'Schrödinger Effect', p. 233.

One's sense of what happened on stage is shaped by perspective, which may be about where in the house you were sitting (to one side, close enough to be spat upon by the cast, peering through opera glasses from The Gods) or it may be about where you happened to be looking at a given moment.[1]

In order to facilitate such multiple audience perspectives – and the interpretive variabilities they potentially make possible – whether in spat-upon or Gods-like, or a range of other proximities and orientations to the staged action, I have, for this chapter, fixed upon a model of interactive sports coverage, whereby the viewer can, by virtue of the remote control red button, appreciate the spectacle from a number of alternative perspectives.[2] On the football (soccer) pitch these include: regular viewing angle; bird's-eye view; goal-to-goal; 'player-cam'; high-lights reel; and 'fanzone'.[3] And in order to exemplify this argument of perspec-tive-informed-interpretation, I have chosen a production from the three-di-mensional and multi-perspectival reconstructed Globe Theatre (or, handy dandy, was it because I chose this theatre that I developed the argument?), Dominic Dromgoole's 2008 revival of *King Lear* starring David Calder as the king. I have focused on the blinding of Gloucester (3.7), the terrible mutilations of which I watched six times in the theatre – from a variety of vantage points, including: in the yard, 'front and centre'; from the upper gallery; side on, middle gallery; and 'behind' the action adjacent to the 'upstage' left and right corners of the stage – and then several times later via archive recordings.

The structural interactivity of the main body of this chapter, which juxtaposes each of these separate viewpoints, is designed to be performative, therefore, in that it evokes the simultaneity and multiplicity of the theatrical event. It is also intended as a challenge to performance criticism that silently elides its sit-uatedness in the best (or sole) seat in the house. That is not to say, however, that my methodology is without limitations. As Hartley continues in the ar-ticle cited above, performance criticism that depends on repeated viewings of the production, either live in the theatre or, more commonly, via the archival recording, distances itself, to some extent, from the experience of the general playgoer. Such a playgoer receives and responds to the production in the mo-ment, without bringing either the same degree of intertextual knowledge (or baggage) to the viewing experience, nor the desire to subsequently excavate the

2. Kim Solga reflects on two separate, and variously perceived (and received), viewings of the 2006 Strat-ford Shakespeare Festival production of *The Duchess of Malfi*. She writes that 'The first time I saw Hinton's production (on 1 June 2006), I confess I was under-whelmed ... I was seated high up on the stage-right side of the Patterson thrust; seeing from above (from a God's-eye view?) I felt somewhat divorced from the visceral pull of the action, inclined to dismiss the scene rather than let it challenge the limits of my expectation ... The next time I saw the show, more than two months later, my seat was downstage left, immediately beside one of the auditorium's two shared entrances; the actors on stage were slightly above me, and their harried entrances and exits lifted the hair on my arms and neck as they rushed on and off ... I felt as though I was seeing the pro-duction a second time with a different body.' *Violence Against Women*, p. 119.

3. Player-cam focuses exclusively on one player (for 15 minutes); Fanzone is a commentary on the game by an extremely zealous fan from either side.

production via its archival traces, nor, indeed, an intention to watch the production multiple times. Hartley thus argues that the academic performance critic's meta-spectatorial awareness might just as well mire, as elevate such criticism.[4] I offer a partial attempt to assuage these concerns: I tried to respond to the scene here discussed, from each of the various perspectives by which I apprehended it, as if I were watching it for the first time (an imaginative energy I would have more invested in had I known before the experiment what I learned during it), but I also acknowledge that the attempt that follows to represent theatrical multiplicity as it happened has only been possible because I have artificially represented simultaneity via omniscient-like reconstruction.

I have, albeit too neatly, aligned details of the production with the various viewing (and listening) perspectives. Thus, watching the production as a 'groundling', front and centre, I have focused on the actions and gestures of the actors. From the upper gallery, not quite the Gods as in the old Royal Shakespeare Theatre (Stratford-upon-Avon), I have concentrated on the overall blocking and movement of the scene. These descriptions are of the type John Russell Brown labels the 'factual details of staging at particular moments',[5] the former notes attesting to the micro-details of the action and the latter to the macro-, almost akin to an extended prompt-book. The left-side view (near to the left-side door of the stage) turned out to be a less than ideal vantage point, at least for the production as a whole. However, not being able to see very well did focus the aural narrative of the production, especially as I was directly beneath the thunder-making machine, so from there I have recorded sound effects, vocal inflections, non-textual vocals and audience responses. From the right-side view I ignored the action on stage and looked only and more closely at the audience, mainly in the yard, as they watched the scene. I have focused, in particular, on three teenagers leaning against the 'front' edge of the stage and have attempted to describe their body language, facial expressions and verbal responses, and on a couple further back in the yard, one of whom sought refuge in the theatre programme during the blinding. The status of such evidence is debatable but I am encouraged by Brown's further observation that 'any full account of performance must go beyond mere quotation or factual description and call upon impressionistic and very personal reconstruction'.[6] Susannah Clapp's review of the production provides an apposite summary of my intentions here:

The audience's ultra-audible reactions to all this – gulps and shudders and gasps and sniggers and bleats of encouragement, as if everything were being seen for the first time – are an amplifying layer to the action, an echo-chamber which demonstrates how quick-changing are the moods and incidents before you. If you recorded their reactions you'd hear the beat of the play. The Globe is Shakespeare's electro-cardiogram.[7]

I have simulated interactive sports coverage, and the facility to perceive the action of the blinding scene from alternative vantage points, via four parallel columns spread across a double page. Column 1 reproduces the text of the scene, including the deletions.[8] Column 2 documents the actions, gestures and movements of the scene; column 3 is the aural or soundtrack recording of

4. 'Schrödinger Effect', pp. 226–233.

5. John Russell Brown, 'Shakespeare's Secret Language', seminar paper, Shakespearean Close Reading, Old and New, International Shakespeare Conference, 2008, Stratford-upon-Avon, p. 2.

6. 'Writing about Shakespeare's Plays in Performance', in Grace Ioppolo, ed., *Shakespeare Performed: Essays in Honor of R. A. Foakes* (Newark, DE: Associated University Presses, 2000), p. 151.

7. 'I do like to be beside the sea. But what's for afters?' *Observer* online, 11 May 2008, www.theguardian.com/stage/2008/may/11/theatre.brightonfestival2008, accessed 10 January 2013.

8. The deletions are 'struck through'; the production was based on the Folio text of the play; the quotations hereafter are from the New Penguin

the scene; and column 4 is descriptions of the audience. Whereas the Sudoku structure of Chapter 2 created non-linearity and temporal dislocation, such that individual boxes sometimes only made (more) sense in relation to other boxes, here the notes in columns 2, 3 and 4 are recorded chronologically and in parallel with the moment that the text is spoken. Thus, the description of the text-in-production is 'thickened' by 'interactive' and parallel cross-references to its delivery, embodiment, staging, acoustic accompaniment and reception, and by select archival information from the music book and show reports.

The editors of *Shakespeare's Globe: A Theatrical Experiment*, Christie Carson and Farah Karim-Cooper, offer an introduction that I might appropriate for the four-column structure of Red Button Shakespeare and, indeed, for *Writing Performative Shakespeares* as a whole. They explain that 'Rather than flattening opposing positions, we have set up a structure that highlights differences in approach in order to propose a new kind of criticism that can incorporate a more complex understanding'.[9] I'm not sure whether this very valuable collection quite achieves those ideals, but applied here, this chapter seeks to raise rather than flatten (this word recalls Pascale Aebischer on the ephemeral nature of performance) opposing or varied spectatorial positions just as this book as a whole, though written by just one person, seeks to provide alternative and contrary critical voices (the next chapter, written in collaboration with someone else, playfully seats seven scholars around a table to discuss multiple viewing perspectives at a Shakespeare production (p. 103)). The performative aims of this chapter include a 'more complex understanding' of how theatrical meaning is contingent on the specificity of the experience of reception and on how documentation of audience response might be incorporated into analysis of such meaning. Carson and Karim-Cooper's book offers further comparative value for this chapter in that the structure of the first part on the 'Original Practices' Project is organised in a very similar fashion to my parallel columns: Stage action; Stage appearance; Music and sound; Actor/audience interaction. Given that Christie Carson goes on to explain that 'the volume has been designed to mimic the theatrical process of creation in that it allows each contributor to speak to his or her area of expertise in order to provide an integrated debate',[10] and that I too am attempting to offer an integrated 'mimic[ry of] the theatrical process', this synchronicity is perhaps not overly surprising. Lastly on this theme, the Globe has sought, as many professional (Shakespearean) companies do, to archive its productions on video/DVD. Unlike most of them, the productions at the Globe have been recorded from three perspectives; the cameras are labelled 'face-on', 'lozenge' (which refers to a diamond shape; the camera is at 45 degrees from face-on) and 'side-on'. The intention has been to preserve some of the three-dimensionality which the theatre architecture demands and which this chapter seeks to replicate.[11]

You have just finished reading the Introduction; what follows is the Interaction; finally, is the Interpretation, the hermeneutic drive of which will be impelled by the various viewing perspectives.

edition of the play, edited by George Hunter (1972) and introduced by Kiernan Ryan (2005).

9. Christie Carson and Farah Karim-Cooper, eds., *Shakespeare's Globe: A Theatrical Experiment* (Cambridge University Press, 2008), p. 6.

10. Christie Carson, 'The "Original Pratices" Project: Introduction', in *Shakespeare's Globe: A Theatrical Experiment*, p. 30.

11. Thus, I have illustrated columns 2, 3 and 4 with screen captures from this archival footage which almost precisely represent the same moment on stage from the three various perspectives (an asterisk in the text column pinpoints the screen captured moment). The face-on images, which offer a clear view both of the groundlings and of the octagonal stage projection (more of that below), illustrate the column dealing with, appropriately enough, the front and gallery view of the production. The lozenge images, which are closer to the stage and show less of the audience, but also, importantly, the balcony spaces, illustrate the soundtrack column. Finally, the side-on images, which are also from considerably above the stage, illustrate the audience response column. Unfortunately every one of these side-on recordings was poorly focused but this does at least preserve the anonymity of those 'photographed' as well as figuring the verticality of the space. I am enormously indebted to Globe Librarian Jordan Landes and Archivist Victoria Northwood for their help with these materials.

INTERACTION

3.7

Enter Cornwall, Regan, Gonerill, Edmund, and Servants　　Through the centre doors, Regan DSR, Edmund DSL

CORNWALL

Post speedily to my lord your husband; show him this　　DSC (with Gonerill), facing outward
letter: the army of France is landed. Seek out the villain　　Back to CS with an arm on Servant
Gloucester.

Exeunt some of the Servants

REGAN

Hang him instantly.　　At the right pillar x CS

GONERILL

Pluck out his eyes.　　DSC

CORNWALL

Leave him to my displeasure. Edmund, keep you our　　x past Edmund to left pillar, Edmund follows him
sister company: the revenges we are bound to take upon　　further left
your traitorous father are not fit for your behold-
ing. ~~Advise the duke, where you are going, to a most~~　　x CS to Gonerill, Regan x CSR
~~festinate preparation: we are bound to the like.~~ Our　　Cornwall kisses Gonerill on the cheek
posts shall be swift and intelligent betwixt us. Farewell,
dear sister: farewell, my lord of Gloucester.

Enter Oswald　　Centre door

How now! where's the king?

OSWALD　　CS

My lord of Gloucester hath convey'd him hence:
Some five or six and thirty of his knights,
~~Hot questrists after him, met him at gate;~~
~~Who, with some other of the lord's dependants~~
Are gone with him towards Dover; where they boast
To have well-armed friends.

CORNWALL

Get horses for your mistress.

GONERILL

Farewell, sweet lord, and sister.

CORNWALL

Edmund, farewell.

Exeunt Gonerill, Edmund, and Oswald

Go seek the traitor Gloucester,
Pinion him like a thief, bring him before us.

Exeunt other Servants

Drums play

Drums stop. Very fast text. Cornwall has a very deliberate speech pattern. He speeds up and slows down for effect. It is a controlled venom.

This is the last scene before the interval, almost 90 minutes into the production. Concentration is perhaps starting to wander. As Patrick Marmion wrote in the *Daily Mail* on 5 May 2008, 'with the interval held back for nearly two hours, the first half is particularly cruel on the £5 "groundlings" forced to stand in the open top arena.'

Indeed, a number of people are leaving before this scene, perhaps with sore feet or backs or perhaps delicate stomachs and aware of what is to come

A woman standing just to the stage right of the octagonal structure checks her theatre programme; she mentions something to her partner

Cornwall responds 'ah'

trA-A-Aitor, long pause, Gloucester …
bring-him, pause, before-us … Then a LONG pause

Though well we may not pass upon his life
Without the form of justice, yet our power
Shall do a courtesy to our wrath, which men
May blame, but not control.* Who's there? the traitor?

Enter Gloucester, brought in by two or three

REGAN
Ingrateful fox! 'tis he.

CORNWALL
Bind fast his corky arms.

GLOUCESTER
What mean your graces? Good my friends, consider
You are my guests: do me no foul play, friends.

CORNWALL
Bind him, I say.

Servants bind him

REGAN
Hard, hard. O filthy traitor!

GLOUCESTER
Unmerciful lady as you are, I'm none.

CORNWALL
To this chair bind him. Villain, thou shalt find—

Regan plucks his beard

GLOUCESTER
By the kind gods, 'tis most ignobly done
To pluck me by the beard.

REGAN
So white, and such a traitor!

GLOUCESTER
Naughty lady,
These hairs, which thou dost ravish from my chin,
Will quicken, and accuse thee: I am your host:
With robbers' hands my hospitable favours
You should not ruffle thus. What will you do?

CORNWALL
Come, sir, what letters had you late from France?

REGAN
Be simple-answered, for we know the truth.

CORNWALL
And what confederacy have you with the traitors
Late footed in the kingdom?

Corn. brings forward a chair, slowly and deliberately

Long, sexual kiss with Regan, near right pillar*
He continues looking at Regan, not at the brought forth
Gloucester

x L and then turns to face Gloucester

Gloucester standing behind the chair
(slightly USC; *locus*)

There are three servants behind Gloucester, Cornwall is
to his left and Regan to his right

With a thick rope, his arms by his side

Gloucester gestures his innocence with his hands
(which should be pinioned)

Cornwall clicks his fingers to motion the Servants back.
He puts his hand on Gloucester's shoulder, almost
comfortingly

He continues the one-man good cop/bad cop act; he
grabs Gloucester by the hair and pulls his head back

Sounds of struggle from off-stage, including Gloucester's muffled cries

The woman starts reading the programme again

The audience switch their focus from the kiss next to the right pillar to the centre doors, through which Gloucester is being brought

An elderly man with a white beard leaves the yard; does he know what's coming next?

Gloucester cries 'oh' as he is pinioned

The woman turns the page, keeps reading

The woman looks up momentarily at the binding of Gloucester

Gloucester emphasises 'UNmerciful lady'

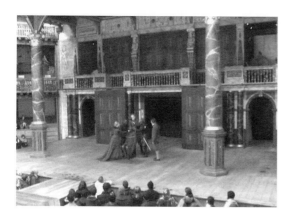

Enter the lute player, Arngeir Hauksson, above right 'Play INTRO & play ever so softly & sparse' (music book)
'Come sir', almost as if to the musician; from above he plays a pleasant tune on his lute. After a considerable pause, Cornwall speaks to Gloucester, 'what letters ...?' Regan stretches the vowel on 'simple'

trA-A-Aitors

Attention in the yard is wandering; my feeling is that many in the audience do not know what is coming next

REGAN
To whose hands have you sent the lunatic king? Speak.

GLOUCESTER
I have a letter guessingly set down,
Which came from one that's of a neutral heart,
And not from one opposed.

Cornwall clips the back of Gloucester's head

CORNWALL
Cunning.

REGAN
And false.

Cornwall and Regan semicircle Gloucester; Cornwall x
right pillar, Regan x left pillar

CORNWALL
Where hast thou sent the king?

GLOUCESTER
To Dover.

REGAN
Wherefore to Dover? Wast thou not charged at peril—

CORNWALL
Wherefore to Dover? Let him first answer that.

GLOUCESTER
I am tied to the stake, and I must stand the course.

REGAN
Wherefore to Dover,* sir?

GLOUCESTER
Because I would not see thy cruel nails
Pluck out his poor old eyes; nor thy fierce sister
In his anointed flesh stick boarish fangs.
The sea, with such a storm as his bare head
In hell-black night endured, would have buoy'd up,
And quench'd the stelled fires:
Yet, poor old heart, he holp the heavens to rain.
If wolves had at thy gate howl'd that stern time,
Thou shouldst have said 'Good porter, turn the key,'
All cruels else subscribed: but I shall see
The winged vengeance overtake such children.

The ferocity of his response makes Regan jump back;
she appears temporarily startled

Cornwall, moving from the right pillar to USC, takes off
his dark jacket to reveal a crisp white shirt. He stretches
theatrically [and gets Gloucester's prop eye from the
upstage ledge of the right pillar]
Regan turns away, seemingly a bit bored

CORNWALL
See't shalt thou never. Fellows, hold the chair.
Upon these eyes of thine I'll set my foot.

Again, Cornwall looks at Regan, not Gloucester, as he
says this

GLOUCESTER
He that will think to live till he be old,
Give me some help! O cruel! O you gods!

Cornwall puts his finger 'in' Gloucester's eye, pulls it
out, complete with lengthy eyestalks, and throws it
backstage. Regan gives an excited shudder

REGAN
One side will mock another; the other too.

Regan claps her hands at the right pillar and then moves

Singing from above accompanies the lute
      Lute player

This text is done very swiftly
Bang

   Bang

Regan cruelly sounds the 'Wherefore to Dover' text as if Gloucester is deaf and stupid

A young woman reels back from the stage, seemingly startled by Regan's venom

Gloucester's reply separates each word of the first two lines, giving special emphasis to his defiance.
Regan gives a surprised laugh

The woman reading the programme looks around at other people in the yard, then back to it again

He-e-e-e-elpppp …. O-o-o-o-o-h … both Cornwall and Regan also wail, simultaneously with Gloucester, though theirs is a triumphant mockery of his pain

She looks up, looks back down; her partner looks at her, she's looking away now

CORNWALL

If you see vengeance—

First Servant

Hold your hand, my lord:
I have served you ever since I was a child;
But better service have I never done you
Than now to bid you hold.

The servant steps in between Cornwall and Gloucester

REGAN

How now, you dog!

First Servant

If you did wear a beard upon your chin,
I'd shake it on this quarrel. What do you mean?

CORNWALL

My villain!

They draw and fight

Cornwall head butts the Servant and then kicks him in
the groin. He takes a sword from the other servant but
is slashed across the belly

First Servant

Nay, then, come on, and take the chance of anger.

REGAN

Give me thy sword. A peasant stand up thus!

Regan takes a dagger from the unwitting other servant,
and stabs 1st servant from behind

Takes a sword, and runs at him behind

First Servant

O, I am slain! My lord, you have one eye left
To see some mischief on him. O!

Dies

CORNWALL

Lest it see more, prevent it. Out, vile jelly!*
Where is thy lustre now?

GLOUCESTER

All dark and comfortless. Where's my son Edmund?
Edmund, enkindle all the sparks of nature,
To quit this horrid act.

Cornwall holds Regan by the thigh as she takes out
Gloucester's other eye. Note the young woman unable
to watch …. Regan puts her hands over, and perhaps
inside, Gloucester's eyes

REGAN

Out, treacherous villain!
Thou call'st on him that hates thee: it was he
That made the overture of thy treasons to us;
Who is too good to pity thee.

Regan throws the eye backstage, wanders near the right
pillar rubbing her hands together, and then wipes her
face with the blood. Cornwall lies back on the floor,
almost post-coital, but then can't get back up because of
his wound

GLOUCESTER

O my follies! then Edgar was abused.
Kind gods, forgive me that, and prosper him!

REGAN

Go thrust him out at gates, and let him smell

Regan points towards the 'front' of the stage

to Gloucester and daubs herself with his blood so that
she has red eye-shadow

Regan lets out an involuntary 'oh' as the eye is produced and then another, more enjoyed and shrieked 'oh'. The audience are a mixture of laughter and 'eurrgh' sounds; mostly laughter, for a good few seconds. This gives way to tittering.

Show Report (8 May 2008):
'The strands on the left eyeball came off during the blinding.'

Backing away from the front of the stage and not leaning on it

Show Report (19 July 2008):
'Rather a lot of fainters today. Three in middle gallery, one in upper and two in lower gallery as well as one in the yard just before interval which then triggered a whole lot of copy cat faints.'

Open-mouthed, and moving up and down, as if to protect themselves but still be able to see

Show Report (17 July 2008):
'Mr Hamilton Dyer made contact with Mr Bishop's face when he head butted him in the G. blinding scene. This is apparently because they lost contact of each other's hands. Mr Bishop has a cut on the inside of his top lip and it is a little swollen but he is ok.'

Shrinking and turning away; again, hands over mouth and then wringing of hands
A father shields his daughter who, right next to the octagon, turns away from the scene

Again, all three of them scream as the other eye is taken out. 'O-o-o-u-u-u-t-t-t' – Gloucester, 'No, no' – 'v-i-i-i-i-l-e j-e-e-ll-y.'
'Where / is / thy / lu-u-u-stre / now? Again, there is laughter, not as much as before, and 'eurrgh' sounds from the audience
Regan is panting, sort of post-orgasmic sighing. 'h-A-A-A-t-es thee'.

Show Report (24 June 2008):
'Mr Mydell lost a contact lens during the blinding scene.'

The woman with the programme turns away again; she holds the programme in front of her, almost as a buffer; now she is clutching the programme

Backing away from the stage again, pointing at the blinded Gloucester

Looking at one another grinning

His way to Dover.

Exit one with Gloucester

This exit takes a very long time, because Gloucester and his aide are the last figures off the stage

REGAN
How is't, my lord? how look you?

From the right pillar

CORNWALL
I have received a hurt: follow me, lady.
Turn out that eyeless villain; throw this slave
Upon the dunghill. Regan, I bleed apace:
Untimely comes this hurt: give me your arm.

Cornwall manages to stagger to the left pillar. Regan crosses to him and they share another long kiss. Cornwall's shirt and Regan's face are covered in blood

Exit Cornwall, led by Regan

Centre doors

Second Servant
I'll never care what wickedness I do,
If this man come to good.

Third Servant
                              If she live long,
And in the end meet the old course of death,
Women will all turn monsters.

Second Servant
Let's follow the old earl, and get the Bedlam
To lead him where he would: his roguish madness
Allows itself to any thing.

Third Servant
Go thou: I'll fetch some flax and whites of eggs
To apply to his bleeding face. Now, heaven help him!

*Exeunt severally**

Gloucester is helped, his hand outstretched, downstage and over the extra thrust, down its steps and through the audience, who part to allow him through. A sword and the chair are left on stage

On the kiss the audience cannot help but laugh
(although not for the very last performance)

The song and lute continue

There is murmuring in the audience
Applause

The song continues into the interval. It is a traditional
Norse song called 'The Wanderer', perhaps speaking for
both Lear and the just-blinded Gloucester:

Indeed I cannot think
Why my spirit
Does not darken
When I ponder on the whole
Life of men
Throughout the world

Starting to discuss what happened

Show Report (6 May 2008):
'A lady fainted on her way out of the theatre at the
interval, then again on West Piazza. She was treated in
the first aid room where she made a quick recovery. She
blamed the lapse on the eye gorging [*sic*]!'
Show Report (11 May 2008):
'As Mr Mydell and Mr Egyiawan were walking DS after
the blinding, a member of the audience fainted just in
front of the SL treads. Naturally, she was surrounded by
people trying to help. Mr Egyiawan calmly steered Mr
Mydell towards the SR treads and they exited through
Door 3.'
Front of House Show Report (11 May 2008):
'Another man fainted soon after the interval began.
Both blamed the combination of the heat and the "eyes
scene". Neither felt able to return to the theatre.'

INTERPRETATION

My argument is that the physical – not to mention emotional, intertextual or ideological – perspective/s of the spectator shapes the way they (are able to?) respond to and interpret the action staged before, besides, below or around them. Therefore, this third section will provide analyses of the play and production that were enabled by the specific vantage points from which I viewed it. Before moving to this interpretive section, though, I will reflect on my choice of the blinding scene as the metonymic engine driving both the production and the following analyses. It is a largely unsurprising choice, I suppose, focal as the scene has proved in both the critical and production history of the play. J. I. M. Stewart's mid-twentieth-century focus on this scene, for example, explores, irrespective, or perhaps even because of, its physical barbarity, the 'disinterested aesthetic concern'[12] which creates a structural, thematic and expressive completeness. More recently, Jay Halio, in a brief note, also focuses upon the structural underpinning and importance of the scene, though the structure he appeals to is mytho-poetic, the scene's 'profound underlying motivation'.[13] These observations are further underlined by the history of the play in performance, where, in many productions, including the one under discussion here, the blinding of Gloucester immediately precedes, and builds up to, the interval, a fact sometimes explained by the desire to prevent audience members coming back late after the break in order to avoid the violence.

Watching the production from the 'front and centre' of the yard focused a particular kind of response. Indeed, the front and centre of the yard was itself focused by an extra thrust, an outcrop of staging made of a short jetty and an octagonal platform which projected another twenty feet into the yard, and from which steps descended into the yard and facilitated entrances and exits through the groundlings (as well as this, an additional facade was inserted on the 'upstage' wall with sliding doors which removed about four foot of the stage depth). One problem of this imposed architecture, at least from my overall, if not front and centre, perspective, was that it reduced the wooden O into a D or perhaps an arc.[14] Thus, as significant amounts of the action occurred on the projected octagon, in the midst of the spectators, as it were, the staging seemed to treat the pillars as a proscenium arch and to leave most of the stage area closest to the exits largely ignored. This meant that the yard areas to the 'side and back' were mostly unpopulated, even when the production was sold out, and that upper gallery seats to the back and side represented very poor viewing value. I will return to the benefits this afforded me for the aural reading of the production, but, by contrast, front and centre, at £5, if you could stand for the pre-interval 100 minutes, represented excellent value.

The discomfort produced by such a long time standing perhaps encouraged the groundlings to empathise with the pain Gloucester was about to go through: and this is the key to my yard interpretation. Here, front and centre, and so often directly appealed to, this position foregrounded the notion of empathy, sympathy and identification with the dispossessed or those suffering within the play. Like Miranda's viewing of the tempest, the groundlings could proclaim of

12. J. I. M. Stewart, 'Blinding of Gloster', *Review of English Studies* 21:84 (Oct. 1945), 266–270.

13. Jay Halio, 'Gloucester's Blinding', *Shakespeare Quarterly* 43:2 (Summer 1992), 223.

14. Tom Cornford discusses this somewhat contentious issue (and more) in 'Reconstructing Theatre: Shakespeare's Globe under Dominic Dromgoole', *New Theatre Quarterly* 26:4 (Nov. 2010), 319–328.

both the blinding and this play's own storm scene, as well as other moments, 'O, I have suffered / With those that I saw suffer!' (*The Tempest* 1.2.5–6). Thus, the key lines of the production, in terms of this perspective/interpretation, were Lear's heartfelt

> Poor naked wretches, wheresoe'er you are,
> That bide the pelting of this pitiless storm,
> How shall your houseless heads and unfed sides,
> Your looped and windowed raggedness, defend you
> From seasons such as these? O, I have ta'en
> Too little care of this.   (3.4.28–33)

This speech was delivered from the octagonal platform and predominantly and directly to the yard audience. The rest of the theatre was still and silent and David Calder's Lear was able to conversationally and empathetically discourse with those just a few feet from him, in stark contrast to the noise of the storm and his almost doomed attempts to shout above it. Unfortunately, each time I saw the production the weather was perfectly clement and thus any of the unique kinds of new Globe frisson which develop from atmospheric serendipities were absent.[15]

Though such bad weather was absent (during my visits), the 'poor naked wretches' were palpably present. At times they were amongst the yard audience with strange sound devices stressing the atavistic nature[16] of the play (I cannot seem to keep the aural reading discrete from this one), and they were sometimes also on stage, in particular during the hovel scene (3.6). Benedict Nightingale observed that 'You won't see many Lears … discover such sympathy for the world's "poor naked wretches", here a swarm of vermicular men'.[17] They came up through the trap with a loud crash and then gathered 'upstage' on pillows as Lear madly arraigned his elder daughters. That these accusations were offered also to the audience forced an incongruity with the words; as Lear shouted and pointed outwardly it made no sense when the Fool joked and also pointed to the audience, 'I took you for a joint-stool' (Q sc. 13.47), when several such stools were on the stage itself. Also up from the trap, and mostly naked and wretched, was Poor Tom and he too did many of his 'set pieces' from the added stage projection. Lear seemed to identify with Poor Tom: as part of the younger man's antic disposition was to wave to imagined creatures in the yard and lower gallery, the older man's genuine lunacy followed suit and mirrored his mad-fellow; he watched him wave and then he, too, waved, comically straining to see at whom he waved. The identification was most poignant after twice (again comically) wondering whether Poor Tom had bequeathed his lands and all to his daughters, Lear appeared to understand their common situation and slowly embraced him. Here, the two men were identified as distressfully dispossessed; the groundlings, and the audience as a whole, were invited to sympathise with them and they did on several occasions via an audible 'aaaah' response.

Gloucester, of course, was about to be included in this fraternity of distress and dispossession and the audience was similarly invited to sympathise with

15. Penelope Woods writes about such 'aleatoric effects', as well as fainting, in 'Shakespeare's Globe Audiences: Old and New', in Bruce R. Smith and Katherine Rowe, eds., *The Cambridge Guide to the Worlds of Shakespeare*, vol. II, *The World's Shakespeare, 1660 to the Present* (Cambridge University Press, 2015). More of that in chapter 5. Victoria Northwood alerted me to the remarkable weather for the production on 1 May; the rain began on Lear's 'I shall go mad', the line prior to Cornwall's 'Let us withdraw; 'twill be a storm' (2.4.281–82), it gathered momentum by the time Cornwall advised 'Come out o'the storm' (2.4.304) and was torrential until Poor Tom was discovered in his hovel.

16. Stewart, 'Blinding of Gloster', 265.

17. Benedict Nightingale, 'King Lear at Shakespeare's Globe' *Times* online, 5 May 2008, www.thetimes.co.uk/ tto/arts/stage/theatre/article1868662.ece 495, accessed 22 July 2008.

18. Nightingale, 'King Lear at Shakespeare's Globe'.

19. 'Feeling his howl of pain', *Evening Standard* online, 6 May 2008, www.standard .co.uk/goingout/theatre/ feeling-his-howl-of-pain- 7406194.html, accessed 20 July 2008.

20. Julie Carpenter, *Theatre Record* 28:9, 496.

him. Ironically enough, Joseph Mydell's Gloucester was presented as so sympathetic that many of the reviewers found it difficult to identify with him. Nightingale thought him 'a Gloucester so mild that you half-expect him to help out at his own eye extraction'[18] and Nicolas de Jongh reckoned somewhat heartlessly that 'Joseph Mydell's Gloucester suffers minimally'.[19] Perhaps the actor had read these reviews because later in the run he seemed to have acquired something of an edge, particularly in this scene. Though he looked back and forth at his interrogators as they spat their questions at him, he stared straight ahead into the audience on that moment when perhaps he moved from being, as Julie Carpenter observed, 'ineffectual',[20] to defiant and determined: 'I am tied to th' stake, and I must stand the course' (3.7.52). It was almost as if he was drawing strength from the yard for what he knew was inevitably coming, a baiting, whipping or worse. And then when his eyes were ripped out the audience responded very vocally (see below). As a final moment of powerful connection before the long-awaited interval, Gloucester staggered with the help of a servant from the chair to the octagonal platform. Arm outstretched and trying to find his newly blinded way, his first steps towards Dover were down into the yard and through the shocked, amused, entertained, not infrequently fainting, and included audience.

From above, the change, in relation to watching the scene and the play from the centre of the yard, was not of inclusion to exclusion but of participant to observer. Thus, whereas the 'poor naked wretches' text exemplified the groundling perspective, from this upper gallery point of view the most resonant part of the play (for me) was Gloucester's Kottian despair, 'As flies to wanton boys are we to th' gods; / They kill us for their sport' (4.1.37–38). And whilst the production might have cast those on the ground as wretches, this architectural perspective cast the viewers, for their much more expensive tickets, as gods watching the action unfold, present but removed. This experience, of witnessing the cruelty at a remove, of watching the movements unfold with far less direct contact or acknowledgement from the actors, reinforced a detached and voyeuristic relation to the mercilessness on display and made an explicit connection (again, for me) to the horrific images of torture from Abu Ghraib. It would have been possible, of course, to interpret the scene in the light of those recent abuses without the advantage of the upper gallery perspective but it served to focus several interesting parallels. Firstly, the notion of experiencing the violence at a mediated remove: in the upper gallery this was as a detached god looking down, akin to the film noir overhead camera; in the case of the Abu Ghraib images their availability was not within touching distance, as for a groundling, but by photographs accessed through the internet. Thus, in both cases was a theatricalised violence moved from a private to a public sphere and, even more disturbingly, a significant aspect of that theatricality was of a masochistic sexuality.

This aberrant sexuality was introduced to the scene by Cornwall. Preparing to torture Gloucester, Cornwall took off his jacket, a gesture half world wrestling and half pornographic film. The kiss he shared with Regan as he rationalised their 'wrath' was prolonged and sexual and it seemed clear (to me) that his ensuing violence was a means of proving and igniting his virility and that it would take the form of a sex game. This fantasy was reinforced by his continuing to stare lustfully at his wife as he declared (to Gloucester) that 'Upon these eyes of thine I'll set my foot' (3.7.66). If, as Jay Halio, after the psychoanalysts, observes, the blinding represents a 'symbolic castration of Gloucester',[21] in this production it also served, albeit briefly, considering Cornwall's imminent death, as an erotic stimulus, a savage Viagra. Regan was very quick to catch on, such that she confirmed what Aebischer has revealed to be almost a theatrical cliché in the middle daughter's portrayal, that of 'ferocious sexuality'.[22] At first, and I am prematurely sampling the aural record of the production again here, Regan's non-verbal response to the removal of Gloucester's first eye was of shock and thrilled surprise but the sound almost immediately developed into a kind of pre-orgasmic moan. From the blood of this first eye she perversely daubed herself with eye-shadow but further indulgences were to follow. Spurred on by the thrill of dispatching the servant, Regan joined Cornwall so that she extracted the second eye herself. She raised her knee and Cornwall gripped her thigh as they both screamed in echoed pleasure at Gloucester's excruciating pain. This time, with the blood on her hands from her own act of violence, she covered her face with it, luxuriating in the bloodlust. When she taunted her victim with, 'Thou call'st on him that hates thee' (3.7.86), she fingered his eyeless sockets and offered a brutal enactment of the castration trope. This godless sexuality, with its all too contemporary (if also Jacobean) confluence of violence and eroticism, was on view to the gods who were either powerless or simply too disinterested, akin to the majority of western liberal response to Abu Ghraib, to intervene.

I have had some difficulty in deferring the soundtrack reading of the scene and play, so integral has it been to the other perspectives, but here I privilege that particular perspective or, perhaps more accurately, hearing. The sounds I am focusing upon include delivery of text, non-verbal sounds, sound effects, music and audience responses; this last series of sounds also blurs my interpretative categories. As mentioned earlier I was alerted to this reading because of my attempt to watch the play from the 'back' and 'left side' of the stage. Not able to see much of the action, which was obscured by the stage-left pillar when relatively static and on the octagonal platform, and beneath the thunder and wind machine, I focused instead on what I could hear; I suppose, to paraphrase the most illustrative text from the rest of the play, from here I was seeing the play 'feelingly'. Or, to push this slightly further, this was a Gloucester-like blind-spot which enabled an other-sensory perspective.

Ironically, the blinding scene itself was perhaps best apprehended from this vantage point; whilst much of the play was obscured from here, the unwatchable was clearly on view, located at the locus. Perhaps the director Dominic Dromgoole had intuitively hit upon Bruce R. Smith's contention that 'An actor may occupy the position of greatest *visual* presence at the geometric center of the playhouse, but he commands the greatest *acoustical* power near the geometric center of the space beneath the canopy'.[23] I have already mentioned the various screams and moans from the stage and I will later return to the various groans and laughter in the audience, but the most striking element of the soundtrack in this scene was of the accompanying lute and song: interestingly, the former sound was diegetic, that is, contained within the world of the play, whereas

21. 'Gloucester's Blinding', 222.

22. Aebischer, *Shakespeare's Violated Bodies*, p. 180.

23. Bruce R. Smith, *The Acoustic World of Early Modern England: Attending to the O-Factor* (University of Chicago Press, 1999), p. 214.

the latter sound was non-diegetic, working in the same way as a film score. As Cornwall prepared to extract the information he required from Gloucester, he gestured to a musician above, perhaps a paid employee of Gloucester's own castle if this is not making of the play too realistic a world, and clicked his fingers to cue a song. The lute player duly obliged with a gentle tune and continued to play throughout the torture scene and until the interval. The singer joined in later but given that she repeated her musical motif at various moments in the production I have described this music as non-diegetic. The website from which I obtained these definitions notes that 'A play with diegetic and non-diegetic conventions can be used to create ambiguity (horror), or to surprise the audience (comedy)'[24] and both of these effects were certainly created in this scene. The instruction and intrusion of the lute, I would argue, even more forcefully than associations to Abu Ghraib, connected this scene to Quentin Tarantino's controversial debut film *Reservoir Dogs* (1992).

The obvious connection here is between the torture – in particular, the severing of the police officer's ear in the film and the extraction of Gloucester's eyes in the play – and also in the way extreme and aestheticised violence uncomfortably juxtaposes with comedy. Stevie Simkin has written similar comparative analyses and observes that 'Early modern tragedies, like graphically violent horror movies, often walk a fine line between seriousness and camp, between shock and laughter'.[25] He continues to provide examples from *The Duchess of Malfi*, *'Tis Pity She's a Whore*, *The Atheist's Tragedy* and especially *The Revenger's Tragedy*. He also notes, appositely for this discussion, that 'At the other end of the spectrum, the blinding of Gloucester in Act 3, Scene 7 of *King Lear* (1604) provokes nothing but shock and horror, unless performed ineptly, or with parodic intentions'.[26] These ideas were, and were not, borne out by the new Globe's staging of the blinding of Gloucester; shock and horror were probably present, although the measuring of such responses might prove difficult, but there was also considerable laughter and the scene was performed neither ineptly nor with parodic intentions. The laughter was an effect, I think, of the appeal to the *Reservoir Dogs* culture, where not just Gloucester, but many of the audience themselves, were stuck in the middle with Cornwall and, Miss Blonde, Regan.

The repeated similarities of the two torture scenes beg the question of whether it is more Tarantino, as famous for his creative plagiarism as Shakespeare, who has influenced the new Globe staging of Gloucester's blinding, or whether he has ripped the scene off, in a demonstration of cycles of violence, from his Jacobean forbear. In any case, the following parallels and juxtapositions may be observed:

1. the victims are both 'tied to a chair'[27] (KL > RD)
2. the torturers both theatrically remove their jackets as if 'getting down to business' (RD > KL)
3. the victims both cue their own torture (KL > RD)
a. Gloucester's protestations that he 'would not see thy [Regan's] cruel nails / Pluck out his [Lear's] poor old eyes' and that he 'shall see / The wingéd vengeance overtake such children [Gonerill and Regan]' (3.7.54–55, 63–64) prompts

24. http://filmsound.org/terminology/diegetic.htm, accessed 2 June 2008.

25. *Early Modern Tragedy and the Cinema of Violence* (Basingstoke: Palgrave Macmillan, 2006), p. 192.

26. Ibid., p. 193.

27. The quotations which refer to the scene from *Reservoir Dogs* are taken from Simkin's description, which highlights parallels with *The Revenger's Tragedy*; see *Early Modern Tragedy*, pp. 194–996. Simon Brown made some helpful observations on these parallels.

his punishment: 'See't shalt thou never' (3.7.65)
b. Marvin, the police officer, probably wishes he hadn't defiantly proclaimed, 'you can torture me all you want'
4. the victims are tortured to playful musical accompaniment (RD > KL)
a. K-Billy's Supersounds of the Seventies plays the Stealer's Wheel tune 'Stuck in the Middle with You'
b. Gloucester's lute player
5. the victims have their faces horrendously disfigured, eyes and ear (KL > RD)
6. the victims' wounds are mocked (RD < > KL)
a. Regan fingers Gloucester's eye-sockets as she reveals Edmund's treachery
b. Blonde speaks into Marvin's severed ear
7. both torturers are interrupted (and eventually killed) by an appalled spectator
8. the appalled spectators who intervene are both killed by accomplices of the torturers

One moment where the two scenes diverge is the actual viewing of the disfiguring violence: the audience at the Globe can decide for themselves where to look; in the film, this decision is made (directorially) for the audience.

There is one detail of this scene, especially well viewed from the 'left back' position, that I have yet to discuss, and it is akin to the perverse, 'black comedy' described above. The Globe's props department, perhaps striving for anatomical authenticity, provided eyes (both of which were hidden on the 'upstage' side of a pillar ledge) with lengthy and blood-dripping eyestalks. In my view, it was these grotesque, tentacle-like sinews that prompted the audience's prolonged laughter and groaning after each gouging, and so exaggeratedly gruesome were they that I cannot believe that they were not intended to produce a mixture, in what was a regularly funny production, of comedy and horror. Perhaps the ambivalent presentation and reception might be theorised along Bakhtinian lines where the dislocation is produced because the comical grotesque of corporeal materiality properly associated within the 'lower bodily stratum' was here relocated to the eyes, more typically figured as windows to the soul. Stewart cites, in order to contest it, Robert Bridges' argument that Shakespeare's frequent depiction, and, regrettably, seeming celebration, of all kinds of debasement, was more a reflection of the audience than the author; he describes, after Bridges, 'the depraving effect of the playhouse public upon Shakespeare's art'.[28] In this production such depravity was staged in order to provoke and appeal to a playhouse public whose appetite for spectacular violence, both shocking but also comical, was fed not by bear-baiting, whipping and hanging but by parallel representations – maiming, dismemberment and decapitation, in cinemas and at home on DVD.

In moving towards a conclusion, I will reflect on some critical writings about Gloucester's blinding, especially as they relate to audience reception, and also as they were either consolidated or challenged by the experience of being in, and watching closely, an audience watching that act at the new Globe. Edward Pechter's argument in relation to this scene that 'In the main our range of response is limited to mental action – sympathy, antipathy, perhaps judgment; and no other play of Shakespeare's … involves an audience so directly and deeply

28. Stewart, 'Blinding Gloster', 264.

29. Edward Pechter, 'On the Blinding of Gloucester', *English Literary History* 45:2 (Summer 1978), 183.

30. Stewart, 'Blinding Gloster', 269.

31. Ibid., 268.

32. Indira Ghose, *Shakespeare and Laughter: A Cultural History* (Manchester University Press, 2008), p. 198. Ghose lists a number of theories of laughter that pertain to the reaction to Gloucester's torture: 'a strategy of self-defence that enables us to face sources of fear or pain', p. 7; 'a hydraulic safety-valve for the unconscious', p. 9; 'Laughter at horror simultaneously invokes and domesticates precisely those aspects of the world that induce terror in us', p. 200.

33. *Shakespeare's Violated Bodies*, p. 159.

34. Ibid.

with its characters'[29] sounds like a Hazlitt-like commitment to the play on the page, but he attributes these responses to spectators, not readers. He omits, lacking the advantage of an open air, reconstructed theatre space, performative responses such as laughter, gasps, groans and chatter or physical movement such as turning away, shifting position, clutching one's belongings, fainting or leaving the theatre altogether. Stewart, also lacking an approximate reconstruction of Shakespeare's theatre, but echoing much recent commentary on the new Globe, supposes that 'the physical conditions of the Elizabethan public playhouse … evoked far stronger suggestions of participation on the part of the spectators than a modern theatre allows'.[30] He also wonders of the 'ruder part of the audience', those in the yard, whether they would respond to the blinding of Gloucester 'with malevolent glee'.[31] Though the 'ruder part' of the new Globe audience laughed at the blinding I detected not a hint of malevolence. In that three of my closely attended subjects were teenagers I might colloquially (and perhaps patronisingly) relate their response as, 'Oh my God, I can't believe they did that; that was so gross.' A measure of this absence of malice was the silence that invariably greeted Regan's callous order, and the best joke of the scene, to 'Go thrust him out at gates and let him smell / His way to Dover' (3.7.92–93). Indira Ghose has written that this line is 'saturated with a savage sense of humour that the play incessantly replays',[32] but not once in the productions I witnessed, either live or recorded, did this line receive even a titter of response. Stewart's surmise about the 'ruder part' of the audience was confirmed to some degree, however, given that the spectators in the upper gallery did not, as far as I could tell, respond with the horrified laughter in the way that their less financially able, and usually somewhat younger, co-audients had. Thus, not only has the new Globe focused further dimensions of audience response, it has also, especially by virtue of the methodology deployed here, revealed the way audience response can be differentiated according to the specific place of reception.

Pascale Aebischer has provided the most recent and concentrated analysis of this scene in the theatre:

It is one thing to know that Gloucester is blinded, but quite another to listen to and, especially, to watch the mutilation, to use our own eyes to watch the removal of somebody else's eyes in a space (the theatre) that is so contained that the audience, if it does not intervene, is made to feel complicit in the violence perpetrated.[33]

Aebischer somewhat overstates her argument when she writes 'that today theatregoers still find the scene literally unwatchable'[34] (although at least one of the audience members I have focused on in this chapter seems to confirm this notion) and I feel there are aspects of this complicity debate that likewise require further teasing out. Simkin has similar reservations about Quentin Tarantino's explication of comedy and complicity in the ear-severing scene:

'I kinda defy anybody to watch Michael Madsen do that dance and not kind of enjoy it', he remarks on the DVD commentary, claiming that the comic lead into the torture implicates the audience: 'You are a co-conspirator.' However, Tarantino makes no attempt to analyse any further what this might mean in terms of audience response, or the audience's *awareness* of its response. Perhaps this lacuna, conscious or not, is simply a recognition that the scene does not have the power to do any such thing.[35]

35. *Early Modern Tragedy*, p. 197. Italics original.

I will return to these ideas shortly. There were occasional gestures in the new Globe audience that attested to the scene being 'literally unwatchable', hands in front of faces, turning away and such, but for the most part people looked on, even if between their fingers, with a mixture of shock and fun. I certainly, as a committed researcher, watched closely and much enjoyed the spectacle, even though I decided years ago, after watching David Fincher's brilliant film *Se7en* (1995), that I would not subject myself to such films, the most recent and particularly joyless incarnation of which has been the torture porn made famous by the *Saw* franchise. I watched, enjoyed, but in no way felt complicit in the stage violence that I witnessed. I must concede that I probably erred in watching the blinding scene from the upper gallery on my third visit to the production: by this time I was fully aware of what would unfold – desensitised, as it were – and thus the potential of the scene to implicate me in its terror was somewhat dissipated. If I had first watched the production from above I might have been appalled not only by the grotesque actions played upon the stage, but also by the barbaric and heartless responses of the £5 'stinkards'.

Perhaps part of the reason for me rejecting the notion of being complicit in the yard (and yet suspecting that I may have felt otherwise in the upper gallery) is explained by Aebischer's use of the word 'contained'; the implication, as I read this, is that the confinement of the theatre space exerts a kind of moral stifling of the ethically compromised spectator. The new Globe, again along Bakhtinian lines, might be thought of as an open and excessive rather than classical and closed space, and one that resists containment in the way that a darkened proscenium auditorium perhaps does not (at least as easily). Accordingly, the upper gallery space might be figured as in between the yard and a darkened auditorium in its capacity to contain (incidentally, sitting in the Gods at the Globe you are protected from the rain but neither can you see much of the sky). Thus, in the least contained (and most exposed to the elements) yard space the visceral impact of the violence is shared by the collective, visible and unruly audience and made comic, perhaps by what Simkin calls 'the audience's *awareness* of its response'. Finally, though, Aebischer is arguably right about complicity if the laughter and groaning exhibited by the yard audience could be said to represent an intervention. Aware of their own response and unable to silently acquiesce to the horrors they see depicted, even as they know they are fictional, but also reflective of real events they have witnessed through hyperreal representations, the audience resist their implication in the events through groans, giggles, laughter, shielding their eyes or turning their backs.

It is not surprising, I suppose, that my analyses should highlight such contemporary readings of the historically staged text given that my interpretative structure has been inspired by relatively recent developments in viewing technology. Perhaps Dominic Dromgoole's background in directing new writing also emphasises the contemporary within the historical in his new Globe productions. Though I would probably have identified the specific intertexts without this structure – and without using Gloucester's extracted eyes as interactive and interpretative red buttons – it has certainly focused, via the priority afforded alternative perspectives, my commentary on identification/sympathy and on complicity/intervention. But I will conclude by returning to reflections on methodological shortcomings and on possible future directions. I can imagine, for example, future 'fanzone' work where the four or more perspectives are contributed by different viewers watching a production at the same time, a project which would mitigate against this chapter's dependence on multiple and inevitably accumulative viewings. At a meeting of performance-focused Shakespeareans in Stratford-upon-Avon to consider the purpose and future of theatre reviews, six separate reflections upon this *King Lear* production, including the first draft of this chapter, were discussed. The most striking observation of all, offered by someone who did not see the production, was that the six papers might have described six different productions. I have here attempted to articulate variance, but I forecast and invite – and, indeed, at one point in the next chapter, begin to stage – more concertedly collaborative, indeed *Rashomon*-like, tellings of theatrical stories.[36]

36. Eve Kosofsky Sedgwick describes her seminar assessment, 'Collaborative Archaeology', thus: 'With your group, settle on a topic that has some autobiographical resonance for each of you ... Don't choose a topic that will disguise the differences among your experiences, but one that will let you explore such differences. Think about good ways of structuring a short but multivoiced, multiperspective, multihistory *archaeology* of this topic.' 'Teaching "Experimental Critical Writing"', in Phelan and Lane, eds., *Ends of Performance*, p. 114.

APPENDIX 3

Cast and Production team:
Goneril – Sally Bretton
Earl of Gloucester – Joseph Mydell
Lear's Fool – Danny Lee Wynter
King Lear – David Calder
Duke of Albany – Fraser James
Regan – Kellie Bright
Duke of Cornwall – Peter Hamilton Dyer
Cordelia – Jodie McNee
Earl of Kent – Paul Copley
Lear's Knight – Kevork Malikyan
Edgar – Trystan Gravelle
Old Man, Doctor – Paul Lloyd
Oswald – Ashley Rolfe
King of France – Beru Tessema
Duke of Burgundy – Ben Bishop
Ballad Singer – Pamela Hay
Bedlamites, Knights, Soldiers – Michael Jarvis, Ben Lee, Richard Marshall, Fabian Spencer and Kurt Egyiawan

Director – Dominic Dromgoole
Designer – Jonathan Fensom
Composer – Claire van Kampen
Choreographer – Sian Williams
Fight Director – Renny Krupinski
Text Work – Giles Block
Movement Work – Glynn MacDonald
Voice & Dialect Work – Jan Haydn Rowles

This production played for 68 performances at Shakespeare's Globe Theatre, London, between 23 April and 17 August 2008.

CHAPTER 4
Graphic Shakespeare

So. You want to use comics to write about Shakespeare. Why?

Hmm.

I want to evoke performance on the page...

... to try to get across a sense of what it was like actually being there...

... to represent different perspectives on the action - close ups, overhead, reverse angles - the materiality of embodiment, atmosphere, audience responses...

Alright, let's do it!

Whoa, whoa, I'm still looking for the right show!

One month later.

RING! RRRING!

Hello?

Bernard? Rob. Got it.

to get into bed with them.

At **Roman Tragedies**, audience perspective, at least for those on stage, is individuated: partial, transitory, autonomous (maybe). As many as 20 screens draw these various, multi-directional gazes. Sometimes live action is closer than a screen but is ignored in favour of the subtitle-providing, televisual mediation.

You denied the people their corn!

Hey! That's **us**!

We **demand** that this request be denied!

Coriolanus is nothing but a beast!

But for all this mediation, we are on stage with the actors.

May hell devour the people!

Actions which had been safely on screen can suddenly threaten to spill your drink.

I witnessed Caius Martius' outburst from the stage at the Barbican. From the auditorium, with its view both of the stage and the action taking place on a large screen above it, it may have read differently, as an embarassing and undignified outburst by someone unable to control himself when given the responsibility of appearing in front of the world on television. From the stage it was an excitingly theatrical expression of anger which suggested the corporate world could not entirely contain political passion...

BRIDGET ESCOLME

96

Scott's point was brought into close (and multiple) focus in the ingenious staging of 2.1 and 2.2 of **Julius Caesar**, the inter-weaving of agonised husband-and-wife conversations.

Brutus sits behind the desk: Portia is 90 degrees to him. Directly facing Brutus, Caesar and Calpurnia sit on a large sofa, hand-in-hand and fingers locked.

Above them, the action is magnified and subtitled on the four-square screen.... Portia looks straight at Brutus as she voices her fears. He's not listening. He looks straight at Caesar.

Dear my lord, make me acquainted with your cause of grief.

Then, frustrated with Brutus' evasions, Portia sits with Calpurnia and Caesar. Not literally, of course, but ghost-like, emblematically. The conversations overlap, the spaces bleed into one another. Three-on-one, Brutus is isolated by his covert ambition.

But then Caesar gets up and sits on Brutus' desk. Now the women faced the men and the couples spoke to each other across scenes, stage and screens. This visual device juxtaposed the two women talking sense to their ears-stopped-by-bravado, deaf-to-them husbands.

Of all the wonders I know, the most strange is that people are afraid...

Impervious to their wives' sensible pleas, the men depart (each to their tragic fates): Calpurnia curls up with cushions and Portia lies foetus-like on the desk-made-bed.

The scene-ending text...

Nothing I can be certain of, but much that I fear, may happen.

...could've been uttered by either or both of them.

GAIUS JULIUS CAESAR   100-44BC

Friends.

Romans.

Countrymen.

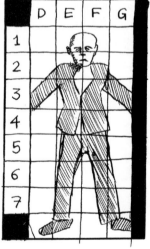

300 minute mark

TWO MORE PAGES UNTIL THE DEATHS OF ANTONY AND CLEOPATRA.

Cleopatra left the stage to chase the Messenger into the auditorium, but Enobarbus, guilt-wracked by his betrayal of Antony, left the building altogether. He leaves the almost-empty stage (we're all back in our seats now), runs through the foyers and out into the street.

The filthiest gutter is too good for what remains of my existence.

He unravels in Dutch, staggering in front of cars and then collapsing like a beggar before bemused Adelaide pedestrians. We follow all this on the screens and cheer his re-entry into the theatre.
Then, a noble Roman, he throws himself into the Death Zone.

Enobarbus' death takes place in the final strange hour of the production. Strange because, after the final set change, we have been asked to vacate the stage. It looks empty and lonely up there without us.

On stage, we were witnesses, our with-ness constitutive of **Roman Tragedies'** performative force.

The set is reduced to a bland, waiting-room banality by our absence.

The deaths of Enobarbus, Antony and Cleopatra take place, literally and figuratively, at a remove from us.

And in the dying moments of **Roman Tragedies**, the Death Zone, which has been carefully preserved all evening ("Kindly do not walk between de glass walls at the centre of de stage") for single deaths becomes overrun

MARCUS ANTONIUS 80-30 BC

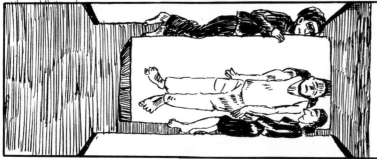

as Iras and Charmian pile in with Antony

and then, Cleopatra herself. Onstage, the dead now outweigh the living. Which would not have been the case had the audience still been up there.

And finally, when Augustus Caesar, silky-smooth media operator, arrives to discover that Cleopatra has cheated her of a trophy-laden victory parade, she sends in a paramedic team (complete with defibrillator) to try to revive her. No dice. The DeathZone is now crowded with the dead and the quick, as Augustus fumes outside.

Documenting this alchemy, Brutus takes **our** picture.

When the curtain call comes, it's a relief to see the stage full once more. The audience stands to cheer, to acknowledge the bravura performances, to confirm their participation in an epic event, and to connect once again with the actors with whom they have shared a stage.

But of course, I'm not trapped in a cramped historical-political-cultural engine like he was.

We spill out into the warm Adelaide night, retracing Enobarbus' steps of an hour earlier.

Am I?

End

CHAPTER 5
Engaging Shakespeare

I conceived the title of this chapter before (consciously) encountering Bruce McConachie's *Engaging Audiences*. Especially coincidental is McConachie's opening sentence: 'I decided to use "engaging" in the title of this book when I was performing a role in a Pittsburgh production of *Richard II*':[1] this chapter emerges from my having performed a role (or three) in a Perth (Australia) production of *Henry IV, Part 1*. This word, *engage*, and its derivatives, which McConachie unpacks via Shakespeare's histories, turns up frequently in discussions of (Shakespearean) theatre, particularly where those discussions focus on audiences. Inviting a mode of performative writing almost thirty years ago, Bert O. States, for example, warns that 'the danger of a linguistic approach to theater is that it is apt to look past the site of our sensory engagement with its empirical objects'.[2] More recently, Matthew Steggle, offering analysis of early modern applause, describes this period's drama as 'a machine of communal, demonstrative, and participatory engagement with literature'.[3] And Bridget Escolme, investigating the excessive emotions of the early modern theatre, both then and now, looks to uncover 'the dramaturgy of the plays and the ways in which they were rhetorically structured to engage audiences'.[4] Each of these quotations helps me to articulate the central concerns of this chapter, but the following two longer quotations are especially apposite. The first is from Anne Bogart's foreword to Erin Hurley's *Theatre & Feeling*, where she writes:

An actor noticing a beeper going off in the back of the theatre or responding to a fellow actor's sudden change in tempo, all the while maintaining the forward momentum of the play, engages the audience in this very balancing act [of intense concentration and awareness] on a moment-to-moment basis.[5]

The second quotation, which echoes the first, is from Stephen Purcell's *Shakespeare and Audience in Practice*:

... when the Globe or an 'immersive' company make claims for a more engaged spectator, it is not an empty boast. The engagement may not be a primarily intellectual one, but involvement in a performance which leaves the heart racing and the adrenalin surging has very real effects on a spectator's moment-by-moment experience, including the process of making meaning.[6]

The focus of this chapter is that this 'process of making meaning' is embedded – or, perhaps more accurately, embodied – within an affective engagement, what I am going to call cumulative performative affect.

1. *Engaging Audiences: A Cognitive Approach to Spectating in the Theatre* (New York: Palgrave Macmillan, 2008), p. 1.

2. *Great Reckonings in Little Rooms: On the Phenomenology of Theater* (Berkeley: University of California Press, 1985), p. 7.

3. 'Notes Towards an Analysis of Early Modern Applause', in Katharine A. Craik and Tanya Pollard, eds., *Shakespearean Sensations: Experiencing Literature in Early Modern England* (Cambridge University Press, 2013), p. 118.

4. *Emotional Excess on the Shakespearean Stage: Passion's Slaves*, p. xix.

5. *Theatre & Feeling* (Basingstoke: Palgrave Macmillan, 2010), p. xi.

6. *Shakespeare and Audience in Practice* (Basingstoke: Palgrave Macmillan, 2013), p. 144.

Here is my argument: the affective force of a Shakespeare play in performance – the way that Shakespearean production engages its audience – is created at the confluence of a number of affective spheres. These affective spheres might include, for a given production: the varying emotional states of the actor (actor affect); the emotional journey undertaken by the character (character affect); the audient's/audiences' response to the emotional vicissitudes of the story (narrative affect); the audient's own emotional stories, especially as they intersect with the concerns of the narrative (personal affect); and, particular, though not perhaps unique to Shakespeare, the dramaturgical orchestrations of the theatre event (here, performative affect). I can express this argument mathematically:

Actor affect
(for example, continuing to perform whilst grieving,
or continuing confidently, as Anne Bogart notes, amid distraction)
+
Character affect
(for example, Rosalind coping with having a banished father,
being banished herself, falling in love and managing a very peculiar forest)
+
Narrative affect
(for example, the audience, having ridden Imogen's emotional
roller-coaster with her, experiences, in Matthew Steggles' phrase,
'communal, demonstrative, and participatory engagement' in
the multiple revelations of the final act of *Cymbeline*)[7]
+
Personal affect
(for example, an audience member recently reunited with
a lost or estranged relative, watches *The Comedy of Errors*, *Twelfth
Night*, *King Lear*, or any of the late plays and re-experiences the 'heart
racing and ... adrenalin surging' described by Stephen Purcell)
+
Performative affect
(for example, the atmosphere specific to a production
perceptible via Bert States' notion of 'sensory engagement', or,
to parse Bridget Escolme, the plays' dramaturgically structured
invitations to traverse player–audience separation)
=
Cumulative Performative Affect

This equation, I suppose, is applicable to any Shakespearean performance event, but it is a sub-argument of this chapter that the affective spheres I outline above, and the potential confluence they create, is most likely, or perhaps most visible, in productions which fall under the very broad categorisation of 'original practices' (OP). Steggles' phrase, 'communal, demonstrative, and participatory engagement', is precisely the kind of marketing discourse – and not an 'empty boast', according to Purcell – deployed by theatre administrations such as those

7. Such as I witnessed at Mike Alfreds' 2001 production of *Cymbeline* at Shakespeare's Globe.

at Shakespeare's Globe or the Staunton Blackfriars theatres.[8] In any case, this chapter will consider cumulative performative affect via an 'originalish practices' production of *Henry IV, Part 1* at the (approximately reconstructed) New Fortune Theatre at the University of Western Australia in Perth, in September of 2011.

First, some details about the production, perhaps the defining feature of which was the use of just five men to stage the play. The use of an abbreviated cast, and the theatrical mischief-making such a decision necessitates, was inspired by Jaq Bessell's 2010 production of *Antony and Cleopatra*, which used only two actors,[9] and the six-actor Globe *Cymbeline* cited on the previous page. Alan C. Dessen documents twenty-five years of five-actor productions which toured the United States as part of the ACTER (A Center for Teaching, Education and Research) / AFTLS (Actors from the London Stage) programs, productions whose numerical minimalism is evaluated 'not [as] a limitation but an asset'.[10] Dessen celebrates the inventive and frequently virtuosic transformations – of properties (8), of bodies and characters (14), and of the stage space itself – required/impelled by this approach. His descriptions of one actor who 'flipped a coin as Orsino and caught it as Feste' (14) and of another doubling Rosencrantz and Guildernstern via a half-turn with one white and one black glove on either hand is paralleled by several moments in the *Henry IV* here discussed. In this production, Chris White doubled Worcester and Douglas and managed to have a confrontational discussion with himself (and Hotspur) in 4.3 via a quickly overturned cloak, which was satin on one side and tartan on the other. One of the other 'magical' effects, as Dessen terms them, of this production was of the doubles buttressed against one another: thus did Hal transform immediately into Kate Hotspur and back again, a transformation mirrored by Hotspur morphing into Poins (and back again), mostly in full view of the audience.

These last few features make clear that this production was both OP and not OP. There was doubling, but there was also trebling, quadrupling and even quintupling! The cast was all male, but while the actor playing Kate was acceptably early 20s, the Hostess was played by an actor in his early 50s. The production was rehearsed in a relatively short space of time after a period of private individual study,[11] and it was a relatively 'open', in-period and non-conceptual production, something of a rarity in Australia, but it was also definitely directed (by me). Notwithstanding Kevin Ewert's reservations about claims for the historical and aesthetic validity of the thrust stage,[12] the production was blocked for an audience on three and even four sides, even if they often initially gravitated to the 'front' of the stage, and it was also designed to be played under shared lighting, though this was achieved with varying degrees of success (depending upon the space in which the production was played). The actors were encouraged to speak directly to the audience, and not exclusively during soliloquy or aside, but the inclusion and use of the audience also extended to actual physical recruitment into certain sections of the play: thus were various audience members required to hand cups of sack to Falstaff, to become the set-upon Travellers and to deliver battle messages.

Two further deferrals before returning to cumulative performative affect:

8. Under 'What we do' on the American Shakespeare Center website, for example, is the following text: **'Universal Lighting**. Shakespeare's actors could see their audience; ASC actors can see you. When actors can see an audience, they can engage with an audience. And audience members can play the roles that Shakespeare wrote for them — Cleopatra's court, Henry V's army, or simply the butt of innumerable jokes. Leaving an audience in the dark can literally obscure a vital part of the drama as Shakespeare designed it. www.americanshakespeare-center.com/v.php?pg=49, accessed 28 November 2014.

9. See Jaquelyn Bessell, 'The Performance Research Group's *Antony and Cleopatra* (2010)', in Andrew James Hartley, ed., *Shakespeare on the University Stage* (Cambridge University Press, 2015), pp. 185–200.

10. 'Portable Shakespeare: Exigencies and "Magic" in Five-Actor Productions', *Shakespeare Bulletin* 29:1 (2011), 1–25.

11. Tiffany Stern, *Rehearsal from Shakespeare to Sheridan* (Oxford University Press, 2000), pp. 61–72.

12. 'The Thrust Stage is Not some Direct Link to Shakespeare', *Shakespeare Bulletin* 29:2 (2011), 165–176.

one, the context of the production itself; and two, a brief discussion of the performative methodology about to be deployed. The performance at the New Fortune Theatre was the production's third incarnation (out of four). Previously it had played at La Trobe University on the floor below three sides of tiered seating and then, in preparation for the New Fortune performance, on a raised platform. For this second stage I replaced the actor playing Hotspur as he had committed to another performance (my presence as a performer is crucial to the analysis that follows). The New Fortune was built in 1964 and not with the same painstaking archaeological and theatre history research that underpinned the reconstructed Globe project.[13] The building is 'sett square', in accordance with the Fortune Theatre contract, and the thrust stage is 12.96 metres wide and 8.24 metres deep (42.5 × 27 feet) by comparison with the stipulated width of 43 feet and a depth half way into the 50 foot yard. The yard is surrounded by three galleries of seating; it is an impressive space, but there are also significant idiosyncrasies and limitations. First of all, the theatre space is surrounded by academic offices, which makes daytime performances (and office-dwelling work) potentially problematic. Secondly, the materiality of the building – 1960s bricks, rendered concrete, office windows (un-double-glazed), green plastic chairs – calls attention to itself in completely different, and not altogether helpful, ways to the timber and plaster of the reconstructed Globe. Third, the theatre is home to several immoveable and quite vociferous peacocks (and peahens).

13. J. M. S. O'Brien, ed., *The New Fortune* (Perth: University of Western Australia Press, 1964).

In my head, before we arrived, I was expecting a beautiful rendition of a theatre with London Globe-like structural characteristics – wooden, rounded. I was quite disappointed with the concrete. I was amazed at the height of the thing. I was not expecting it to be that tall, without some form of a roof **(RD'A)**.

I feel it is a great shame that people, especially visitors, want to alter it so that it looks like a fake 'Globe Theatre'. What is wrong with taking it as it is, especially for Studies and Experiments and Research purposes … I regard it as a challenging non-traditional open space where theatrical things can happen … It was such an accident that the space even arrived! And never would have if Prof Edwards and then Phil Parsons hadn't spotted the intriguing measurement of the one big rectangular courtyard which was planned **(JP)**.

I think it's fair to say that there are unavoidable conflicts of interest in terms of a multipurpose building, especially where a performance venue is concerned. In the long past there used to be regular lunchtime performances which were well attended and didn't seem to lead to problems **(BW)**.

This may actually be helpful – an advantage – when it comes to the affective power of a performance, I think. From my experience, the authentic material conditions at the New Globe often create an additional implicit and invisible pressure on spectators to 'perform' as an early modern audience … The New Fortune audience, by contrast, does not experience any immediate cultural pressure from the architecture. As former or current students or performers, of course, they bring other emotional memories of the space but this is different from the expectations imposed by the building itself **(AF)**.

I was invited to bring the production (by Bob White) for a research 'collaboratory' hosted by the Australian Research Council Centre of Excellence for the History of Emotions 1100–1800. The three-day event was entitled 'Performing Old Emotions on the New Fortune' and began with talks, three of which are especially relevant here. First, Andrew Gurr spoke about anti-Dominicanism, the frustration produced by current Globe Artistic Director Dromgoole's turning of that space into a faux-proscenium. Next was Penelope Woods' investigation into audiences at the new Globe and especially of what she labelled the 'aleatoric' effects particular to that space. She made the observation that an actor gesturing to, for example, the sun when she or he speaks that word in the text is almost guaranteed a laugh: if it's sunny, 'look, it's sunny'; if it's not sunny, 'it's never sunny.' Last was Ralph Alan Cohen's marvellous explication of transhistorical audience behaviour, particularly in spaces where the audience, such as at the Blackfriars in Staunton, is in the same light as the players. This discussion included: direct address, especially

I think I talked about weather, and particularly pigeons as 'aleatoric' performance agents at the Globe. These chance interruptions can threaten to disrupt a performance, but they also have the potential to be interestingly co-opted by actors who acknowledge them in the moment. This produces a kind of excess of meaning that informs the performance in strange and intense ways, as if the natural world is temporarily in alignment with the performance world **(PW)**.

actors making sustained eye contact with spectators; distracted and inattentive audience members; the body language of audience members and its effect on (OP) performance; and the added investment an audience makes when it has to overcome various obstacles, such as problems with sightlines or physical discomfort. The audience for the production of *Henry IV, Part 1* included: Grant Malcolm, enthusiastic president of the graduate dramatic society at the New Fortune, 9 o'clock (that is, to the left of the stage from the actor's point of view), middle gallery; Bill Dunstone and Joan Pope, veteran NF performers/audience members, 11.30, yard; Rosemary Gaby, editing the play, closely attuned, 11.45, yard; Joanne Tompkins, inscrutable behind dark glasses, 12 noon; Ralph Cohen, open, grinning, expectant, 12.02, yard; Kate, his daughter, smiling, interested, in front of Joanne, 12, yard; Peter Reynolds, the convenor of the 'collaboratory', also behind dark glasses, 12.15, further back in the yard; Danijela Kambaskovic-Sawers, with baby in front harness, 12.30, still further back in the yard; Alison Findlay, resplendent in a purple suit and moving around both the clock face and the vertical levels (cheeky northerner); Andy Gurr, his eminence, 2 o'clock, middle gallery; Pen Woods, shivering, 3 o'clock, middle gallery; and Bob White, session organiser, cheery benevolence, 3 o'clock, upper gallery. One last important contextual detail: I was sick with a throat infection.

'Memory', writes Bruce R. Smith, at once providing both an ideal segue to this last detail of my throat infection and offering an enscapsulation of the methodology here deployed, 'resides in lungs, throat, mouth and ears'.[14] Thus, the remembering of performance that this chapter performs could not have been possible without my explicitly (disabled) embodied practice-as-research involvement. The specific inclination of this performative and practice-led writing is, after Bert O. States, part 'phenomenological attitude', which seeks 'a transaction between consciousness and the thickness of existence',[15] and, via McConachie, part cognitive studies. Introducing, summarising and defending the aims of phenomenological enquiry, Stanton B. Garner's *Embodied Spaces* helps to flesh out my particular phenomenological attitude. He describes such enquiry as 'to pursue the thing' – in this case, the performance event of *Henry IV, Part 1* – 'as it is given to consciousness in direct experience; to return perception to the fullness of its encounter with the environment'.[16] Even more helpful for the performative (post)structuring of this chapter, and for the entire project that is *Writing Performative Shakespeares*, is Garner's later assertion:

Instead of presence, the theater asks to be approached in terms of *presencing*; theatrical phenomena are multiply embodied, evoked in a variety of experiential registers, refracted through different (and sometimes divergent) phenomenal lenses.[17]

14. 'Speaking what We Feel About *King Lear*', in Holland, ed., *Shakespeare, Memory and Performance*, p. 35.

15. 'The Phenomenological Attitude', in Janelle G. Reinelt and Joseph R. Roach, eds., *Critical Theory and Performance* (Ann Arbor: University of Michigan Press, 1992), p. 378.

16. *Bodied Spaces: Phenomenology and Performance in Contemporary Drama* (Ithaca, NY: Cornell University Press, 2000), p. 2.

17. *Bodied Spaces*, p. 43.

I approach presencing *Henry IV* below via several layers, severally refracted. This chapter began, I think, in the after-show discussion of the production. Its next iteration was as a seminar paper. I circulated that paper – its phenomenological attitude signalled by first-person, embodied description – almost three years after the performance to several of the participants (on stage and off) and asked for their memories and observations (such as are incorporated on the previous two pages).[18] Finally, I have viewed (and will include insights gleaned from) both the photographs and DVD recording of the production in order to either confirm or problematise the various remembrances, perceptions and mis-remembrances and misperceptions that the variety of experiences register.

18. My respondents are: Tom Considine (TC), actor; Remi D'Agostin (RD'A), Stage Manager; Bill Dunstone (BD), audience; Alison Findlay (AF), audience; George Lingard (GL), actor; Bob Pavlich (BP), actor; Joan Pope (JP), audience; Joanne Tompkins (JT), audience; Bob White (BW), audience; Chris White (CW), actor; Penelope Woods (PW), audience. I am enormously indebted to them all.

* * *

The sun is beating down on my back, which, at this stage appears something of a miracle, given that the weather has been inclement right up until thirty minutes before the production began. The production is more than halfway through and I am glad of this hiatus, given that my voice is constantly breaking. At 3.2 when Bob's King says 'Lords, give us leave; the Prince of Wales and I must have some private conference' (lines 1–2), those of us not included in the scene – my Hotspur, Tom's Falstaff and Chris' Bardolph – turn our backs to the action and the majority of the audience. Up until now any actor not involved in the scene sits on his stool in front of the *frons scaenae* and watches the action, in a liminal space between character and actor, on stage and off. But this royal request for privacy, suffused with a barely suppressed frustration, means that we turn away. The scene plays along a long diagonal. It plays. The house is absolutely silent. Harriet Walter writes, echoing Anne Bogart above, and probably with more relevance for Royal Shakespeare than for Globe or New Fortune Theatres, about the way actors sense audience, but her observations illuminate the following discussion:

I felt that this was a particularly interesting moment, both for the performers and also – perhaps more so – for the audience. Up to this point, the actors, even when 'off stage' on the stools, had been a part of the scene by viewing it, just as the audience was doing. In fact to some degree, our very visible presence on the stage made the audience the subject of OUR gaze. As soon as we turned our backs, the audience would simultaneously have registered that (a) they were no longer being watched, and (b) they were privy to a scene that we were not a part of. That moment undoubtedly altered the audience's perception of both our and their interaction with the action of the scene **(CW)**.

> To perform well we have to be in a state of alertness and sensitivity not only to our fellow players but to the audience's mood, and in 'listening out' to gauge the quality of their attention we cannot filter out the negative bits. One cough or sweet-wrapper rattle can throw the timing of a line or drown out a vital word. It takes only a few bored fidgets to undermine the quality of concentration of the whole audience. They may not even be consciously disturbed, but subliminally the actor–audience connection is derailed and the actors have to fight to get things back on course.[19]

19. *Other People's Shoes: Thoughts on Acting* (London: Nick Hern Books, 2003), p. 144. See also McAuley, *Space in Performance*, p. 246.

I sit there, getting really hot, straightening a little, pushing my shoulders into the adjusted but still too tight jacket, when Hotspur is mentioned, and wonder, truly, whether everyone in the audience has left; my 'listening out' hears nothing. It is dead silent. The New Fortunate actors do not have to compete, as their northern Global cousins do, with planes and helicopters, but there is still plenty of noise. The wind buffets the makeshift cyclorama curtain, there are the rustles of the audience and the theatre itself is a thoroughfare. But it is SILENT. On my cue to turn – Blunt's 'Douglas and the English rebels met' (165) – I wheel around with some trepidation and then am genuinely surprised that the whole audience is still there.

This issue speaks to one of the important ways that open-air, shared-lighting theatres disrupt certain theatrical conventions and learned expectations. The learned mechanisms for 'listening out' are all wrong in these spaces because the audience is highly visible ... When audiences are visible I feel that there is a greater responsibility (or requirement) placed on them by the actors to 'perform' attentiveness, fulfilling their side of the performance exchange, although I think this is not always sensed or responded to by the audience. Activity, such as perhaps Alison's roving around for the best spot and my nail-biting, offers evidence of particular moments and repertoires of audience engagement and attention that have significance, that might be attended to in a similar but different way to 'listening out' **(PW)**.

Scene 3.2 is unique in our production relative to all the other scenes. Most importantly, it is the only scene in the production not played outward, the only time the audience is not directly addressed. Parts of most of the play have been cut – as many as 800 lines – but this scene, even though the King has a very long dressing down of Hal, is relatively untouched. Whereas the pace of the production as a whole borders on the breakneck, here the language and narrative is allowed a bit more space to breathe. But the most important factor is the inwardness of the scene. For the rest of the production we play out and invite the audience in; here, they are ignored but, if the silence is anything to go on, they are more desperate to get in; perhaps the fact that the space is, for once, divided, rather than united, into player and audience means that they press hard against the division. And here, via this particular scene, is an initial illustration of cumulative performative affect: in terms of actor affect, Bob had spoken to me on a number of

3.2. The actors not in the scene face away from the action. Bob White looks down from the upper gallery. Photograph courtesy of Remi D'Agostin.

occasions about his kids during the rehearsal, of his daughter being able to parrot the opening speech of the play back to him without really understanding it (which now strikes me as an unconscious expression of his own difficulties with that particular speech), and of his occasional battles with his teenage son. For George, playing Hal, his father was in the audience, a Perth-bound father seeing his Melbourne-living son in a real, grown-up role. These personal contexts may each have informed or inflected this particular performance of 3.2. Bob

During Hal's and dad's big scene I felt blinded by the sun and couldn't really see Bob's face for most of it. At one point I adjusted my gaze, to look at the audience, and I could see my real dad on the middle balcony. I agree with your comments about my dad being there. He had never really seen me act before and that definitely informed the show/that scene **(GL)**.

also spoke to me after the production of feeling very early in the scene that 'we've got them [the audience]' as he sensed the deep concentration in the spectators that I was hearing as silence. This actor emotion, a thrilling security in the face of other uncertain anxieties, clearly aided the playing and reception of the scene. In terms of character affect, this is very much an emotionally driven scene. Bob's King choked – at the text's instruction – on 'Not an eye / But is a-weary of thy common sight, / Save mine, which … doth that I would not have it do, / Make blind itself with foolish tenderness' (89–91) and George here played Hal as an undissembling Prince whose emotional journey in the scene was from recalcitrance to petulance to penitence to obedience, such that the King's eventual response, 'A hundred thousand rebels die in this' (159), was convinced and heartfelt.

> I do think that I'd be a better actor if I was more on top of the struggle to keep this mental space under control. A fear of it overwhelming me during performance and thus leading to a stage freeze or line stumbles or the end of the world does diminish my abilities to convince others that I ought to be on this stage – that for a moment I am a plausible King of England … I know from experience that when I am truly on top of this struggle and can devote almost my entire attention to the precise moment on stage it is then that I most enjoy acting. This did happen for me in Henry – possibly a few times … I do remember that it occurred during 3.2, where, for whatever reason, we did truly hold the audience's attention. But what caused this experience – was I particularly focused from the start or did the audience's attention force me into that place? I do know that it was a moment that was free of struggle, that the emotions that Henry needs to feel were there in me, and the words were in me and Hal was my son **(BP)**.

It should be clear by now that each of the affective spheres I am describing entail significant degrees of overlap and thus these actor and character affects just described inevitably inform the audience's experience of, and engagement with, the narrative affect, chiefly here in their investment in Hal's maturation and in his stop-start reconciliation with his father. In turn, each of these other dimensions is responded to by the individual audience members in terms of the personal stories they bring into interaction with the narrative. Perhaps the most forceful demonstration of this personal affect is the story recorded in the new Globe's publicity materials for the season following their production of *Julius Caesar* (1999). Though Mark Rylance's one-and-only directing assignment at the Globe received critical condemnation, it obviously struck a chord with at least one spectator, whose story of her son being the victim of a knife attack prompted an especially visceral reaction to the murder of Caesar:

> I wept openly and revealed my inner emotions affiliated with my son's incident the previous week. Yes, I did well and truly get involved. Not superficially, but 'for real'. I explained my emotions to both my husband and my son. For me, the pent-up emotion of the previous week's true life drama was released within the contexts of the William Shakespeare play of 400 years ago.[20]

20. McConachie could be offering a cognitive explanation of this very incident when he writes, on p. 36 of *Engaging Audiences*, 'If the memory is recent, the viewer has an added incentive to transfer it from private life and project it into the fictional play.' See Stephen Purcell's *Shakespeare and*

Like Bob describing the 'audience's attention' above, this woman uses the word *truly* as an attempt to articulate the affective force of the performative moment. This story is especially demonstrative of what I am labelling 'personal affect' but also encapsulates at least two of the other affective states here described, and lends further weight to my argument that a confluence of character, narrative and personal affects (it's there, but I can't access actor affect in this anecdote) produce what I am calling cumulative performative affect.

* * *

In order to theorise both the success of 3.2 (as I have described it) and the last affective sphere of my equation above, that of performative affect, I turn to Nicholas Ridout's provocative study of theatre as failure and fiasco: thus, by fiasco will I (attempt to) find engagement out. Canvassing unsettling theatrical encounters such as stage fright, audience embarrassment, animals on stage, and corpsing and fiasco, Ridout argues of theatre that: 'Failure, then, is constitutive. That there is something wrong with theatre is the sign that it is theatre.'[21] This is from the end of the Introduction: in the last chapter he goes even further, describing theatre as 'a huge machine designed expressly to break down – reverse-engineered, as it were, from these moments of failure, and the pleasures they occasion, which are its true aim'.[22] Even more apposite as a potential theorisation of the theatrical engagement that this chapter's production of *Henry IV, Part 1* – and perhaps other original/ish practices productions, too – produced (and produce) is Ridout's analysis of Tommy Cooper's stand-up comedy. Ridout, via Adrian Heathfield, writes that, with all of the inbuilt disasters of his act, Cooper achieves that which Darwin had pronounced imposible, 'namely tickling himself', a notion extended to the audience as well:

The audience might reasonably be said to be doing the same. In performances in which fiasco is sustained in this way an affective relationship between audience and performer seems to be generated, in which both appear to be caught up in a cylindrical bubble of mutual convulsion and stupefaction, each party astonished at the other's (and their own) capacity to make so much out of nothing, dazzled by their own stupid complicity in this patently senseless and stupid performance. The circularity of this infection, its self-tickling aspect, might suggest that the relations of masochism, if they are present as in other tickling scenarios, are internalised on either side of, rather than played out across the metaphorical footlights of the laugh-encounter. Everyone is equally baffled amid the feedback loops.[23]

Before unpacking and applying this analysis to the New Fortune *Henry IV*, here is Jeremy Lopez's correlative summation of the early modern theatre. In *Theatrical Convention and Audience Response in Early Modern Drama*, Lopez writes that 'Elizabethan and Jacobean drama was extremely self-conscious, but … demanded an equal self-consciousness from its audience as well' and, further, that this audience was 'very much aware of the limitations of the early modern stage, and that the potential for dramatic representation to be ridiculous or inefficient or incompetent was a constant and vital part of audiences' experience of the plays'.[24]

Was the early modern audience awareness of playhouse limitations, identified here by Lopez, disposed towards or against the plays? Did they, for example, want to see incompetence in order to laugh at it, such as the royals watching the mechanicals' *Pyramus and Thisbe*? Or, were they, as the Prologue to *Henry V* (to whom I will return below) requires, determined, co-operatively, to make up for the perceived shortcomings of representation? The Prologue's repeated requests might lend equal weight to either side of this discussion: the appeals

Audience in Practice, p. 119, for a quite different account of audience experience at this production.

21. *Stage Fright, Animals, and Other Theatrical Problems* (Cambridge University Press, 2006), p. 33.

22. Ibid., pp. 150–151.

23. Ibid., p. 149.

24. *Theatrical Convention and Audience Response in Early Modern Drama* (Cambridge University Press, 2006), p. 2.

for concerted imaginative participation endow the audience with significant creative agency in the production's success, but the repeated – here and elsewhere – conferments of gentility on that audience perhaps also speak to an uneasiness that playgoers might treat the performance before them as something akin to a staked bear. However the early modern audience behaved, audiences at original practices Shakespeare have tended to be raucously, self-ticklingly, partisan. Such audiences seem to come both wanting the performers to do well and to do well themselves. Our New Fortune audience, of course, didn't pay, didn't expect professionals, are interested in original practices Shakespeare and have sat, discussed, eaten and drunk with us over the course of the collaboratory: they are on our side. But I have observed and heard of similar types of response at the new Globe and Staunton Blackfriars Theatres. Paying five pounds to stand at the Globe is next to free and the audience that watched Mark Rylance with script in hand fill in for the ailing actor playing the Abbess at one performance of *The Comedy of Errors* (2006) seemed to derive special pleasure from the title-appropriate chaos of the occasion (this is also to do with Rylance's mythic status in the building, the drag comedy on offer and perhaps the fact that he was able to partly, but not wholly, obscure the script within a prop Bible). The onsideness of the audience can, however, make it somewhat difficult to assess the success of a particular moment in a production; lovers of psychologically nuanced Shakespeare often despairingly shake their heads at raucously appreciated, though, to their minds, pantomimic Globe Shakespeare. Michael Billington, making the same mistake as Henry V proclaiming 'We are no tyrant, but a Christian king' (1.2.241), wrote of the above *Errors* production: 'The audience however, loved it … It would be curmudgeonly and ungenerous to deny the production's genuine gaiety. But when the Syracusan Antipholus says "I to the world am like a drop of water That in the ocean seeks another drop" we should feel a quiver of emotional longing which here gets lost amidst the pervasive merriment.'[25] Via Ridout, Billington is here stupefied by 'stupid complicity'. So, how does thinking about the New Fortune production of *Henry IV* as failure or fiasco, and yet the beneficiary of this kind of generous, if not stupid, complicity, help to explain the circularity of its particular infection, the special bafflement of its feedback loops?

Two specific elements of the New Fortune *Henry IV* that might be described as fiasco and failure – respectively the presence of the peacocks and my failing voice – prompt an understanding of the whole production, of original practices Shakespeare in general, and, indeed, perhaps all Shakespearean production, according to these terms. Before attending to these specifics, though, in what ways might the overall production be thought of as fiasco and failure? First of all, this particular production represents a resources fiasco. Using five men to

Even though it was free, I wonder if maybe this could make audiences more, rather than less critical – there was a hard core that stayed right through with apparent signs of genuine absorption. If they could vote with their feet (or their voices) as it was free, staying and being quiet seemed to be tacit endorsement. That's how it felt, though hard to prove – but I've heard other directors confirm that 'free' audiences are often the most unruly and critical and even hostile to performances **(BW)**.

Although interestingly people [at the Globe] have asked for their money back, in a way that I think would be more unusual at other theatres in London (the incident I'm thinking of in particular was when a production wasn't in period dress) **(PW)**.

25. www.guardian.co.uk/stage/2006/aug/02/theatre, accessed 25 June 2012. With the New Fortune *Henry IV*, how do you judge, for example, the affectiveness of a quietly attended 'I do, I will' (2.4.468) when the majority of the audience know that the poignant, anthologised moment is coming and collectively hold their breath, a factor not necessarily relevant at the Globe where unknown and unforeseen exposition sometimes causes gasps?

play not the thirty-three speaking parts of the text, but sixteen of those roles, and with audience members filling in for three others, represents something of a fiasco, especially when the actors change costume in front of the audience, sometimes during the scene.[26] Resource fiasco, of course, is what the opening Prologue of *Henry V* attempts to mitigate (and perhaps celebrate) in his request to the audience to compensate imaginatively for the production's limitations of representation. He twice asks for 'pardon' (Prologue 8, 15), apologises specifically for 'unraiséd spirits' (9), an 'unworthy scaffold' (10), a 'crookéd figure' (15), and 'imperfections' (23), twice confers gentility upon his auditors (8, 34) as well as humility, patience (33) and kindness (34), and five times directs them to consider the imaginative force of their thoughts (18, 19, 23, 26, 28). These resources (and attendant aesthetic) fiascos that the Prologue addresses for the 1599 Globe Theatre *Henry V* are amplified for a 2011 New Fortune Theatre *Henry IV, Part 1*. What could be more definitive of fiasco than five men performing a play designed for three times that number, in costumes approximating those worn four centuries ago, waving pretend swords in the air, in a reconstructed theatre plonked in a university quadrangle (with peacocks) on the other side of the planet. For all of the 1599/2011 differences, though, the fiascos have a common ground, perhaps common to all Shakespearean production, at least to some degree: a shared, performer/audience acceptance and enjoyment of demonstrable artifice.

In the seminar paper draft of this chapter I supposed that the audience were quiet at the beginning of the production in a very different way to the almost rapt silence I described for 3.2. I thought they were too quiet and, via comments made in the post-show discussion, hypothesised that this was due to anxiety about the peacocks and my ailing voice. The responses to the right, one from off-stage and one from on-, offer more seasoned and reasoned (and less needy) explanations for this quietness. Alison's comment is neatly applicable, I think, to the above discussion of fiasco. Though I am less persuaded by the language of codes and semiotics, wary, as this study is, of 'reading' the stage, I can recast this notion thus:

26. Geoffrey Milne, encyclopedic titan of Australian theatre, pithily observed after watching the first iteration of this production that we 'were probably a man short'.

I do not think spectators – certainly any of the ones I was sitting next to – were unsettled by your voice or 'worried' by the peacocks to the extent Ralph notes. However, getting the measure of the show takes intense concentration – to learn the codes governing performance and how they should respond as spectators means they are fully occupied in absorbing and processing all those different semiotic codes and so were quiet **(AF)**.

Personally I think it was more to do with the peacocks, than any major concerns about your voice. They were an audience familiar with the space watching a troupe that they knew were NOT familiar with it. Perhaps they had experienced productions that were negatively affected by the problems inherent in the space (peacocks, etc.). I found them a little slow to warm up – but nothing unusual for a matinee audience **(CW)**.

getting the measure of – concentrating on, absorbing and processing – an originalish practices Shakespeare production requires becoming acquainted with and either accepting, perhaps embracing, or otherwise rejecting its particular brand of fiasco. Besides noting (in the post-show discussion) that he thought the audience found it difficult to relax initially because of concerns about how we would deal with the on-stage and voluble peacocks, Ralph Cohen also confessed that he had, also initially, thought that Tom's Falstaff fat-suit, the demonstrable artifice of which was especially evident because it had to be taken on and off regularly for role switches, was 'ghastly'. Soon, he continued, he began to regard its simplicity as beautiful: this, it seems to me, represents an absorbing, processing and, thankfully, embracing of fiasco.

The peacocks for me were a delight – their colour beautifully added to the stark concrete and brick. The peacock is quite a sexual bird, a very masculine bird, which is interesting. Their noise was the bother, entertaining at first, a little funny, then repeatedly frustrating **(RD'A)**.

Peacocks – the worst problem is that they are incontinent, or rather not toilet-trained – which raises difficulties over cleaning responsibility. But I think what you say about them in the performance is spot-on – you used them sparingly as an opportunity, and it worked **(BW)**.

I didn't think they were very anxious! Apart from me ... and I felt anxious that I had licensed everyone precisely NOT to worry about the peacocks by having named this sort of effect earlier on. I felt that I had enabled them to supersede what would be a more normal imported theatre etiquette of trying very hard to pretend to focus on the show. This is what Globe audiences generally do, I would say, with the pigeons until they make themselves un-ignorable. The peacocks were always going to be un-ignorable, but I felt that I had created a new awareness of birds, and other chance events, as agents operating within the performance text, and a new licence for relishing this, rather than resisting it. When I saw how the peacocks were behaving and when people started laughing at them I felt this was informed by the way I had established birds as agents in open-air performance. Perhaps this was just my imagination, but I felt that people actually looked over to me as they laughed, to indicate: 'See! This is exactly what you were talking about! What a great joke' and I was trying NOT to make eye contact. I didn't want to collude with this response that I felt really threatened the show. I just wanted everyone to ignore the peacocks and get back to concentrating on the performances **(PW)**.

During 'I know you all', we, as a cast, hadn't yet acknowledged/incorporated the peacocks, to my knowledge. And as their squawks permeated the space, I remember quite vividly sensing the anxiety the audience had for me, or for the show in general (as you mention). I could see people biting their nails as I delivered the text, interrupted occasionally by the peacocks, I even saw someone wince each time a squawk happened. I thought perhaps during the later comedic scenes we'd be able to incorporate them, but during that speech I chose to ignore them. But I recall an almost tangible sigh of relief amongst the audience when Tom acknowledged them **(GL)**.

The stairwells and chairs and railings are so peafowl fouled it is quite unpleasant. I wish they had been persuaded to stay in the Great Court and the Tropic Garden opposite the Library! **(JP)**

At least one audience member (Ralph) was anxious about how we would cope with the presence of the peacocks and at least one audience member (Alison) thought their significance overstated. Rewatching the production on the DVD recording I count 42 squawks in the first 30 minutes (and none in 3.2). Whatever the range of other feelings towards them in the audience, and some are recorded to the left, we, in the cast, are very comfortable with the peacocks. We like to embrace what Pen Woods has named (for us) the aleatoric effects and are glad of opportunities to improvise. In the previous day's rehearsal we incorporated the peacocks whenever there was any reference to birds in the text. But for the performance we decide not to overdo this in-house joke and to neither ignore, nor reference them too much; we will play around them. It is, though, as Ralph observes later, only when Falstaff condemns Hal's seeming cowardice with 'If I do not beat thee out of thy kingdom with a dagger of lath and drive all thy subjects afore thee like a flock of wild geese' (2.4.130–32), whilst simultaneously shooing a serendipitously proximate peacock at this line's conclusion, that the audience break into a hearty, and relaxed, laugh. At least, that's how I (and Ralph and George) remember it. The DVD shows George's Hal instructing Falstaff about their robbery of the Travellers, and, appropriately enough, stage whispering, 'Lie down, lay thine ear close to the ground' (2.2.31–32). Interrupted by a squawk from above, he looks over his shoulder and enjoins the bird to 'sshh'. Cue, of course, audience laughter.

If responses to the first of my fiasco and failure markers, the peacocks, were

122

various, responses to the second, my failing voice, seem almost uniform. I remembered, in my seminar paper: 'My voice is another matter. I'm terribly unwell and it gives way not infrequently, especially as I am too shouty in the role anyway and neither my voice nor body is trained for acting.' And based on this 'lungs, throat, mouth and ears' memory I hypothesised that the audience were almost inevitably, and to the production's disfavour, 'affected by my physical and emotional discomfort'. My respondents offer a counter perspective, right. The most obvious explanation for this disparity of perception (and reception) is, as Chris wisely suggests, the specific differences of perspective of performer and audience member, but I am going to prise at the disparity a little further in the hope of explicating some of the specific features of (original practices) Shakespearean theatrical failure.

Here, for example, is an annotated transcript, courtesy of the DVD recording (which I could only bear to watch some time after the event) of 1.3.212–24: my voice giving way is represented by bold capitalised text struck through:

I honestly don't remember this to have been a problem. It's not in my memory at all about this production **(JT)**.

I think you overestimate the anxiety caused by your voice. Most spectators did not know you were ill and were not worried that you would not complete the performance **(AF)**.

Whilst I remember other points of the performance in vivid clarity, I don't remember your voice being an issue, at all **(PW)**.

It is likely that, in this instance, as in most others, the audience – even if they noticed the vocal problems you were experiencing, which is by no means certain – simply accepted them as present and engaged with the performance on that basis ... I think it likely that your own awareness of the difficulties you faced in that performance made them much more apparent to you than to the audience. For you, they were a mountain to be scaled – for them, they were just another part of the experience **(CW)**.

Rob mentions, perhaps a dozen times (yawn, yawn, too many matey!) the condition of his throat and how it affected him and, he assumed, the audience. Strangely I hadn't realised that anyone was crook **(JP)**.

HOTSPUR
I'll keep them all;
By God, he shall not have a Sc~~O~~t of them; [peacock squawk]
No, if a Scot would save his s~~OU~~l, he shall not:
I'll keep them, by this hand.

WORCESTER
You start away
And lend no ear unto my purposes.
Those prisoners you shall keep.

HOTSPUR
Nay, I will; that's flat:
He s~~AI~~d he would not ransom Mortimer;
F~~O~~rbad my tongue to sp~~EA~~k of Mortimer;
But ~~I~~ will f~~IN~~d him when he l~~IE~~s asleep,
And in his ear I'll holla 'Mortimer!'
N~~AY~~, I'll have a starling shall be taught to speak
Nothing but 'Mortimer,' and give it him
To keep his anger still in motion.

[after the third 'Mortimer', rather desperately, I take an unplanned drink from an on-stage goblet]

[I'm drained of confidence here and only half-commit to this moment of pretending to be a chirping starling]

123

This section of the DVD runs from 18.44–19.18: 9 cracks of the voice in 34 seconds. With a croak – in this admittedly quite short, shouty section – every 3.8 seconds, I can ask with (the self-indulgent) Leontes of the disbelieving courtiers on the previous page: 'Is whispering nothing?' (*The Winter's Tale* 1.2.286).

Let me restate the overall argument of this chapter, that, at a given moment in a Shakespeare production, a confluence of affective spheres – actor + character + narrative + personal + performative – add up to a cumulative performative affect. Here, I am considering the last of these spheres, what I am calling performative affect, a broad category that incorporates elements such as the dramaturgical make-up of the play and production, the environmental or aleatoric effects, the eventness of the occasion. I am now (sub)arguing that, particularly within originalish practices Shakespeare productions, this affective force potentially founds upon, and is able to exploit, performative defects, namely, via Ridout and Lopez: failure, fiasco, ridiculousness, inefficiency and incompetence. My voice is the present failure test case, which I remember ailing and failing badly. This produced a range of emotional states in me, such as anxiety and despair, which, in turn, drained me of confidence and energy. My respondents, especially those off stage, do not remember this aspect of the production in anything like the same way, claim that my illness, such as it was, did not adversely affect their reception of the production, and suggest that I overstate its significance. Rewatching the DVD recording of the production, however, confirms (for me) that my recollection of my voice breaking is not overstated to the degree that they suggest. It was relatively straightforward to argue that the peacocks, exemplars of ridiculous fiasco, could be used to the production's advantage: once they were acknowledged, the audience could relax about our capacity to cope with them, and even enjoy the playfulness and skill of those incorporations. Can I, though, make the same argument about a defective voice? Can an inefficient, failing voice be absorbed, processed and turned to a(n original practices Shakespeare) production's credit?

I turn to Gay McAuley for the beginning of an answer to these questions. Reflecting on the repercussions to reception of an actor being visibly injured on stage, McAuley records a pertinent theatrical anecdote:

My recollection of the occasion when Georges Bigot sprained his ankle toward the end of the Théâtre du Soleil's *Henry IV* is of my concern for the injured actor, admiration for the way the other actors handled the situation and for his fortitude, and my apprehension that something else would go wrong. The disjunction between fiction and reality was accentuated, and as a consequence it is this that dominates my memory of that performance. The subtle balance and interplay between the different orders of reality that is an essential part of theatre's mode of operation was brutally disrupted.[27]

27. *Space in Performance*, p. 253. See also, States, *Great Reckonings*, p. 119.

The significance (for me) of this moment is in its difference from the one I am attempting to analyse. McAuley notes, contrary to my respondents, that she was clearly cognisant of the 'injured actor', a cognisance which admitted other, perhaps unwanted, distractions. Also of significant difference between this moment and mine is the shape and arrangement of the respective performative affect spheres. The (outer) Paris *Henry IV*, performed in the 'Cartoucherie, a disused cartridge factory', was end-on, its ornate design beautifully lit in the darkened 'large hangar-like warehouse'.[28] The Perth *Henry IV*, by contrast, was performed in a (quite narrow) thrust space in daylight with the actors actively acknowledging the presence of the audience (and various aleatoric effects). I suggest, via this direct comparison, that the 'disjunction between fiction and reality was accentuated' especially by the modernist aesthetic of the Théâtre du Soleil, which perhaps may not have been such a problem at the originalish practices New Fortune. Suppose I had visibly sprained my ankle rather than less perceptibly strained my voice. In this space, and according to a dramaturgical arrangement that fuses or overlays, creates a junction of, not a space between, 'fiction and reality', the injury, if not too serious, could be acknowledged and shared and then incorporated and exploited. Another way to frame this is via McConachie's (borrowed) notion of 'conceptual blending', the cognitive science used to explain the way an audience member 'makes possible the doubleness of actor/characters'.[29] I further suggest, therefore, that in original practices productions of Shakespeare especially, an audience member is invited – most blatantly by Fabian in *Twelfth Night*[30] – to conceptually blend fiction and reality. If such blending occurs, the brutal disruption McAuley describes is potentially mitigated: reality cannot crash the fiction if the dramaturgy dictates blending rather than disjunction. I didn't, though, sprain my ankle: my voice was strained and my respondents claim not to have noticed. How, then, can these arguments be applied to a phenomenon that appears to have gone unnoticed? McConachie's cognitive studies offer further ways of explicating this less visible dimension of performative affect and audience engagement.

One of the key concepts of *Engaging Audiences*, and one which resonates especially with early modern open-air playhouses, is of 'emotional contagion'. McConachie writes that 'Emotional contagion in a theatre is automatic and usually very quick', and especially in 'lighted auditoriums', in which audience members can see each other's 'facial expressions and bodily movements'.[31] These expressions and movements are termed 'visuomotor representations' and, applied to actually watching the play, rather than audience fellows, 'provide spectators with the ability to "read the minds" of actor/characters, to intuit their beliefs, intentions, and emotions by watching their motor actions'.[32] Moreover, such cues are neither purely visual. Offering some validity to my (tentative) claims that the audience was indeed affected by my failing voice, McConachie explains that 'the voice is largely a product of muscles and manipulated air; spectators can feel muscular tension in the voice just as they experience it in the tension of other muscles that are more available for visuomotor perception'.[33] And, just as usefully, 'Our muscular, chemical, and neurological responses to others' emotions are often so small that they escape conscious recognition, but they can have a significant impact on our behaviour.'[34] Suppose the Conkie via McConachie position has, indeed, validity: that the New Fortune spectators, perhaps beyond 'conscious recognition', felt the 'muscular tension' of an occasionally breaking voice and intuited, perhaps, e'en so quickly, caught, the emotional state of the speaker of that voice. How, in this case of performative affect,

28. Kennedy, *Looking at Shakespeare*, p. 287.

29. *Engaging Audiences*, p. 42.

30. 3.4.125–26.

31. *Engaging Audiences*, p. 97.

32. Ibid., p. 65.

33. Ibid., p. 75.

34. Ibid., p. 67.

might inefficient failure be recuperated? Perhaps my vocally challenged performance enabled the audience to reflect, consciously or otherwise, on physical vulnerability, mine and theirs (this could be an expression of the self-conscious audience Lopez describes). These kinds of thoughts might affectively contextualise other thoughts and feelings, for example, on this Hotspur's defective and compromised attempts to articulate his fervour which therefore anticipate the rebels' inevitable failure. Or, indeed, my turning my back for 10 minutes, and not speaking, means that the audience can relax into the vocally consistent 3.2 (this is akin to Lopez's argument that unwieldy exposition produces in the audience the desire for action).[35] Perhaps, given their general onsideness, there is a mixture of concern and admiration, such as McAuley notes. In all of these possibilities failure is made good (not success): defect-affective, Polonius might say.

35. *Theatrical Convention*, p. 94.

* * *

I open the final section of this chapter, a discussion of the overt strategies of audience engagement deployed in the New Fortune *Henry IV*, and the kinds of emotional contagion they spread, via, once again, Gay McAuley on theatrical space. Building on Barbara Freedman's view that 'it is the return look that constitutes theatricality',[36] McAuley discusses the 'Play of Looks', which includes the spectator/actor look, the returned actor/spectator look and the less discussed spectator/spectator look,[37] all of which contribute to what she calls theatricality's 'energy exchange'.[38] Applying these ideas to the New Fortune *Henry IV*, it is impossible to isolate an originary look, but, for three reasons, I am going to start with Penelope Woods. First, Woods, as her annotated comments in this chapter attest, is an expert on audience behaviour in reconstructions of early modern theatres, an expertise confirmed by her selection as Stephen Purcell's last chapter interlocutor in *Shakespeare and Audience in Practice*.[39] Second, because she generously records

36. *Space in Performance*, p. 260.

37. Ibid., pp. 255–270.

38. Ibid., p. 246.

I was not feeling relaxed, I was a bit cold and a little preoccupied – the final edits of my PhD thesis were on my mind. And I was nervous because as the play opened and I realised what a big focus-pulling effect the peacocks were going to have, I actually felt somewhat queasy about the talk I had given that morning. I sat stage right on my own and bit my nails throughout the performance **(PW)**.

39. *Shakespeare and Audience in Practice*, pp. 157–172.

being in a uniquely emotional space flown out to the University of Western Australia for the research 'collaboratory' on performing emotions, with only eight days to go until submitting her not quite finished doctorate, and with the possibility of taking up a post-doctoral position at UWA (which she subsequently did), jetlagged and a little culture-shocked, as an audience member, she was inevitably somewhat distracted. The third reason is that the ubiquitous visuomotor representation she performs of biting her nails, if not an originary moment, can at least be identified as having a knock-on effect.

To 'Play of Looks' I add 'pinball effect' to describe this particular 'energy exchange'. The first look/pinball is Pen sitting at stage right, a little hunched up because she is cold, worried about having licensed peacock foolery and biting her nails. George/Hal sees this during his soliloquy (1.3) and is a little concerned; he's also worrying about the peacocks, not so much about whether they will squawk or not, but how to use them if they do. Now he's blinded by the sun (I'm collapsing chronology here for dramatic effect) so he looks out at the second gallery and spies his father just as Bob/King is reprimanding him for his, like Richard's, 'skipping' (3.2.60) behaviour. Bob can see Grant Malcolm (stage left, middle gallery) generously intent on the performance and directly across from him is Andy Gurr, whose default audience position appears to be leaning forward expectantly. And thus the pinball/play of looks creates McAu-

It's true to say that our emotional states during performances shift around a lot ... sometimes it's about summoning up feelings that are needed for the scene to work, sometimes it's relaxing into a moment that is light and doesn't demand much, sometimes it's dealing with a moment that is maybe just beyond one's range. Frustration, pleasure, fear – these the actor feels while trying to summon up anger, love, terror – these the actor must feel on behalf of the character. And all the time there's this fucking peacock sitting on the edge of the stage and it might start raining again and Rob has a sore throat and will he make it to the end of the show? And I am glad that they found Mistress Quickly funny but will they approve of how I play Henry in the next scene (because I've just remembered that there are some serious Shakespeare experts out there in the audience and they've probably seen this play many, many times before) **(BP)**.

ley's 'energy exhange', McConachie's 'emotional contagion' and Ridout's 'circularity of ... infection'.[40] The most effective (and affective) actor (and audience member) might be he or she who generates the most looks or shoots off the greatest number of pinballs. Our leader Tom clearly relishes this prospect. Most of us are too scared to look directly at Andy but Tom/Falstaff clearly refers to him on 'An old lord of the council rated me the other day in the street' (1.2.83–84). In the mock king play Tom/Falstaff turns the whole house into the tavern audience, shooting pinballs in all directions. He's the only one who consistently looks to the upper gallery. I didn't even know, until I saw the photographs later, that Bob White, the session organiser, is sitting stage right in the upper gallery. In almost every one of those photos he's leaning forward and smiling, but I do not think many looks or pinballs were directed squarely at him. From this position, perhaps, an audience member can observe the play of looks/pinball trajectory: this provides, for a session organiser, almost a supervision[41] – and this word takes on added resonances within the context of a play of looks – of audience engagement.

40. One potentially problematic aspect of this analysis is that the theatre was nothing like full – about 100 people – and thus I am able to identify individuals. Suppose the 'play of looks' could be traced at a sold out matinee at the new Globe, that 'ocular proof' was identifiable: would there be hundreds of criss-crossed individual lines or would they merge more into a collective?

The games you played with vertical space, actual and metaphoric, helped to amplify dramatic tensions ... This staging fits into the bigger picture in which Hal plays his own games of 'high' and 'low' with Falstaff and the King **(BD)**.

McAuley's compelling analysis enables fascinating conjecture about how the New Fortune *Henry IV* might have affectively engaged audiences but the 'play of looks' also, I think, needs to be extended to account for the way this originalish practices Shakespeare production operated. Original practices Shakespeare has been characterised, as was this *Henry IV, Part 1*, by audience-inclusive practices such as: direct address of soliloquies, asides and other textual parts of the play to the audience, such as when Mark Rylance's Globe *Hamlet* (2000) demanded an answer to his question of 'Am I a coward?' (2.2.506), and then adapted his performance depending on the answer and its delivery;[42] making sustained eye contact with the audience; endowing and implicating individual or collective members of the audience within the fiction of the play,[43] such as the groundlings as English soldiers in the Globe's *Henry V* (1997) or gesturing at certain people when insults are made; and physical recruitment into various scenes (more ish than original, of course, and mostly in the yard, such as the wrestling scene in

41. This analysis resonates with my earlier discussion of spectating from the Gods at the Globe (see above, pp. 84–85).

42. See Escolme, *Talking to the Audience*, pp. 70–72.

43. Ralph Alan Cohen, 'Directing at the Globe and the Blackfriars: Six Big Rules for Contemporary Directors', in *Shakespeare's Globe: A Theatrical Experiment*, pp. 218–222.

the Globe *As You Like It* (1998)). The New Fortune *Henry IV* deployed each of these practices and required more than a play of looks to sustain its 'energy exchange'. Indeed, a play of exchanges or a play of engagements, such as the *Hamlet* moment above illustrates, might more accurately represent originalish practices theatrical dynamism: this movement from looks to engagements is one of acknowledgement, perhaps communication, to collaboration, and for the remainder of this chapter I will sample the New Fortune *Henry IV*'s play of engagements in order to further explore cumulative performative affect.

We address the audience directly several times in the first act of the production. Having been terrified by Ralph's talk of trochaic rhythms, Bob channels his anxieties about playing to Shakespearean luminaries into the first scene; that is, the King addresses his Council with some trepidation about committing to a holy war (1.1.1–33). George is far more comfortable with 'I know you all' (1.2.185–207), taken at a measured pace and spoken directly to various people, mostly in the yard. On the DVD Tom seems, perfectly naturally, to speak as many lines outward as to the other characters. But still the production is warming up; it is perhaps still being 'absorbed', in Alison Findlay's phrase. It is only with the robbery of the Travellers (2.2; 2.1 is cut in its entirety) that we powerfully engage, or absorb, the audience; indeed, we literally capture (two of) them.

Use of the yard has been a particular bugbear for some Globe academics, including at least one of the New Fortune spectators, such that notes were included in the programmes of the offending productions disavowing the practice as without historical precedent. But having only five actors, the solution of using audience members in this scene (and elsewhere) occurred when the stage manager, Remi D'Agostin, was – again, literally – roped into the scene; moreover, I was intrigued by Tiffany Stern's recording that 'Killigrew told Pepys that as a child he would go to the Red Bull and "when the man cried to the boys, 'Who will go and be a divell, and he shall see the play for nothing?'" he would take the role and get into the play free.'[44] This is how it works for us: before the production starts Remi asks (without shouting) the assembling audience members if they would like to be involved in the show. For this scene the lines of the Travellers are printed on the top of the small, bottle-top-laden chest they carry. In rehearsal we deliberated about getting them to actually walk across the stage, but favoured the bandits instead going into the yard. In the brief history of the production we have had some memorable Travellers – ailing pilgrims desperately seeking Canterbury, bold nincompoops, terrified teens – but Bill and Joan are the nonpareils of the excellent adventure. They are vocal in ways I can only dream of, and their characterisation and enthusiasm is irresistible. Part of the reason for the 'collaboratory' is to try to revive interest and investment in the New Fortune, which has been criminally underused, both as a site of theatrical and academic endeavour, and Bill and Joan have been at the centre of its rise, fall and desire to rise again; perhaps this embodied history also informs the cumulative performative affect of this moment. In any case, from here the audience are with us, physically, intellectually and emotionally.

44. Rehearsal from Shakespeare to Sheridan, p. 77.

It was a privilege to be asked to partner up with Bill Dunstone and stand by, ears on tenterhooks, as it were, for the cue for OUR BIT. This proved to be a nice little buzz of improvisation, and there is no doubt that afterwards, as we were roughly, though courteously, directed to our front row chairs, that I felt both warmer, considerably muscle-relaxed and quite pleased with how we had been able to be helpers in the event; not just spare members of a small but attentive audience ... I was made to feel alive and aware of what was happening; pleased to notice all sorts of cunning details of the play-game. I have always had an interest in the way children 'play': inventing things, making up extra bits, condensing time and space, using their energy to do three things at once ... No mucking around; no waiting ... And this is what you lot gave me **(JP)**.

Joan and I had learned our lines, collected our stage prop, and had a brief word from the SM about our cue. We knew nothing about the action that would happen on stage; in the spirit of things, we drew on our experience of the NF and responded spontaneously to the moment ... The deployment of playing spaces was simplicity itself, but it energised our performances. The audience didn't know we were actors. We sat in our everyday clothes at the end of the front row of seats, just below the DL corner of the stage. We stood up on cue and 'travelled' DR along the yard floor, parallel to and immediately below the lip of the stage, till the actors bound and 'robbed' us DC. At the end of the scene we simply returned to our seats. This transformation of the yard as Gad's Hill opened up transactions between the text, the playing space, and our bodies and intentions as actors. Our ambiguous position in relation to the audience made us closely attentive to their response. I think this proximity surprised and energised them, too. We also had to compensate in our physical acting for being off-stage ... As I recall, Joan and I felt elated the moment we left our seats, and this elation developed into an intense bodily presence throughout the short scene. We exaggerated the scale of our bodily responses partly in keeping with the comedy, but also to establish our position as actors in the yard. Our surprise entry into the action as 'audience-cum-victims' made the audience laugh ... I think all of us were exhilarated by what we were getting away with as actors and audience ... The dialogue also worked for us. The brief lines were virtual stage directions for rapid changes of embodied interiority; 'we'll walk a while and stretch our legs' (easing tired muscles, companionable inattentive walk); 'Stand' (startled, immobilised, roped back to back); 'we are undone, both we and ours for ever' (mouths and eyes dilated, faces upwards, emotionally and physically trapped in the moment) ... the comedy was in the embodied responses rather than the words. I seem to remember making another physical adjustment, not quite relaxed, as we returned to our seats and the action continued above us **(BD)**.

Yes – they are the mother and father of the emotional temperature – providing a visible/audible and now tactile lead for the responses of other spectators **(AF)**.

Gad's Hill robbery. Photographs courtesy of Tanya Tuffrey, ARC Centre for History of Emotions, UWA.

129

The grand success of the robbery does not mean, however, that the production is all smooth sailing from here. In the very next scene I deliver the letter-reading soliloquy; the voice is just about okay. But I have concocted some business that I screw up the letter and throw it away in disgust before asking an audience member to return it to me, somewhat ashamed of myself, on 'Let me see some more' (2.3.6). I have a good arm. I screw the ball too tight. I throw. The yard audience must be twenty feet away but it goes like a bullet and hits Ralph's daughter Kate smack on the nose. She looks momentarily stunned. We've struck up a friendship over the last couple of days, exchanging stories of families coping at home without us, and she looks a bit hurt. I gesture something of an apology, she collects herself and throws the letter back. Then George comes out with a skirt on and I go from braining Kate to kissing Kate. This double isn't effected in front of the spectators and for every audience except this one his entrance raises a few laughs and our kiss some uncomfortable exclamations.

I was surprised by the lack of laughs during Kate's entrance. I found this encouraging and it further convinced me that the audience silence was an engaged and respectful one **(GL)**.

Here, once this has been played, we change back to Hal and Poins for 2.4. Tom requests cups of sack from various spectators, some of whom are glared at by Bob's Peto as the culprits of lime-infestation, and Falstaff's recounting of the botched robbery, the trading of insults, the explanation of the running away and the play-within-the play all works its irrepressible magic. This scene, 2.4, the heart of the play, is especially illustrative of the play of engagement I am describing. On lines like Hal's incredulous 'I'll no longer be guilty of this sin' (235), or Falstaff's ingenious 'I was now a coward on instinct' (264) or self-preserving 'I'll hide me' (490), the actors' delivery takes in both the characters in the scene and (those in) the audience. Thus these lines are offered somewhere between conversation and aside, both and neither, a third way of communicating which straddles representation and presentation, theatre and metatheatre, locus and platea, fiction and reality. The audience both partakes in and dictates the cumulative performative affect of the scene, primarily one of hilarity, because of the play of engagement that the dramaturgy demands. Yes, we play to the audience; but like the peacocks we play with and around them too.

There were other notable instances of such engagement in the second half of the production: chiefly, in Alison Findlay's purple-suited messenger (4.1.12), who, both timid and bold, actually came up on to the stage with her errand, and then in Falstaff's casting of the (seated) groundlings as his soldiers, 'ragged as Lazarus' (4.2.25), which, for Rose Gaby, who was editing the play, resonated with the line about 'They'll fill a pit as well as better' (4.2.65–66). But I will conclude, by considering how the play of engagement facilitates cumulative performative affect via reflection on actor, character, narrative, personal and performative affects experienced during Hal and Hotspur's battle.

I'm looking forward to the fight, an example of actor affect. I don't have to speak so much. It's an enjoyable routine, although, like previous Hotspur David Harewood's playful resentment at having to lose the final duel to Michael McFadyen's Hal,[45] I slightly bristle at being defeated by someone twenty years younger than me. Why have I only applied Just for Men™ to my head and not

45. Bella Merlin, *With the Rogue's Company: Henry IV at the National Theatre* (London: Oberon Books, 2005), p. 9.

also to my hopelessly greying beard?! I'm fit, but not quite as fit as I'd like, and, unlike the boy-player Desdemona for 1610 Oxford *Othello*, as Scott McMillin supposes,[46] I breathe very heavily after being vanquished. There's one more thing. Last time we played George forgets to close my eyes as I stare dead out at the audience and he waffles on about unblinking honour. Close my eyes, damn you, close them. He does. All of this closely dovetails with character affect. We begin the fight with Hotspur arrogantly sure of success and Hal cowering somewhat, but determined to go through with it. And then, when I am slain, disbelief at first and then despair of those lost titles. As I die, I look out to the audience to prophesy and then I eyeball Ralph on 'food for-' (5.4.85). The narrative affect perhaps turns on heroism, respectively misplaced and belatedly achieved. When characters lose their life we leave their tunics on the stage – not sure where I pinched this probably well-worn convention from – so that the cost of the battle accumulates. Perhaps this resonates with the personal affect of certain members of the audience. Or maybe the Englishwomen and men in the audience are struck by their history, a history of death, being played down under, a concrete example of an o'er-played scene in 'states unborn and accents yet unknown' (*Julius Caesar* 3.1.113). Or, perhaps the Australian Shakespeareans in the audience rejoice at an at least temporary death for Directors' Shakespeare. Some of these answers are provided in the post-show talk. I hear myself talking about the emotions I was feeling during the show, about my character's emotions (especially why Hotspur is so angry), about the emotional journey of the story and of the emotions I could sense coming back from the audience.[47] And I say I think they are all interrelated and could someone please write that down …

46. Scott McMillin, 'The Sharer and His Boy: Rehearsing Shakespeare's Women', in Peter Holland and Stephen Orgel, eds., *From Script to Stage in Early Modern England* (Basingstoke: Palgrave Macmillan, 2004), pp. 233–234.

47. In 'Intuition in Practice: Emotion and Feeling in the Artistic Process', p. 128, Harry Feiner writes: 'Though this may seem contradictory, it may be common to the nature of experience that ideas are originally intuited emotionally which are later explicated rationally with theory. We come to understand what has already happened to us on a more primal level.'

APPENDIX 5

Cast and Production team:
Falstaff / Blunt / Glendower – Tom Considine
Prince Hal / Kate Hotspur – George Lingard
King Henry / Hostess / Peto – Bob Pavlich
Westmoreland / Worcester / Douglas / Bardolph / Sheriff – Chris White
Hotspur / Poins / John of Lancaster – Tom Davies / Rob Conkie

Director – Rob Conkie
Designer – Romanie Harper
Fight Director – Chris Serong
Stage Manager – Remi D'Agostin

Production details:
This production played for 18 performances.
Union Hall, La Trobe University, 4–12 March 2011
New Fortune Theatre, University of Western Australia, 16 September 2011
45Downstairs, Melbourne, 28 February–11 March 2012.

CHAPTER 6
Ghosting Shakespeare

I acknowledge the Wurundjeri people of the Kulin Nations as the traditional custodians of the land upon which the work of this chapter was conducted. I recognise their ongoing connection to the land and value the unique contribution the Wurundjeri people and all Indigenous Australians make to the wider Australian society. I pay my respects to their Elders, past, present and future.

Remember me

This chapter is prompted by a mural painted on a shed wall backing on to a communal path in North Fitzroy, Melbourne, Australia.[1] The subject of the mural is the Australian Aboriginal Flag, black above to represent the Aboriginal people, red below to represent the spiritual, but bloodied earth, and with REMEMBER ME stencilled onto the yellow sun at the flag's centre. The mural was painted by

My photograph of 'Remember Me', by Reko Rennie.

Reko Rennie, a Melbourne-born Kamilaroi/Gamilaraay/Gummaroi street artist of international repute. In the text that accompanies Rennie's photographic essay documenting the production of the mural (for a Master of Arts at RMIT University), he frames the (research) project thus: 'in what ways does my artwork reveal my identity as an urban Indigenous artist and raise awareness about contemporary Indigenous issues?' After this, the various stages of the mural as a work-in-progress are labelled: 'I want to make images that will cause people to: … Reframe … Rethink … And be re-educated … I want people to remember.'[2]

1. In 'Introduction: Making Indigenous Place in the Australian City', *Postcolonial Studies* 15:2 (2012), 135–136, Emily Potter observes of the Fitzroy (and neighbouring Collingwood) area that 'From the 1930s to the 1970s particularly, these suburbs became hubs of Aboriginal social services (educational and medical, for instance) as well as activism and political agitation.' Lee-Anne Hall notes in Sylvia Kleinert and Margot Neale, eds., *The Oxford Companion to Aboriginal Art and Culture* (South Melbourne: Oxford University Press, 2000), p. 281, that the 'Nindeebiya Aboriginal Workshop was an early example of a community-based art workshop serving an Aboriginal population. Based in Fitzroy, in inner Melbourne, Nindeebiya began operations in 1976 with small grants from several funding bodies. Offering a program of arts and crafts, the workshop sought to reduce the effects of social problems such as alcohol and drug abuse. Activities included screen-printing, mural design, and painting.'

2. Reko Rennie, 'Remember me', *Creative Approaches to Research* 1:1 (2008), 73–79.

3. Chris Healy, *Forgetting Aborigines* (Sydney: University of New South Wales Press, 2008).

4. Mark Finnane writes, in '"Payback", Customary Law and Criminal Law in Colonised Australia', *International Journal of the Sociology of Law* 29 (2001), 293, that 'Satisfaction of a grievance, such as **death** or **wife-stealing**, may be sought through ritual ceremony, gift-giving, corporal punishment and ordeal, or even killing (my emphasis)'.

5. See note 43, p. 152. All quotations from *Hamlet* are taken, unless otherwise noted, from Ann Thompson and Neil Taylor's Q2 Arden 3 edition of the play (London: Arden Shakespeare, 2006).

6. For an Indigenous appropriation (by an Indigenous artist) of a canonical theatrical text, see Wesley Enoch's *Black Medea*, in *Contemporary Indigenous Plays* (Sydney: Currency Press, 2007). On Shakespeare productions in Australia featuring Indigeneity, see Elizabeth Schafer, 'Reconciliation Shakespeare? Aboriginal Presence in Australian Shakespeare Production', in Elizabeth Schafer and Susan Bradley Smith, eds., *Playing Australia: Australian Theatre on the International Stage* (Amsterdam: Rodopi, 2003), pp. 63–78, and Emma Cox, '"What's past is prologue": Performing Shakespeare and Aboriginality in Australia', *Multicultural Shakespeare: Translation, Appropriation and Performance* 8:23 (2011), 71–92.

7. 'Mo(u)rning in America: *Hamlet*, Reagan, and the Rights of Memory', *Theatre Journal* 59:1 (2007), 3, 5.

I am not claiming that Reko Rennie is ventriloquising Hamlet's father's Ghost; neither am I claiming, Harold Bloom-like, that Hamlet is ventriloquising Reko Rennie. But I am using the mural in order to reframe and rethink a reading of Shakespeare's *Hamlet*, a reading impelled by both contemporary and historical Indigenous issues. My use of the term 'reading' reveals how this chapter does something different to the previous chapters: where previously I have attempted to re-perform already-played productions through performative writing, here I reread the play to imagine a new performative iteration of it. Thus, my aims here are: one, to re-energise engagement with *Hamlet* via contextual dialogue with Indigeneity; and, two, to rehearse scenes from Indigenous Australian history as a particular intervention in the oft-replayed narrative identified by Chris Healy of remembering, but then forgetting, Aborigines.[3]

My Indigeneity-focused reading of *Hamlet*, at its most basic, is this: the play is a story of dispossession, where a murdered father returns to demand that his son exact payback, an Aboriginal law of retribution and/or restoration, both for the murder and for the stealing of his wife.[4] A cursory reading of the first scene reveals the multiple resonances of such an approach. The sentinel Barnado's famous first-line anxiety about a possible reappearance of the ghost – 'Who's there?' – becomes, in this reading, an analogue of a society haunted by the spectre of its usurped and murdered forebears. Francisco's reply, 'Stand and unfold yourself' (1.1.2), in its original context a request for identification, becomes, for me, indicative of the unfolding or upheaval of identity that the remembering of Indigenous history potentially entails. Shortly after this initial exchange, when Horatio enters (with Marcellus) and has to offer his identification, he says that they are 'Friends to this ground' (13): being friends to the ground resonates powerfully within an explicitly Indigenous context. Horatio is there, as the academic sceptic, to offer a rational perspective on their 'fantasy' (22), but when he sees the ghost for himself he declares, 'It harrows me with fear and wonder' (43). The Arden 3 edition of the play glosses this line with 'The metaphor [of harrowing] derives from the agricultural implement that breaks up the ground after ploughing',[5] a continuation of the ground trope introduced by Horatio, a signal of how omnipresent images of ground, earth and soil will be within the play as a whole, and the establishing of a connection between ethereal ghostliness and material harrowing: Horatio's spirit is figured as broken matter. Horatio, however, who is non-Indigenous here, can elicit no answer from the ghost, irrespective of his 'I charge thee speak' (48–49) and is left to summarise Aboriginal deaths in custody, prime ministerial refusals to apologise, backtrackings and evasions on native title legislation, Stolen Generations and other too numerous examples, as boding 'some strange eruption to our state' (68).

I am not the first, of course, and shall not be the last, to appropriate *Hamlet* for a contemporary context.[6] In the recent past Timothy Raphael has, perhaps surprisingly, read Ronald Reagan's highly successful presidential strategy of 'mimetic and political re-membering of catastrophic bodies' via *Hamlet*. He further suggests, appositely for my project, that Hamlet's desire to have the Murder of Gonzago staged before his uncle is motivated by 'the capacity of performance to compel the living to acknowledge the dead'.[7] In an example from a diametric, if not unlinked, politics, Ewan Fernie's proof that *Hamlet* 'stands provocatively apart in the present' and that 'Like Shakespeare's ghost, [it] breaches and disrupts successive presents' is that the play's 'dramatization of spiritualized violence compels us to confront the defining issue of our present [2005]: terrorism'.[8] Who is 'me' in Reko Rennie's 'Remember me'? Who is 'we' in Kevin Rudd's same year (2008) 'We apologise'?[9] And who is Fernie's under-compulsion 'us'? On the last one, at least, it 'aint me. Fernie begins by citing Jacques Derrida's meditation on *Hamlet* whereby 'A masterpiece always moves, by definition, in the manner of a ghost' and that 'The thing haunts, for example, it causes, it inhabits without residing, without ever confining itself to the numerous versions of this passage, "The time is out of joint"'.[10] Perhaps Fernie shouldn't have, therefore, confined the play to the particular – although it can feel near universal – out-of-jointness of terrorist attacks. I enjoy his description of Sulayman Al-bassam's The *Al-Hamlet Summit* (2004), and lament not having seen it, with its eponymous prince 'as a diffident, Europeanized Arabic playboy' dressed 'in the robes of Islamic fundamentalism',[11] but my compulsion – both authors above use the word *compel* – is to apply what John J. Joughin has described as *Hamlet*'s 'radical legacy for the future allegorization of a political present'[12] to matters more local.

Taking a lead from Thomas Cartelli, Craig Dionne and Parmita Kapadia, the editors of *Native Shakespeares: Indigenous Appropriations on a Global Stage*, assert that 'The most important form of appropriation for our [localised and Indigenised] purposes is the transpositional mode, where the reader seizes upon a voice or grain of the text and brings it to light.'[13] Cartelli's explication of this mode is exemplary of the method here attempted: it 'identifies and isolates a specific theme, plot, or argument in its appropriative objective and brings it into its own, arguably analogous, interpretive field to underwrite or enrich a presumably related thesis or argument'.[14] My theme – a series of parallels, of arguable analogues, between Shakespeare's *Hamlet* and Australian Indigenous experience, historical and present – opens on to an expansive, and not easily navigable, interpretive field. The argument that follows is methodologically miscegenous; part literary presentism, part performative meditation, part anti-colonial politics and part, as a respectful stranger to the philosophy, critical Indigenous studies. A further illumination of this method is provided by Hamlet's conception of the Mousetrap, the play-within-the-play designed 'to catch the conscience of the king' (3.1.540): he says that 'I'll have these players / Play something like the murder of my father / Before mine uncle' (3.1.529–31). This short phrase 'something like', noted by Marvin Carlson in *The Haunted Stage*, as evocative of 'the inevitable slippage in all repetition' but which also 'at the same time acknowledges the congruence that still haunts the new performance',[15] is, again, highly apposite for my project. As the Mousetrap stands in relation to the play, as an exposé of wrong-doing, so my something like appropriation of *Hamlet* attempts a haunting unsettling of the play and, via Reko Rennie's plea to 'Remember me', the raising of 'awareness about contemporary Indigenous issues'. Thus, the tragedy of the First Australians, is, in this reading, something like a play called *Hamlet*.

8. 'Shakespeare and the Prospect of Presentism', *Shakespeare Survey* 58 (Cambridge University Press, 2005), p. 169.

9. Gay McAuley addresses this question in 'The National Apology Three Years Later', *Australian Studies* 3 (2011), 13-15.

10. 'Shakespeare and the Prospect of Presentism', p. 169.

11. Ibid., p. 182.

12. John J. Joughin, 'Shakespeare's Memorial Aesthetics', in Holland, ed., *Shakespeare, Memory and Performance*, p. 50.

13. *Native Shakespeares: Indigenous Appropriations on a Global Stage* (Aldershot: Ashgate, 2008), p. 10. In *Decolonizing Methodologies: Research and Indigenous Peoples*, 2nd edn (London: Zed Books, 2012), Linda Tuhiwai Smith describes (on p. 147) one of 'Twenty-five Indigenous Projects' thus: '*Indigenizing* ... similar to that which has occurred in literature, with a centring in consciousness of the landscapes, images, languages, themes, metaphors and stories of the indigenous world, and the disconnecting of many of the cultural ties between the settler society and its metropolitan homeland. This project involves non-indigenous activists and intellectuals.'

14. Thomas Cartelli, *Repositioning Shakespeare: National Formations, Postcolonial Appropriations* (London: Routledge, 1999), p. 17.

15. *The Haunted Stage: The Theatre as Memory Machine* (Ann Arbor: University of Michigan Press, 2003), p. 4.

Dramatis Personae

HAMLET — *an elder's son*
GHOST — *Hamlet's father, an elder recently deceased*
KING Claudius — *a powerful land-'owner', 'brother' of the deceased elder*
QUEEN Gertrude — *Hamlet's mother and his father's widow, now married to Claudius*
POLONIUS — *Claudius' chief of staff*
LAERTES — *Polonius' son*
OPHELIA — *Polonius' daughter*
HORATIO — *Hamlet's friend and fellow student*
ROSENCRANTZ / GUILDENSTERN — *also students and friends to Hamlet*
OSRIC — *land-'owner'*
GRAVEDIGGER — *a clown*
YORICK — *another clown*
FORTINBRAS — *a warrior*

1 **HAMLET** The hero is an Australian Aboriginal man living in the present day. He is about thirty years old and is doing a PhD in Philosophy. His thesis is on Derrida and 'Undecidability'.

2 **GHOST** Hamlet's father is an Indigenous elder from the eighteenth or nineteenth century. Hamlet and the Ghost are the men on either side of Byron Pickett's painting *Aboriginality* (1996), which 'comments on the changing life of Aborigines over the last two hundred years. On the left is the traditional elder, in the middle a station hand, and on the right an Aborigine of today, a self-portrait of the artist' (*Oxford Companion to Aboriginal Art and Culture*, p. 282). Who is the middle figure? Fortinbras, perhaps?

Ken Gelder and Jane M. Jacobs's *Uncanny Australia: Sacredness and Identity in a Postcolonial Nation* (Melbourne University Press, 1998) provides a fascinating discussion of Indigenous ghost stories.

It argues that 'the postcolonial ghost story speaks not so much about possession as (dis)possession, coming as it does after the fact of settlement. It deals with postoccupational matters' (32). Of one particular agitated bunyip narrative the authors write, 'The creature itself is highly unsettled, highly mobile, marauding, his whereabouts now even more difficult to predict than before' (35) and of Tracey Moffatt's film *BeDevil* they observe, 'these are ghost stories which refuse the fantasy of a fully embodied reconciliation' (38).

Mudrooroo's *Aboriginal Mythology* (London: Thorsons, 1994) does not mention ghosts, but in his novel *Master of the Ghost Dreaming* (Sydney: Angus & Robertson, 1993), a satirical reworking of George Augustus Robinson's hagiographic self-construction, the dying Aborigines confined to an island that is not their home, look to the shaman Jangamattuk to enter the dreaming of the invading ghosts in order to prevent more deaths and deliver healing. But it is not just the blacks who consider the whites ghosts: the unhappy missionary's wife complains, 'I'm not staying on. What with the natives dying off like flies, soon all that'll be here are ghosts. Just wandering ghosts hungry and pitiful' (43).

Commenting on his then forthcoming film *The Darkside*, a follow up to the award-winning *Samson and Delilah*, Warwick Thornton says:

I want to use ... contemporary stories to help other people understand that there is an amazing connection us Aboriginal people have with the afterlife – a connection to family that have passed on. I have seen ghosts in my life. I don't think I could go into this film being cynical ... the thing that was running through them all was that connection of family and the searching for meaning to life and death ...

3 **KING** The King is transhistorical. Janet Carsten writes in *Ghosts of Memory: Essays on Remembrance and Relatedness* (Oxford: Blackwell, 2007) that 'the presence of ghosts speaks not only of unresolved griefs and excessive losses, but that these manifest themselves in parallel temporalities in which the past takes on a more than usually vivid existence' (11). Claudius is thus any number of historical whitefellas who have murdered/dispossessed/ignored the traditional owners of the land they/he seize and exploit. He is Governor George Arthur; he is A. O. Neville; he is various Australian prime ministers. He is Hamlet's father's 'brother' and thereby Hamlet's 'father' by virtue of having married the widowed Gertrude.

4 **QUEEN** The Queen is also transhistorical. She is any of the number of Indigenous women taken by non-Indigenous men. Sometimes she performs this role in order to protect her people – she is Truganinni – and sometimes she is only able to make the best of the situation – maybe Evonne Goolagong-Cawley – in which she finds herself.

5 **POLONIUS** A white politician. Not as bloodthirsty as Claudius but prepared to support the regime for material advantage.

6 **LAERTES** He's a bit of a bogan.

7 **OPHELIA** A young white woman dissuaded from a relationship with an Indigenous man. A political pawn.

8 **HORATIO** Also a student, Horatio is what is sometimes referred to in the literature as 'an Aboriginal sympathiser'. He is Watkin Tench and John Green. Is he Governor Arthur Phillip? He is anthropologist Peter Sutton. I want to be Horatio.

9 **ROSENCRANTZ / GUILDENSTERN** Two more student friends of Hamlet's, the latter is Indigenous, the former not.

10 **OSRIC** Of this 'water-fly' sycophant, someone who has cashed in on the colonial designation of *terra nullius*, Hamlet says 'He hath much land, and fertile ... 'Tis a chough but, as I say, spacious in the possession of dirt' (5.2.69–75).

11 **GRAVEDIGGER** He might be Indigenous, much experienced in, and desensitised to, death. He might be non-Indigenous, a director of contemporary and literal Shakespeare productions.

12 **YORICK** A joker, an interpreter, a go-between; he is something like Bennelong.

13 **FORTINBRAS** An Indigenous man of Hamlet's age from sometime in the past, he is trying to assert a claim to land.

A place from which to speak

Attacking Bain Attwood for his critique of Sally Morgan's *My Place*, a critique with which she expresses considerable sympathy, Jackie Huggins writes: 'Foremostly I detest the imposition that anyone who is non-Aboriginal can define my Aboriginality for me and my race. Neither do I accept any definition of Aboriginality by non-Aboriginals, as it insults my intelligence, spirit and soul and negates my heritage.' Further, she writes that 'There are no books written by non-Aboriginals that can tell me what it is to be Black as it is a fiction and an ethnographic presumption to do so.'[16] Earlier in the same volume, Ian Anderson frames this issue as a more open question: '"how" is it possible', he asks, 'for non-Aboriginal academics to "know" Aboriginal people and issues in order to constructively and truthfully represent them?' This is obviously a fundamental question for my undertaking, as is Huggins' trenchant dismissals of white definitions of blackness. The answer Anderson proposes is that 'What is needed is an active engagement with some of the core issues raised by Indigenous critical writers who have called into question the basis of traditional systems of "western" knowledge.'[17] Two of those core issues raised by Michael Dodson (in the same volume) are: one, understanding the motivations behind historical constructions of Aboriginality; and two, the related necessity of subverting such constructions which are both hegemonic and insidious.[18] My 'active engagement' with such issues has included consulting and dialoguing about this project with Indigenous academics such as Julie Andrews and Phillip Morrissey, and, some time after this, workshopping the first act of the play with Indigenous actors Gregory Fryer and Justin Grant. Any production growing out of these ideas, discussions and the workshop would, of course, include a cast of both Indigenous and non-Indigenous actors and would need to be co-directed by an Indigenous artist: indeed, perhaps a better model would have an Indigenous director, to whom I could serve as dramaturg.[19] In this collaborative model, in which many of the readings posited here would be discussed, negotiated and contested, the dialogue, the active engagement over the politics of representation could be continued. On this notion, Marcia Langton writes that Aboriginality, an unfixed thing, 'arises from the intersubjectivity of black and white in a dialogue.'[20] If the ideas here expressed, however, meet with the sort of disapprobation with which I opened this paragraph, then the dialogue would need to be stopped, and the project abandoned or reconceived, but that is the risk that non-Indigenous intervention in Indigenous affairs entails, irrespective of attempts at respectful and ethical engagement.

Part of my solution to these problems is to position myself for this project in the role of Horatio, the observer and scholarly commentator. Horatio is a useful analogue in this regard on several levels. He is, as I am, an outsider to the action, not a direct agent in it. Moreover, as John Kerrigan notes, Horatio's capacity to fulfil the task required of him by the dying prince, the relating of Hamlet's story, is limited. Kerrigan writes that despite Horatio's admirable qualities he 'is simply not equipped by circumstance to inform the yet unknowing world'[21] of numerous facets of the story and this is a reminder of my incapacity to relate the whole, in this particular reading, of Hamlet's story. What does Horatio do?

16. 'Always was Always Will Be', in Michelle Grossman, ed., *Blacklines: Contemporary Critical Writing by Indigenous Australians* (Melbourne University Press, 2003), p. 60.

17. 'Introduction: The Aboriginal Critique of Colonial Knowing', in *Blacklines*, p. 21.

18. 'The End in the Beginning: Re(de)finding Aboriginality', in *Blacklines*, pp. 31-42.

19. This would represent a reversal of the power structures revealed respectively by Elizabeth Schafer and Emma Cox, cited above in note 6: the majority of the Indigenous–non-Indigenous Australian Shakespeare productions they discuss have non-Indigenous directors and Indigenous supporters/facilitators/enablers of that director.

20. '*Well, I Heard it on the Radio and I Saw it on the Television*': *An Essay for the Australian Film Commission on the Politics and Aesthetics of Filmmaking by and about Aboriginal People and Things* (North Sydney: Australian Film Commission, 1993), p. 31.

21. 'Hieronimo, Hamlet and Remembrance', *Essays in Criticism* 31:2 (1981), 121.

Twice he is called upon to confirm other opinions: firstly, the existence of the Ghost; and secondly, Claudius' guilt-revealing reaction to having witnessed the Mousetrap. And twice he is called upon to report: first, to Hamlet that he has seen his dead father; and second, that

> So shall you hear
> Of carnal, bloody and unnatural acts,
> Of accidental judgements, casual slaughters,
> Of deaths put on by cunning, and for no cause … (5.2.364–67).

To confirm and to report is not to explain or, as Huggins detests, to define. My task is to best approximate the qualities Hamlet finds in Horatio which make him an effective witness and reporter. He describes his friend with the words 'blest are those / Whose blood and judgement are so well co-meddled' (3.2.64–65) and, indeed, this project represents equal parts affect and intellect. Finally, when Hamlet first sees Horatio in the play, just after his first despairing soliloquy, and just before Horatio informs him of the Ghost, the prince's question of why Horatio is there is met with, 'a truant disposition, good my lord' (1.2.168): the reading that follows below might be characterised as a truant disquisition.

The counterfeit presentment of two brothers

Old Hamlet and Claudius are not, in this reading, biological brothers; the former is black and the latter is white. In the play, when Hamlet juxtaposes their respective pictures in order to chastise his mother's choice in remarrying, he likewise figures the brothers as white and black, and is incredulous that Gertrude could prefer the latter to the former:

> Have you eyes?
> Could you on this fair mountain leave to feed,
> And batten on this moor? Ha! have you eyes? (3.4.63–65)

In the antipodean reversal posited here, black is fair. In what sense, then, according to this performative reading (and writing), are Old Hamlet and Claudius brothers? First, they are brothers of the land: Old Hamlet is the traditional owner and custodian of that land and Claudius is the invader, settler and appropriator of it. Second, they are brothers via marriage to Gertrude: Claudius becomes Old Hamlet's brother and young Hamlet's father once he has married into the family. Lastly – and this was a discovery of having workshopped the first act of the play with Indigenous (and non-Indigenous) actors, something to which I will return in more detail below – Claudius, is invited, in the manner extended to white anthropologist Peter Sutton, to become fully kindred (with Victor Wolmby and his family).[22] Unlike Sutton, but something like the many white figures in colonial Australian history who have initially or ostensibly appeared sympathetic to the plight of Indigenous Australians, such as A. O. Neville or George Augustus Robinson, but have then proved ultimately self-serving and destructive, Claudius, once embraced as family, repays the privilege with

22. See Peter Sutton, *The Politics of Suffering: Indigenous Australians and the End of the Liberal Consensus* (Melbourne University Press, 2009), pp. 1–5.

138

treachery. As figurative brothers, Old Hamlet and Claudius figure two specific notions in this reading: the former figures ghostliness and haunting, the way both Indigenous, but also non-Indigenous, Australians are haunted by murdered and dispossessed forbears; and the latter figures forgetfulness, what the oft-cited W. E. Stanner calls 'the Great Australian silence' and a 'cult of forgetfulness practised on a national scale'.[23]

Analyses of Australian Indigenous histories are suffused with ghostliness and haunting. When Marcia Langton describes Ricky Maynard's photographs of Tasmanian Aboriginal people, some of whom might visually suggest Old Hamlet's Ghost in this reading, she says:

It's as if the past is the heaviest burden for Tasmanian Aboriginal people and it's as if they were long ago condemned to death and they live in a kind of netherworld because of the racism, the historical racism and a peculiar hateful kind of racism that they suffered.[24]

The netherworld of the play – purgatory – is described by the Ghost as a place of 'sulphurous and tormenting flames' (1.5.3). More apt, perhaps, as a description of the faces photographed by Maynard is Horatio's description of the Ghost to Hamlet: 'A countenance more in sorrow than in anger' (1.2.230). Extending 'clinical and theoretical work' on trauma, and applying it to Australian Aboriginal history, Bain Attwood writes that 'trauma is inherently incomprehensible or unrepresentable in any realistic sense' and 'that it can only be represented, inadequately, in highly symbolic terms that necessarily distort it in some sense or another'. Further, trauma 'reveals itself in its belatedness, and … it returns to haunt the psyches of those party to it – especially victims, but also perpetrators, bystanders, collaborators and so forth. It can affect not only contemporaries but also those born later'.[25] Even more resonant with *Hamlet*, such that I must quote it at considerable length, is anthropologist Deborah Bird Rose's account of 'Dead Bodies' in relation to the Yarralin people of Australia's north:

The most salient feature of this part of the dead person – *manngyin* … – is that it can be dangerous. My understanding is that this is because it is the unique individual with intimate ties to people and all the passions of life. Unless a person dies shortly after birth or at an extraordinarily advanced age, Yarralin people believe that death is almost certainly caused through malevolent human agency, and that the dead person is angry about having died. They long for the people they love and want to kill those who made them die. Yarralin people believe that out of love and loneliness a *manngyin* may return to take its relations or spouse with it on its journey to the sky country, thereby causing them to die. Conversely, if a *manngyin* feels that its family has not shown proper concern to prevent or avenge its death, it will turn its anger on its own relatives, killing them one by one.[26]

History, art, anthropology and, next, cultural studies: the theme of haunting also suffuses, in particular, Chris Healy's account of *Forgetting Aborigines*. He cites Klauss Neumann's rebuttal of Keith Windschuttle's denialism, which focuses not on the disputed numbers of murders, but on the seizing of the land in the first place: 'It is the initial act of dispossession, more so than settler–indigenous conflict, that had a lasting impact on settler-colonial society and keeps

23. These phrases are cited by, among others: Healy, *Forgetting Aborigines*, p. 16; McAuley, 'National Apology Three Years Later', p. 16; and A. Dirk Moses, 'Genocide and Settler Society in Australian History', in A. Dirk Moses, ed., *Genocide and Settler Society: Frontier Violence and Stolen Indigenous Children in Australian History* (New York: Berghahn Books, 2004), p. 9.

24. *First Australians: Her Will to Survive* (SBS Corporation, 2008). Episode 2. Speaker: Marcia Langton, 49 minutes, 35–55 seconds.

25. Bain Attwood, *Telling the Truth about Aboriginal History* (Crow's Nest: Allen & Unwin, 2005), p. 177.

26. *Dingo Makes us Human: Life and Land in an Australian Aboriginal Culture* (Cambridge University Press, 2000), p. 72. On the previous page, Rose records an interview with Old Tim describing manngyin: 'When him dead, his body, he leaves his bones, he get up from hole longa grave … He get up, look around country, up to chest, the rest underground … Talks to himself in graveyard place … "Where my wife? I like to go down to my wife." Nother little boy come along back behind. Dead man [talk]: "I've gotta go back to my wife." Little boy talk: "No. You gotta go that way."'

27. *Forgetting Aborigines*, p. 21.
28. Ibid., p. 23.

29. Ibid., p. 219.

30. Ibid., p. 91.

haunting Australia to the present day.'[27] Healy continues with passages such as 'the achievement of civic rights is haunted by dispossession and genocide'[28] and 'Aboriginality is always there for settler and indigenous Australians. It haunts both those who are prepared to disinter unpalatable memories and those enamoured with amnesia, repression or denial.'[29] He celebrates 'Leah King-Smith's haunting ghost pictures',[30] described elsewhere as having achieved

King Billy 5. Artwork and Permission to print by Leah King-Smith.

atmospheric, almost dreamlike, effects by overlaying nineteenth-century photographs of Aboriginal subjects with her own contemporary painted and photographed images of the Australian bush. The artist's subtle layering, which is not unlike the ghosting created by double exposure in nineteenth-century spirit photographs, attempts to encourage the audience to 'activate their inner sight to view Aboriginal people.'[29]

29. *The Oxford Companion to Aboriginal Art and Culture*, p. 289.

King-Smith's symbolic (perhaps, as Attwood writes above) art is especially relevant to my reading (like Rose's ethnography) because of its explicit, spectral engagement of past and present, but Maynard's realist images no less represent a present request to 'remember me' from the past.

Some requests, though, however important and insistent, go unheeded. Claudius, for example, practises the 'cult of forgetfulness' identified by W. E. Stanner, even as he speaks (for the first time in the play) of 'memory', 'grief', 'woe', 'sorrow' and 'remembrance':

> Though yet of Hamlet our dear brother's death
> The memory be green, and that it us befitted
> To bear our hearts in grief, and our whole kingdom
> To be contracted in one brow of woe,
> Yet so far hath discretion fought with nature
> That we with wisest sorrow think on him
> Together with remembrance of ourselves. (1.2.1–7)

There needs no Ghost come from the grave to report statesmen duplicitous, or, indeed, backstabbing, but the confidence of Claudius' text implies, to me, and perhaps especially for this reading, that he has begun to believe his own narrative, that even in remembrance he is forgetting. Later in the scene, when he is upbraiding Hamlet for 'obstinate condolement' (1.2.93) in not tempering his two-month-old grief, Claudius charges him with 'A fault against the dead' (102). Claudius is obviously the antithesis of Macbeth, whose face 'is as a book where men / May read strange matters' (*Macbeth* 1.5.61–62): he is either brazen or amnesiac enough to admonish Hamlet with words which describe his, Claudius', literal fault against the dead.

Claudius' capacity for self-deception develops into self-obsession. When Gertrude reports Hamlet's slaying of Polonius his first thought, a not inaccurate one, is, 'It had been so with us had we been there', and then, 'It will be laid to us' (4.1.13, 16). His seemingly unselfconscious and repeated use of the royal we, and of the ownership that it implies – six times in the opening seven lines quoted above – is demonstrative, especially in this reading, of: one, a split in his subjectivity into which he can displace and erase responsibility for past actions; and two, of the appropriative motivation and result of those actions. This arrogant and possessive amnesia finds full expression when Gertrude protests his innocence of Polonius' death to Laertes. Claudius does not require Gertrude's intervention; he says:

> Let him go, Gertrude, do not fear our person.
> There's such divinity doth hedge a king
> That treason can but peep to what it would,
> Acts little of his will. (4.5.122–25)

Claudius' cultlike devotion to forgetting means that he is here somehow able to invoke divine providence in support of his reign; there appears no memory of his own peeping treason, nor that such a hedge failed to protect Old Hamlet. I do not hear dissemblance in these lines, nor guilt, though the latter is clearly evident when Claudius is earlier at prayer (3.3.36–96). I do not hear a disavowal or denial of the past, which is at least some kind of acknowledgement. I hear a sense of entitlement and right founded on forgetfulness.

Though Old Hamlet's Ghost and Claudius do not coincide or meet in the play, the twin figures of ghostly haunting and forgetfulness continually overlap and work cyclically to reproduce one another. Thus, John McIntyre, something like Claudius, was speared (in 1790) as payback for killing the sisters and brothers of the something-like Old Hamlet warrior, Pemulwuy. Pemulwuy's exploits – waging guerrilla warfare against the invaders, leading a hundred-strong force against the British at Parramatta and surviving multiple gunshot wounds before finally getting shot and made a trophy – are ghosted by Eric Willmot's novel, *Pemulwuy: The Rainbow Warrior*.[30] Or, William Barak (1824–1903), something like Old Hamlet, called 'King William, last chief of the Yarra Yarra tribe', go-between his people and the inaccurately named, Claudius-like, Board for the Protection of Aborigines. He is ghosted by legendary Indigenous actor Uncle Jack Charles in Andrea James and Giordano Nanni's Ilbijerri Theatre Company production of *Coranderrk*,[31] the story of Aboriginal self-determination in the face of inestimable odds at Coranderrk reserve. The desire to forget is interrupted by unwanted spectres, sometimes in the form of novels or plays, the sightings, readings or spectatings of which produce anew the desire to forget.[32] And he who begins the play by agonising, 'Must I remember?' (1.2.143, 161), but then affirms that 'from the table of [his] memory / [He'll] wipe away all trivial fond records' so that the Ghost's 'commandment all alone shall live / Within the book and volume of [his] brain / Unmixed with baser matter' (1.5.99–100, 102–04), he, Hamlet, is the key site for this convergence of father/uncle and haunting/forgetting. He is both the son to whom the dead brother must appeal for payback and the 'son' through whom the live brother is reminded of his crime.

Hamlet, Spear-shaker

Hamlet to Horatio: I am native here. (1.4.14)

Hamlet to Rosencrantz and Guildernstern: I have of late, but wherefore I know not, lost all my mirth, forgone all custom of exercises and, indeed, it goes so heavily with my disposition that this goodly frame the earth seems to me a sterile promontory, this most excellent canopy the air, look you, this brave o'erhanging firmament, this majestical roof fretted with golden fire, why it appeareth nothing to me but a foul and pestilent congregation of vapours. (2.2.261–69)

Hamlet confides with Horatio but isn't being entirely truthful with his other university friends, of whom he later says (especially pertinent in Australia), 'I will trust as I will adders fanged' (3.4.201). He is not, actually, like *The Merchant of Venice*'s Antonio, claiming 'In sooth I know not why I am so sad' (1.1.1). He knows what is wrong and it is eating him from inside. Highly educated, self-aware, self-determined, he is radically troubled – mirth-lost – by the history of his people, and he feels an uneasy guilt about no longer observing traditional rites, having 'foregone all custom of exercises'. His relationship to the land is 'sterile'; his urban existence is a 'congregation of vapours'. Neither is he concentrating as diligently on his philosophy studies as is required. He is distracted by student theatre, by travelling players, and, in particular, by Indigenous theatre. It nourishes him; it oppresses him:

30. *Pemulwuy: The Rainbow Warrior* (Moorebank: Bantam Books, 1998).

31. See http://ilbijerri.com .au/productions/project/ coranderrk/, accessed 17 November 2014.

32. Chris Healy makes something like this point on p. 131 of *Forgetting Aborigines* when he asserts that 'To think of Aboriginality as a space of memory and the vernacular is to imagine the forgetting of dispossession as the spectre haunting Australian heritage.'

With Uncle Jack Charles about fifteen minutes before he went on in *Coranderrk*, Belvoir St Theatre, Sydney (2 January 2014).

22 Plea

The Woman carries the Suitcase with her as she approaches the audience.

You know there has always been this grieving,
Grieving for our Land, our families.
Our cultures that have been denied us.
But we have been taught to cry quietly
Where only our eyes betray us with tears.
But now, we can no longer wait,
I am scared my heart is hardening.
I fear I can no longer grieve
I am so full and know my capacity for grief.
What can I do but . . . perform.

These are my stories.
These are my people's stories,
They need to be told.

The Woman places the Suitcase down at the feet of the audience.[33]

DESERT SANDS

That's how the desert sands were created. My mum used to laugh 'n laugh at that story. She was always laughing, my old mum. Had a sense of humour.

The kids creep back into their beds and SANDY *is left to finish his story alone.*

She used to say that when you walk on the sand, the wind can blow away your footsteps, like you had never made them, and the earth would become pure again. The sand could heal itself. The land where my people come from is covered in red sand and in the old days, the women, to try and stop the white men from raping them, would shove sand inside themselves. Anything to stop the men from raping them, anything. [*He becomes quieter.*] And that's what my mother did, but it didn't stop them and so I came along. My mother, she loved me, but she called me Sandy anyway. She sure had a sense of humour, that one.

Lights fade to black.[34]

being exacted in reprisal. On the twenty-seventh of October, 1834, Governor Stirling led a detachment of soldiers and civilians to the Murray River at Pinjarra. In the early morning they came across a camp of some sixty or seventy natives. The detachment took up positions on both sides of the river. Rain, which had been threatening for some time, began to fall heavily. The party opened fire and more natives appeared from shelters. The men defended themselves with spears, while the women and children sought shelter in the river. For one hour they were subjected to crossfire from twenty-four guns from both banks. The official estimate was fifteen to twenty dead, but only eight women and several children were finally rounded up.[35]

MUST I REMEMBER?

33 Wesley Enoch and Deborah Mailman, *The 7 Stages of Grieving* (Brisbane: Playlab Press, 1996), p. 73.

34. Jane Harrison, *Stolen* (Sydney: Currency Press, 1998), pp. 22–23.

35. Jack Davis, *No Sugar* (Sydney: Currency Press, 1986), p. 81.

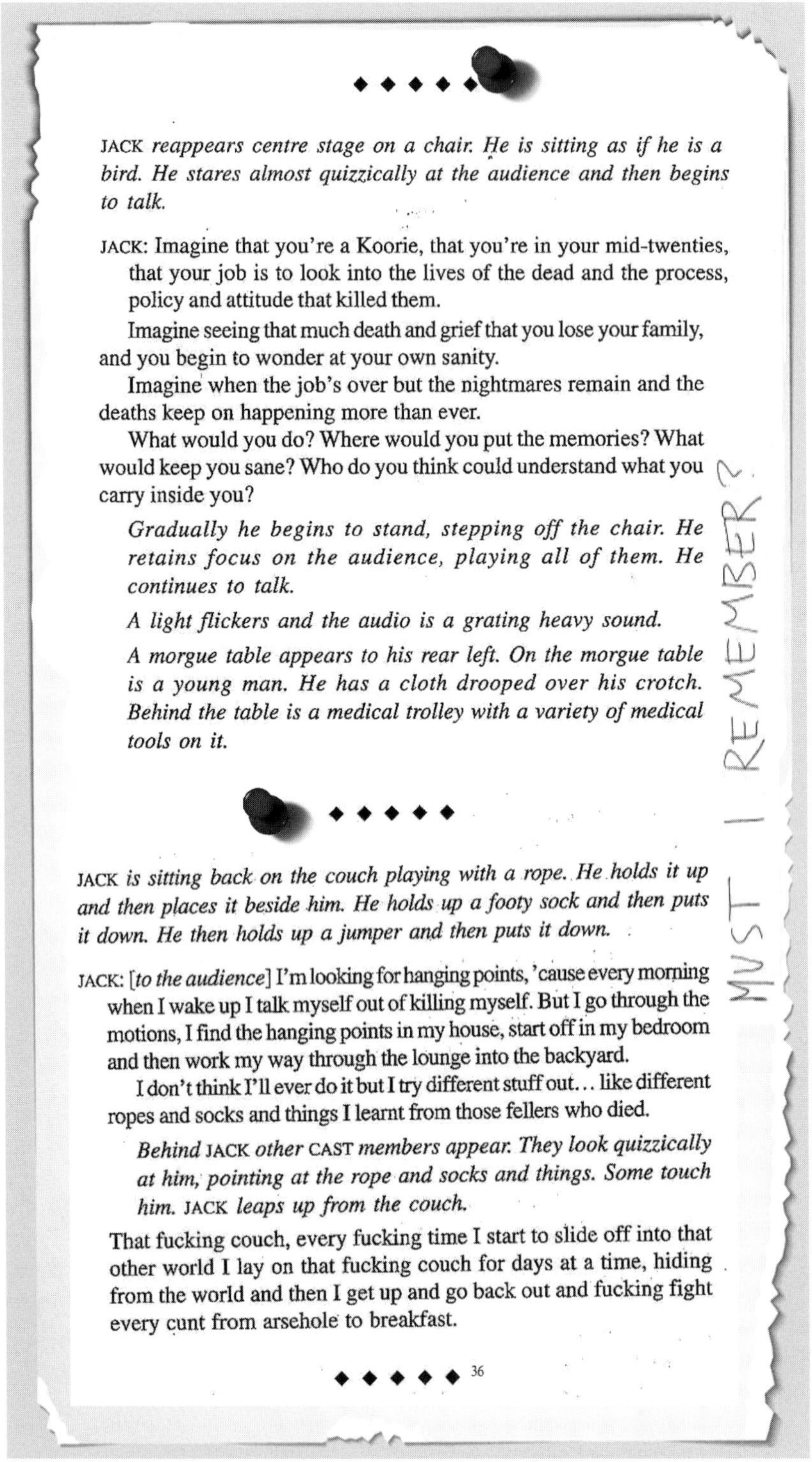

JACK *reappears centre stage on a chair. He is sitting as if he is a bird. He stares almost quizzically at the audience and then begins to talk.*

JACK: Imagine that you're a Koorie, that you're in your mid-twenties, that your job is to look into the lives of the dead and the process, policy and attitude that killed them.

Imagine seeing that much death and grief that you lose your family, and you begin to wonder at your own sanity.

Imagine when the job's over but the nightmares remain and the deaths keep on happening more than ever.

What would you do? Where would you put the memories? What would keep you sane? Who do you think could understand what you carry inside you?

Gradually he begins to stand, stepping off the chair. He retains focus on the audience, playing all of them. He continues to talk.

A light flickers and the audio is a grating heavy sound.

A morgue table appears to his rear left. On the morgue table is a young man. He has a cloth drooped over his crotch. Behind the table is a medical trolley with a variety of medical tools on it.

JACK *is sitting back on the couch playing with a rope. He holds it up and then places it beside him. He holds up a footy sock and then puts it down. He then holds up a jumper and then puts it down.*

JACK: [*to the audience*] I'm looking for hanging points, 'cause every morning when I wake up I talk myself out of killing myself. But I go through the motions, I find the hanging points in my house, start off in my bedroom and then work my way through the lounge into the backyard.

I don't think I'll ever do it but I try different stuff out… like different ropes and socks and things I learnt from those fellers who died.

Behind JACK *other* CAST *members appear. They look quizzically at him, pointing at the rope and socks and things. Some touch him.* JACK *leaps up from the couch.*

That fucking couch, every fucking time I start to slide off into that other world I lay on that fucking couch for days at a time, hiding from the world and then I get up and go back out and fucking fight every cunt from arsehole to breakfast.

◆ ◆ ◆ ◆ ◆ 36

(handwritten, right margin) MUST I REMEMBER?

36. Richard J. Frankland, *Conversations with the Dead,* in *Blak Inside: 6 Indigenous Plays from Victoria* (Strawberry Hills: Currency Press, 2002), pp. 221–222, 264.

The significance of the Ghost's demand to 'Remember me' changes, in this reading, from 'do not forget me' to 'make sure I am remembered' and, indeed, to 'imitate me'. Not his literal father, or perhaps both his literal father and also a series of elders from before and after white occupation, when the Ghost of Old Hamlet charges his son to 'Remember me' there is a lot to take on. Thus, when Hamlet informs Horatio of his plan to 'put an antic disposition on' (1.5.170), he is committing himself to a re-engagement with his history: colloquially, he is going to 'go native'. From this moment on Hamlet wears traditional dress and body markings and sometimes carries a spear. He has, of course, read Homi K. Bhabha on mimicry. On his bedroom wall he scrawls:

Mimicry is … the sign of the inappropriate … a difference of recalcitrance which coheres the dominant strategic function of colonial power, intensifies surveillance, and poses an immanent threat to both 'normalized' knowledges and disciplinary powers … Mimicry is at once resemblance and menace.[37]

Hamlet mimics Bennelong, the Yorick figure of 'infinite jest' (on the shores of what would be renamed Botany Bay as the renamers arrived), and of 'most excellent fancy' (5.1.175) (when transported to England as a curiosity from the colony). Hamlet is most interested, mimicry-interested, in the returned and dispossessed Bennelong. 'He takes to drink,' says Inga Clendinnen, 'in fury. He stalks through the streets of Sydney naked with his spears threatening [yes, he shakes spears] to kill the Governor.'[38] This describes Hamlet's behaviour during the word games with Polonius (3.2.365–77), now laden with far more threat, especially given that later that spear will pierce through both the arras and the old man's chest. And Hamlet mimics another mimic, Yorta Yorta man Glen Angus Atkinson. The *Age* newspaper reported on 20 December 2007 that Glen Atkinson contested drink-driving offences by attending Melbourne Magistrates Court wearing 'traditional dress', including having 'his criminal record number painted in white' across his back and 'his wardship number' likewise across his chest. Atkinson's defence was based on his depredation as a member of the Stolen Generations and the further claim that 'I don't believe they have the jurisdiction to adjudicate Aboriginal people under law.' Further, in a paraphrase of Hamlet's lament that 'I could be bounded in a nut shell and count myself a king of infinite space, were it not that I have bad dreams' (F 2.2.254–56), Atkinson claimed outside the court, 'It's not about the drink-driving charge, the magistrate can lock me away, it doesn't matter, this country is my jail.'[39]

Hamlet deploys other strategies of mimicry, for instance, when haranguing Ophelia about entering a nunnery (3.1.95–160), or when he is remonstrating with his friends for playing upon him like a pipe (3.2.287–363). Sometimes he carries a bottle of VB in a paper bag. He swigs from it mid-conversation, staggers a bit and slurs his words. But the bottle is filled with water; if Hamlet is drunk it is when he is on his own. Sometimes he mimics 'Jacky Jacky', 'disadvantaged and trapped in a cultural void … a "primitive" among "moderns"',[40] such as when Claudius interrogates him about where Polonius' body has been stowed. These behaviours disorient Polonius, make Claudius nervous

37. 'Of Mimicry and Man: The Ambivalence of Colonial Discourse', in Philip Rice and Patricia Waugh, eds., *Modern Literary Theory: A Reader*, 4th edn (London: Arnold, 2001), pp. 381, 382.

38. *First Australians: They Have Come to Stay* (SBS Corporation, 2008). Episode 1. Speaker: Inga Clendinnen, 49 minutes, 27–37 seconds.

39. Sarah-Jane Collins, 'Traditional Way to Court Appearance', *The Age*, 20 December 2007: www.theage.com.au/news/national/traditional-way-to-a-court-appearance/2007/12/19/1197740380534.html, accessed 31 March 2013.

40. Ian Anderson, cited in Healy, *Forgetting Aborigines*, p. 97.

and torment Gertrude but the moment when Hamlet mimics to most menacing effect (and affect), of course, is through the staging of the Murder of Gonzago. In the stage production of the *Mousetrap* within the stage production of *Hamlet: Remember Me*, the Player King is doubled, as often happens in the theatre, by the actor playing Old Hamlet's Ghost. In fact, he is a one-man band – it's Uncle Jack Charles touring his show *Jack Charles versus the Crown*[41] – and Polonius must announce in the singular that 'the actor is come hither' (2.2.329). Given this resources fiasco

41. See http://ilbijerri.com
.au/productions/project/
jack-charles-v-the-crown/,
accessed 17 November 2014.
Uncle Jack, of course, does
not offer Priam's slaughter,
but something from *Black
Medea* (see note 6).

Indigenous
Male: Hamlet
Male: Ghost / Player King / Gravedigger
Female: Gertrude / 2 Gravedigger
Female: Francisco / Guildenstern / Fortinbras
Non-Indigenous
Male: Claudius
Female: Horatio
Female: Ophelia / Barnardo
Male: Marcellus / Laertes / Rosencrantz
Female: Polonius / Osric

Hamlet recruits his friends into the *Mousetrap*: Lucianus is played by Rosencrantz and the Player Queen by Guildenstern. When the latter realises, too late, what she's been duped into she wants to leave the stage but Hamlet intervenes, desperate that the 'necessary question of the play … be considered' (3.2.40–41). On 'Madam, how like you this play?' (3.2.223) he gets on to the stage – he has studied Augusto Boal's Joker figure within the Forum Theatre of the Oppressed[42] – grabs Guildenstern's Player Queen and forces her to continue with 'Sleep rock thy brain / And never come mischance between us twain' (3.2.221–22). When Gertrude replies to his question, her much anthologised answer, 'The lady doth protest too much, methinks' (224) refers, in part, to the actress struggling physically against Hamlet's unwarned and unwanted interruption. This Gertrude, though, has long suspected Claudius of foul play and has married him to try to protect her son. Thus, the line on protesting too much also suggests an anxious warning from mother to son not to agitate too much lest he suffer something like his father's fate.

42. Augusto Boal, *Games for
Actors and Non-actors*, trans.
Adrian Jackson, 2nd edn
(London: Routledge, 2002),
ch. 5.

To play's the thing
In the last week of September 2013, we (see the appendix for individual details) workshopped the first act of *Hamlet* according to the ideas presented here. The workshop took place in the Playroom, a medium size rehearsal/performance space in the Union Building at La Trobe University. After four days of rehearsing the staged reading (our Ghost only materialising in the afternoon of the third day), a small group of invited guests watched the performance, many of whom stayed behind to participate in the Long Table discussion afterwards.[43] It was only through this practice, and, as Marcia Langton argues above, the

43. This was dramaturg
and collaborator Penelope
Woods' idea drawn from
Lois Weaver's concept.

dialogue that took place, that the following observations about *Hamlet: Remember Me*, as more than an imaginative, well-intentioned and theoretical exercise, could be made.

Act 1, Scene 1 begins with the security guards, Barnardo and Francisco, outside a homestead somewhere in the Pilbara region of northern Western Australia. This place has been suggested in discussions around the rehearsal table, especially in the context of fracking, a practice we suppose our Claudius has imposed upon the land he has 'inherited'. This has resulted in environmental protests and therefore he has need of added security. Justin, who plays Hamlet, spent his early years in Darwin and is invaluable for such speculation. These background, contextual discussions inform the imaginative playing of the scene, but are not represented visually: it is a bare, slightly raised thrust stage, 3.6 metres wide × 6 metres deep, with a further raised step at the upstage end.

The Ghost, carrying a spear, enters through a gap in the upstage wall and walks through the midst of the guards and the now arrived Horatio and exits at the downstage left corner to walk behind the audience ready for his next entrance in the downstage right corner. In the film version I imagine of the production, the security guards' walkie-talkies are reduced to crackly static when the Ghost is proximate (which must be a well-worn cinematic cliché).

The second scene is staged as the ending of a party celebrating the marriage of Claudius and Gertrude. Moreover, it's a costume party and the theme, hopelessly insensitive on the new King's part, is early nineteenth century colonialism. I'm wanting to suggest that the Hamlet/ Old Hamlet/Claudius/Gertrude story has multiple, transhistorical iterations in colonial, Indigenous Australia. Thus, the newly married couple are intended to visually infer George Augustus Robinson and Trugannini, the former professing his intention to protect Aboriginal people, the latter desperately trying to make up for the former's shortcomings. But the costumes come off as stateswoman Polonius preps Claudius for a statement to the press. The world of the production is present day, but will be haunted by a Ghost from pre-invasion Australia privy to the colonial repetitions of his tragedy.

The fourth and fifth scenes are, of course, the most important for the workshop. It's in these scenes that Gregory (Ghost) and Justin's participation makes the most impact. Hamlet's discussion with Horatio about yet another Claudius-thrown party takes on a new resonance: disgusted, he says, 'they clepe *us* drunkards' (1.4.19), a bitter commentary on the stereotype, at least as old as *The Tempest*, of the drunken Indigene. When the Ghost urges Hamlet to follow him into the night, Gregory shows us a local beckoning gesture, a simple nod of the head in the direction that they will go. And when Hamlet declares 'Speak! I'll

The Long Table Etiquette

There is no beginning

It is a performance of a breakfast, lunch or dinner

Those seated at the table are the performers

The menu is up to you

Talk is the only course

There is no hostess

It is a democracy

To participate take an empty seat at the table

If the table is full you can request a seat

Once you leave the table you can come back

There can be silence

You can break the silence with a question

You can write your questions on the table

There can be laughter

There is no conclusion

'The Ghost speaks'. Detail from the Long Table (cloth). Illustrations by Long Table guest, Bernard Caleo.

go no further' (1.5.1), Gregory invites him to sit just as Justin has explained the young men do to listen to Elders in his community in Darwin. The story that the Ghost has to relate has obstinately refused to accommodate my reading – that the Ghost of Old Hamlet is in purgatory, the Catholic liminal netherworld – but a potential solution presents itself through the discussions and rehearsals. The tragedy of this Ghost 'confined to fast in fires' (1.5.11) is that his murder, unnatural on so many counts, has shunted him into the wrong afterlife.[44] The in-

vaders, and even the man he welcomed into family as a full brother, have brought a new religion and the Ghost finds himself not just in flames, but in the flames of the invader. Only in the right afterlife can the Ghost find rest and thus his appeal is doubly urgent. Once the story is told the Ghost, on 'If thou hast nature in thee bear it not' (1.5.81), hands his spear to his son, a crossing from the other side. But Hamlet is urban, urbane: he looks at the spear as if to say, 'what am I going to do with this?' The Ghost senses his reticence, enjoins him once more, and then departs with his famous farewell.

44. On p. 69 of *Dingo Makes Us Human,* Deborah Bird Rose notes that 'Some [Yarralin] people have accommodated Christian teachings within a general framework of ideas about spirits, but few people use Christian ideas in precisely the same way, and people have no interest in such accommodation.'

DVD still: Gregory Fryer (Ghost) farewells Hamlet (Justin Grant). Kate Flaherty from the Australian National University and Bob White from the University of Western Australia, two very generous Long Table participants, look on with students and colleagues from La Trobe University.

He poisons him i' th' garden for's estate

As rewarding as staging the ideas of *Hamlet: Remember Me* proved, it was not until I discovered a specific place, and imagined the action actually happening there, that an even greater enthusiasm for the ideas emerged. The Gumbi Gumbi gardens at the University of Southern Queensland (USQ) in Toowoomba tell, the sign at its entrance records,

the story of the journey of this land's original inhabitants whose ancient traditions and cultural values were focused on interconnectedness, through the dark times of dislocation and disempowerment and on to the People's return.

Two specific features of the Gumbi Gumbi garden make it an ideal site for a new version of the other story the gardens tell, that of 'the transition of non-Indigenous peoples from a position of ruthless domination and ignorance to a more enlightened position of wishing to understand and coming to appreciate the value of partnership'. This is a story, the sign continues to inform, 'that is still far from complete'. The first feature (below left) is the Yarning Circle, a place for the informal sharing of Indigenous stories. This particular circle will accommodate about 40 people sitting on its circumference of rocks. The second feature (below right) is the fifty metre long watercourse, which 'reflects the centrality and importance of water to life, both in the past and today'. I imagine the pro-

My photographs of the Yarning Circle at USQ.

duction happening here. It's dark, the security guards inhabit the circle and face away from the watercourse. There's just a suggestion of a (rabbit-proof) fence, perhaps with a danger symbol on it because of what's being extracted from the ground. The Ghost starts at the top of the watercourse – it hasn't, in my visits to USQ,[45] had any water in it – and walks ever so slowly, his feet disturbing the stones. The spectators hear him, but the too spooked security guards do not. Later, when the Ghost enjoins Hamlet to follow him, he walks along and atop the circle, forcing those sitting on the stones to make way for him and his not-far-behind son. And after the Ghost has commanded Hamlet to revenge and started the long walk back up the watercourse, Hamlet draws Claudius' face in the dirt with the spear tip, saying 'So, uncle, there you are' (1.5.110), before hastily erasing it with his foot when his companions find him.

Such a production might fulfil Judith Rugg's notion that 'site-specific artworks can be places in which to reconceptualize the garden as a focus for environmental [in this case, in a very wide sense] concerns'.[46] Even more apposite, though about site-specific performance more generally and not gardens in particular, Joanne Tompkins writes that 'space, place, site, landscape, and location are regularly characterized by ambiguity, contingency, and unsettlement'.[47] It is this last word, unsettlement, potentially representing a reversal of the euphemism of settlement, that resonates more clearly. And even more apposite and

45. On a second visit to USQ for the Australia and New Zealand Shakespeare Association Conference, Will West, Penelope Woods and Lyn Tribble offered a workshop in the Gumbi Gumbi garden on 'Historical Phenomenology'. Woods' section on aleatoric effects features Lyn and David McInnis performing the Hamlet/Polonius cloud routine in the Yarning Circle.

46. *Exploring Site-Specific Art: Issues of Space and Internationalism* (London: I. B. Tauris, 2010), p. 71.

47. 'The "Place" and Practice of Site-Specific Theatre and Performance', in Anna Birch and Joanne Tompkins, eds., *Performing Site-Specific Theatre* (Basingstoke: Palgrave Macmillan, 2012), p. 1.

resonant than this is Mike Pearson's formulation of site-specific performance, via scenographic collaborator Cliff McLucas, as a host/ghost dynamic: here, site-specific performance is characterised

> as the coexistence and overlay of two basic sets of architectures: those of the extant building or what he [McLucas] called the host, that which is at site – and those of the constructed scenography and performance, or the ghost, that which is temporarily brought to site. The site itself became an active component in the creation of performative meaning, rather than a neutral space of exposition or scenic backdrop for dramatic action.[48]

One danger, or 'trouble',[49] to use Nick Kaye's phrasing of the relationship between site and performance, of this production might be the potential reinscription or overdetermining of essentialist notions of the relationship of Indigenous peoples to the land. This is an opportune moment to remember that such a production could not take place without the consultation of, and collaboration with, not just other Indigenous artists – directors, dramaturgs, designers, actors – but also local Elders. By such dialogue, perhaps those ontological aspects identified by Marcia Langton might be creatively explored: she writes that for the Lakefield-Cliff Island peoples, 'being is constituted by being-in-place, [and] that, in their world, being and place are constituted simultaneously as being-in-a-place'; further, this ontology is enabled by 'the relationship between embodiment and emplacement: how beings are embodied in place and emplaced in body'.[50] The tragic flipside of this personal-environmental integration, of course, is its post-invasion disintegration: that displacement, and this is the Ghost of Old Hamlet's story here, results in disembodiment. And not just the Ghost, but Hamlet and Gertrude, too.

Forgetting history

Displaced, a/trophied, appropriated, Gertrude never forgets her history. Even before the full knowledge that the Mousetrap affords, her participation in Claudius' reign has been muted and grudging. In the production history of the play Gertrude has been played somewhere between almost willing accomplice to Claudius' crime and, therefore, sensuously enjoying her new marriage, to, at the other end of the spectrum, being unsure of whether her new husband had something to do with her first husband's death and then, as the awareness develops, of being actively hostile to Claudius. In the reading (and imagined performance) proposed here she exceeds even this latter position. From the beginning her role as Claudius' Queen has been under sufferance. Her comments in support of him, such as the exhortations to Hamlet to forego his grief (1.2.64–128), are motivated by her desire to protect Hamlet from potentially suffering the same fate as his father. She is subversive in order to survive and to enable the survival of her lineage. Her response to Hamlet after he has chastised her so brutally for remarrying, 'O Hamlet, thou hast cleft my heart in twain' (3.4.154), is an acknowledgement of her painful dividedness, of being split, something she has kept from him for his own sake. After Hamlet's outburst at her Gertrude

48. 'Haunted House: Staging *The Persians* with the British Army', in Birch and Tompkins, eds., *Performing Site-Specific Theatre*, p. 70.

49. *Site-Specific Art: Performance, Place and Documentation* (London: Routledge, 2000), p. 11.

50. 'The Edge of the Sacred, the Edge of Death: Sensual Inscriptions', in Bruno David and Meredith Wilson, eds., *Inscribed Landscapes: Marking and Making Place* (Honolulu: University of Hawai'i Press, 2002), pp. 259, 260.

temporarily lapses into numbness: her discussion with Claudius after Polonius' death and her dealings with Ophelia's madness and suicide are insensate; she is spiritually dispossessed by the material dispossessions into which she has been implicated. But she gathers herself for the play's end. Gertrudes at the knowing end of the spectrum often drink the poison in defiance of Claudius' protective, 'Gertrude, do not drink'. Here, this is amplified. Claudius physically intervenes but the Queen wrests the goblet back from him, fully aware of its contents, and replies with venom, 'I will, my lord. I pray you pardon me' (5.2.273–74).[51] Her efforts, like Trugannini's attempts to confound those who would make a keepsake of her skull, are somewhat in vain. Like his father, and now his mother, and many of his kin, Hamlet dies by poison.

Neither does the Gravedigger – in this reading also Indigenous – forget his history: he can't, he's standing six feet deep in it. But unlike Jack from *Conversations with the Dead*, another sort of gravedigger, he has become de-sensitised to it. When Hamlet and Horatio come across him apparently merrily digging they observe:

> HAMLET
> Has this fellow no feeling of his business? 'A sings in grave-making.
> HORATIO
> Custom hath made it in him a property of easiness. (5.1.61–64)

Later, though, when Hamlet asks him whose grave it is he is digging, the reply 'Mine, sir' (112) signals that if Denmark's a prison, then Indigenous Australia's a graveyard. The Gravedigger's literal reply, to this and other questions, also prompts an alternative reading of his identity. I also read the Gravedigger as the kind of Australian theatre director who creates contemporised and sometimes doggedly literal[52] Shakespeare productions. Marion Potts argues that 'Productions that update so specifically are often reductive',[53] to which I would add cluttered, gimmicky and illogical, but my chief objection to such productions, in the context of this argument, is the way that they – set RIGHT NOW!, with smart technologies, designer clothes and chic decors – forget, or, like the Gravedigger, have 'no feeling of' history. Though near ubiquitous in recent Australian Shakespearean theatrical production, the forgetting of history might not always be a bad thing, as the Bell Shakespeare Company's vibrant *Twelfth Night* (2010) set in the context of bushfire tragedy attested, but this same company's twenty-year orthodoxy of contemporising the plays in production seems to me endemic of the desire to dehistoricise Shakespeare on these shores. Such a strategy might be read as a political act, especially in its infancy as British fetters required breaking. But as a later orthodoxy of its own what is the political significance of forgetting Shakespeare's history? Such an approach fits into the notion espoused in Simon Palfrey's 'Ghostly Selections':

Australians of my generation tended to think that history happened elsewhere; that somehow we were liberated from it, on account of growing up in the greatest bloody place on earth, and that for us there would be no serious consequences.[54]

51. Perhaps, as a reversal of this image, there are moments in the production when Gertrude is enjoined to drink (at Claudius' celebrations) which she feigns to do and then pours the contents disdainfully on the ground when he is not looking.

52. See Stephen Greenblatt, *Hamlet in Purgatory* (Princeton University Press, 2001), p. 172.

53. Cited in Cox, '"What's past is prologue"': 86.

54. Simon Palfrey, 'Ghostly Selections', in *Shakespeare and I*, p. 251.

This chapter rests on an analogue: *Hamlet*, I have suggested, is something like the tragedy of the First Australians. Here, in conclusion, I'm suggesting that the forgetting of history in recent Australian Shakespearean theatrical production – where the past is not a foreign country but a kind of *terra nullius* – represents a metonymic play-within-a-play of wider historical forgetfulness. Moreover, the disengagement from the ideological ruptures of the early modern period that such a strategy entails, one of the most prominent ruptures of which, of course, is racial, is likewise something like the contemporary disengagement from ideological and material ruptures identified by critics from Stanner to Healy. Even Simon Phillips' post-colonial *Tempest* (1999), with Indigenous actors playing Caliban and Ariel and an Indigenous dance company representing other spirits of the isle, ended, for example, with the sentimental, 'no serious consequences' resolution of Caliban reinheriting the island.[55]

I have tended, in the past, to interpret Joseph Roach's oft-cited observation that 'memory is a process that depends crucially upon forgetting'[56] in terms that Hamlet describes: needless memories are jettisoned (or purposely forgotten: 'I'll wipe away', he says, cited above) so that other memories have space to exist. Thus, the clutter of a Phillips contemporised production seems to me to strangle the possibility of contemplation (maybe that's his point). But in the context of this reading I understand or appropriate Roach slightly differently. The memory that this reading attempts to recall, the cry of 'Remember me' which it attempts to amplify, is that of Australian Indigenous pasts and presents: the mnemonic that I have deployed is Shakespeare's *Hamlet*. But if *Hamlet* is something like the tragedy of the First Australians it is also, of course, something not like it. When the prophet Nathan confronts King David with having stolen by murder the beautiful Bathsheba he uses a story like and not like the real story and he relies on the King having (wilfully) forgotten the story in order to be powerfully remembered of it. Likewise, Claudius is viscerally impacted by the something like / something not quite like memory of his crime because of his wilful forgetting. And, if the reading (and foretaste of a production) that I have provided here has any force at all, it will be because it is something not like enough to get past its initial target audience – ooh, an Aboriginal Hamlet, how interesting, 'it touches us not' (3.2.235) – but also something like enough to register, to seize on forgetfulness and insist on remembering.

APPENDIX 6

Cast and Production team:

Hamlet – Justin Grant

Ghost – Gregory Fryer

Gertrude – Kristy Lillyst

Claudius – Tom Considine

Polonius – Meredith Rogers

Ophelia – Stef Falasca

Laertes – Nathaniel Shaw

Barnardo – Kurt Mottershead

Francisco – Leigh Ormsby-Langdon

Horatio – Helen Mayers

Director – Rob Conkie

Dramaturg – Penelope Woods

This staged reading workshop took place in The Playroom, Union Building, La Trobe University, on 27 September 2013.

---

55. See Cox, '"What's past is prologue"', 74–77.

56. Joseph Roach, *Cities of the Dead: Circum-Atlantic Performance* (New York: Columbia University Press, 1996), p. 2

CONCLUSION

I'd start seeing a lot more plays if they'd start making those in 3D, too. Cos they're pretty boring the way they are now. Just a bunch of people standin' around talkin' ... Don't you think it'd be nice if they made a 3D book, it's about time, isn't it? You just open up the book and a structure pops up between the pages. Well, guess what, it's not gonna happen, not in our life time.

Arj Barker, *Heavy*

Some time before hearing Arj Barker's stand-up routine, *Heavy*, I had an idea, which I still long to pursue, of a Shakespeare production pop-up book. In it, iconic Shakespeare productions pop out from the page. Sally Dexter's white box set for Peter Brook's *Dream* opens up and Alan Howard's Oberon is levered up and down perhaps followed by William Dudley's cathedral setting for Antony Sher's Richard III to scuttle across.[1] In the meantime I submit *Writing Performative Shakespeares*, an attempt to evoke, with a nod back to Pascale Aebischer at the beginning of this book (p. 4), perhaps 2½ dimensions of the Shakespearean performance event. And here I offer some concluding remarks on the form and content of those Shakespeares and the various modes and methods by which I have performatively written them.

One of the most insistent themes of this book has been that of failure, a theme perhaps in closest alignment with Della Pollock's characterisation of performative writing as nervous. I have described the genesis of this project as a failure to be able to represent Shakespearean performance via linear form and needing to find an alternative. Most of the productions discussed in this book instance some kind of failure or limitation. I suggested that the very best moments of the productions described in Chapter 1 occurred during the rehearsal processes and did not fully translate to the finished productions, when the vast majority of their audiences encountered them.[2] The productions I have worked on and that have featured in this book have been described at times as either hopelessly wayward in terms of the effects and meanings I was hoping to generate, or defective of execution or prone to unintended and sometimes quite (similarly unintended) comic effects. Chapters 3 and 4 focus the notion – in one instance via a series of frustratingly unfocused photographs – that you can't see everything in a production: you miss bits, people laugh inappropriately, as an audience member you sometimes lose concentration (especially, perhaps, in a six-hour production). This theme of failure, most explicitly explored by Nicholas Ridout and Jeremy Lopez (discussed in Chapter 5), is offered, especially in the context of materialising Shakespeare, as an antidote to idealising

1. Having written this, I find P. A. Skantze has beaten me to it: 'As an author I wish for a critical form somethiing like a pop-up book where every time the words seem to sink the bodies into the sea of the abstract, a bit of paper would jump out of the text and make Blackfriars Theatre into a 3-dimensional space, setting before us the close proximity of audience to thrust stage, for example.' *Stillness in Motion in the Seventeenth-Century Theatre* (London: Routledge, 2003), p. 3.

2. I discuss rehearsal as potentially exceeding performance as a means of engaging with Shakespearean production in 'The Pleasures of the Flesh', *Shakespeare Bulletin* 30:4 (2012), 411–429.

Shakespeare. The writing of performative Shakespeares, which takes note of split britches, broken voices, varieties of viewing perspective, temperatures, textures, etc., resists the notion, and the production histories that emerge from it,[3] that a Shakespearean production could or should be an ideal, whatever that means, version of the text.

3. I address these kinds of idealised production histories in 'Surveying *Survey*'.

A second preoccupation of this book, guided by the productions I have selected, has been of audience engagement. The productions discussed here of *Romeo and Juliet* (Chapter 1), *Othello* (Chapter 2), *King Lear* (Chapter 3) and *Henry IV, Part 1* (Chapter 5) all featured the use of direct address to their respective audiences. This is a reflection of the recent impact of original practices Shakespeare which, of course, does not have any overriding claims to such modes of address. The productions of *Pericles Punished* and *Othellophobia* were both end-on in darkened auditoria, both attempted specific politicised interpretations of the play (more of that below), which is perhaps also reflected by their changed titles. The *Roman Tragedies* production discussed in Chapter 4 perhaps represents a more complex form of audience engagement, straddling, as it does, the emerging forms of immersive and mediatised Shakespearean production. The imagined *Hamlet* production of Chapter 6 combines the emergent, or recently theorised, form of site-specific Shakespeare with direct address and political engagement. Related to this theme of engagement, and signalling an alignment to Pollock's articulation of the subjective and citational dimensions of performative writing, has been this book's staging of scholarly discussion. Most obviously via the round table at the heart of Chapter 4, which was inspired by the Shakespeare in Practice Network, but also gestured to via the feedback mechanisms of Chapters 2 and 5, the invitation to collaborative criticism at the conclusion of Chapter 3 and the centrality of dialogue to Chapter 6, this book has sought to, to return once more to Escolme, talk to its audience.

Writing Performative Shakespeares has tried to be evocatively, metonymically visual. Ranging from spatially rearranged pages and different uses of font and typeface, to pinboards offering the juxtaposition of a range of archive materials, to photographs of rehearsals, production moments, other artwork, and landscapes, this visuality has been designed to evoke aspects of performance such as atmosphere, embodiment and motility. In Chapter 4 the visual form of the comic book/graphic novel facilitates representation, even of (intertextual) musings, my remembering of Mark Rylance's Cleopatra, even as I am watching Chris Nietvelt's. This production, the visuality of which has been much scrutinised, was geopolitical in scope, concentrated, as the round table discusses, on mediatisation and its political discontents. Other productions are discussed throughout the book according to my interpretation of how they were attempting to intervene (consequentially) in political matters (with big and small Ps). These interventions concern race (Chapters 2 and 6), sex and violence (Chapter 3) and, in the very first chapter, the use of Shakespeare to comment on the issue of asylum seeking, subjectivities shaped in border crossings, war zones, and, in the very last image of the production (p. 45), detention.

Finally, and these observations are more about form than content, the chapters of this book have sometimes been subject to multiple iterations.[4] The most

4. Jacques Derrida discusses

obvious example of this iterative multiplicity is the Sudoku chapter (the example with which I started this book). The work began as a production (although, relevant in-class discussions at University College Winchester preceded the production) which then became the Sudoku article. I then turned the article into a performative installation which had iterations at conferences, research symposia, in class, and, even, at an (ill-fated) job interview. The installation itself was developed so that the participants wrote (back to it) rather than just read it. And then it was reworked for this book with the inclusion of three extra pages documenting the new production of *Othello*, as well as boxes representing both the installation and one of the student responses (p. 63, middle and lower right boxes). By the time this book is produced a performance event of Graphic Shakespeare devised by Bernard Caleo and myself will have occurred. It is planned, like the production of *Roman Tragedies*, to be globally mediatised, whereby the round-table discussants will read/perform their published words (and go off script to discuss the production more informally) via video-link technology. Engaging Shakespeare began as a performance, then became a seminar paper entitled 'The Play of Engagement', that seminar was then distributed and the feedback commentary I received was incorporated into the current chapter 5. Ghosting Shakespeare reversed this sequence: it began as an essay, 'Remember Me', was then workshopped as performance and then reworked into chapter 6. The writing of performative Shakespeares, it seems, especially in pedagogical contexts, generates performances in excess of the re-performance of the chosen productions and, perhaps, discussions of those performances in excess of those invited by more conventional modes of writing. That, at least, has been my hope.

performativity, via J. L. Austin, and iteration in 'Signature Event Context', in *Limited Inc* (Evanston, IL: Northwestern University Press, 1988), pp. 13–21.

Bibliography

Aebischer, Pascale, *Shakespeare's Violated Bodies: Stage and Screen Performance* (Cambridge University Press, 2004)

Anderson, Ian, 'Introduction: the Aboriginal critique of colonial knowing', in Michelle Grossman (ed.), *Blacklines: Contemporary Critical Writing by Indigenous Australians* (Carlton: Melbourne University Press, 2003), pp. 17–24

Attwood, Bain, *Telling the Truth about Aboriginal History* (Crow's Nest: Allen & Unwin, 2005)

Barker, Roberta, *Early Modern Tragedy, Gender and Performance, 1984–2000: The Destined Livery* (Basingstoke: Palgrave Macmillan, 2007)

Barrett, Estelle and Barbara Bolt (eds.), *Practice as Research: Approaches to Creative Arts Enquiry* (London: I.B. Tauris, 2010)

Barthes, Roland, *S/Z: An Essay*, trans. Richard Miller (New York: Farrar, Straus and Giroux, 1975)

Belsey, Catherine, *The Subject of Tragedy: Identity and Difference in Renaissance Drama* (London: Methuen, 1985)

Benedetti, Jean, *Stanislavski and the Actor* (London: Methuen, 1998)

Berry, Cicely, *The Actor and the Text* (London: Virgin Books, 2000)

Bessell, Jaquelyn, 'The Performance Research Group's *Antony and Cleopatra* (2010)', in Andrew James Hartley (ed.), *Shakespeare on the University Stage* (Cambridge University Press, 2015), pp. 185–200

Bhabha, Homi K., 'Of Mimicry and Man: The Ambivalence of Colonial Discourse', in Philip Rice and Patricia Waugh (eds.), *Modern Literary Theory: A Reader*, fourth edition (London: Arnold, 2001), pp. 380–86

Billing, Christian M., 'Introduction: Rehearsing Shakespeare: Embodiment, Collaboration, Risk and Play...', *Shakespeare Bulletin* 30:4 (2012), 383–410

'The Roman Tragedies', *Shakespeare Quarterly* 61:3 (2010), 415–39

Bloom, Harold, *Shakespeare and the Invention of the Human* (London: Fourth Estate, 1999)

Boal, Augusto, *Games for Actors and non-Actors*, trans. by Adrian Jackson, second edition (London: Routledge, 2002)

Bogart, Anne, 'Foreword', in Erin Hurley, *Theatre & Feeling* (Basingstoke: Palgrave Macmillan, 2010)

Borbonesa, *Othello – A Bestiary (with Floral Additions)*, illus. Ian Whitmore (Baskerville: Borbonesa, 2011)

Bristol, Michael, 'Race and the Comedy of Abjection in Othello', in Robert Shaughnessy (ed.), *Shakespeare in Performance* (Basingstoke: Macmillan Press Ltd, 2000), pp. 142–70

Brown, John Russell, *Shakespeare and the Theatrical Event* (Basingstoke: Palgrave Macmillan, 2002)

'Writing about Shakespeare's Plays in Performance', in Grace Ioppolo (ed.), *Shakespeare Performed: Essays in Honor of R. A. Foakes* (Newark: Associated University Presses, 2000), pp. 151–63

Carlson, Marvin, *Performance: A Critical Introduction* (London: Routledge, 1996)

The Haunted Stage: The Theatre as Memory Machine (Ann Arbor: The University of Michigan Press, 2003)

Carnicke, Sharon Marie, 'Stanislavsky's System: Pathways for the actor', in Alison Hodge (ed.), *Twentieth-Century Actor Training* (London: Routledge, 2000), pp. 11–36

Carson, Christie and Farah Karim-Cooper (eds.), *Shakespeare's Globe: A Theatrical Experiment* (Cambridge University Press, 2008)

Carson, Christie, 'The "Original Practices" Project: Introduction', in *Shakespeare's Globe: A Theatrical Experiment* (Cambridge University Press, 2008), pp. 29–34

Carsten, Janet, *Ghosts of Memory: Essays on Remembrance and Relatedness* (Oxford: Blackwell, 2007)

Cartelli, Thomas, *Repositioning Shakespeare: National formations, postcolonial appropriations* (London: Routledge, 1999)

Cohen, Ralph Alan, 'Directing at the Globe and the Blackfriars: Six Big Rules for Contemporary Directors', in Christie Carson and Farah Karim-Cooper (eds.), *Shakespeare's Globe: A Theatrical Experiment* (Cambridge University Press, 2008), pp. 211–25

Conkie, Rob, 'The Pleasures of the Flesh', *Shakespeare Bulletin* 30:4 (2012), 411–429

'Surveying *Survey*', *Cahiers Élisabéthains*, 40th Anniversary Special Issue, '"Nothing if not Critical": International Perspectives on Shakespearean Theatre Reviewing' (2012), 37–44

Cornford, Tom, 'Reconstructing Theatre: Shakespeare's Globe under Dominic Dromgoole', *New Theatre Quarterly* 26:4 (2010), 319–328

Coursen, H. R., *Reading Shakespeare on Stage* (Newark: University of Delaware Press, 1995)

Cox, Emma, '"What's past is prologue": Performing Shakespeare and Aboriginality in Australia', *Multicultural Shakespeare: Translation, Appropriation and Performance* 8:23 (2011), 71–92

Culler, Jonathan, *Literary Theory: A Very Short Introduction* (Oxford University Press, 1997)

Daileader, Celia R., 'Casting Black Actors: beyond Othellophilia', in Catherine M. S. Alexander and Stanley Wells (eds.), *Shakespeare and Race* (Cambridge University Press, 2000), pp. 177–202

Davis, Jack, *No Sugar* (Sydney: Currency Press, 1986)

Dawson, Anthony, *Hamlet*, Shakespeare in Performance (Manchester: Manchester University Press, 1995)

Derrida, Jacques, 'Signature Event Context', in *Limited Inc* (Evanston: Northwestern University Press, 1988), pp. 13–21

Dessen, Alan C., 'Portable Shakespeare: exigencies and "magic" in five–actor productions', *Shakespeare Bulletin* 29:1 (2011), 1–25

Dionne, Craig and Parmita Kapadia (eds.), *Native Shakespeares: Indigenous Appropriations on a Global Stage* (Aldershot: Ashgate, 2008)

Dodson, Michael, 'The End in the Beginning: re(de)finding Aboriginality', in Michelle Grossman (ed.), *Blacklines: Contemporary Critical Writing by Indigenous Australians* (Carlton: Melbourne University Press, 2003), pp. 25–42.

Dollimore, Jonathan, 'Desire is death', in Margreta De Grazia, Maureen Quilligan and Peter Stallybrass (eds.), *Subject and Object in Renaissance Culture*, (Cambridge University Press, 1996), pp. 369–86

Drucker, Johanna, *The Century of Artists' Books*, second edition (New York: Granary Books, 2004)

Enoch, Wesley, *Black Medea*, in *Contemporary Indigenous Plays* (Sydney: Currency Press, 2007)

Enoch, Wesley and Deborah Mailman, *The 7 Stages of Grieving* (Brisbane: Playlab Press, 1996)

Escolme, Bridget, *Talking to the Audience: Actors, Audiences, Selves* (London: Routledge, 2005)

Emotional Excess on the Shakespearean Stage: Passion's Slaves (London: Bloomsbury Press, 2013)

'Being Good: Actors' Testimonies as Archive and the Cultural Construction of Success in Performance', *Shakespeare Bulletin* 28:1 (2010), 77–91

Ewert, Kevin, 'The Thrust Stage Is Not Some Direct Link to Shakespeare', *Shakespeare Bulletin* 29:2 (2011), 165–76

Feiner, Harry, 'Intuition in Practice: Emotion and Feeling in the Artistic Process', in Megan Alrutz, Julia Listengarten and M. Van Duyn Wood (eds.), *Playing with Theory in Theatre Practice* (Basingstoke: Palgrave Macmillan, 2012), pp. 125–38

Fernie, Ewan, 'Shakespeare and the Prospect of Presentism', in *Shakespeare Survey* 58 (Cambridge University Press, 2005), pp. 169–84

Finnane, Mark, '"Payback", Customary Law and Criminal Law in Colonised Australia', *International Journal of the Sociology of Law*, 29 (2001), 293–310

First Australians: They Have Come to Stay (SBS Corporation, 2008)

First Australians: Her Will to Survive (SBS Corporation, 2008)

Fischer, Susan L., *Reading Performance: Spanish Golden-Age Theatre and Shakespeare on the Modern Stage* (Rochester, NY: Tamesis, 2009)

Fitzpatrick, Tim, *Playwright, Space and Place in Early Modern Performance: Shakespeare and Company* (Farnham: Ashgate, 2011)

Flaherty, Kate, *Ours As We Play It: Australia Plays Shakespeare* (Crawley: UWA Publishing, 2011)

Frankland, Richard J., *Conversations with the Dead*, in *Blak Inside: 6 Indigenous Plays from Victoria* (Strawberry Hills: Currency Press, 2002)

Gale, Maggie B. and Ann Featherstone, 'The Imperative of the Archive: Creative Archive Research', in Baz Kershaw and Helen Nicholson (eds.), *Research Methods in Theatre and Performance* (Edinburgh University Press, 2011), pp. 17–40

Gannon, Susanne, 'The (Im)Possibilities of Writing the Self-Writing: French Poststructural Theory and Autoethnography', *Cultural Studies ⇔ Critical Methodologies* 6:4 (2006), 474–95

Garner, Stanton B., *Bodied Spaces: Phenomenology and Performance in Contemporary Drama* (Ithaca: Cornell University Press, 2000)

Gay, Penny, *As She Likes It: Shakespeare's Unruly Women* (London: Routledge, 1994)

Gelder, Ken and Jane M. Jacobs, *Uncanny Australia: sacredness and identity in a postcolonial nation* (Melbourne University Press, 1998)

Gerstle, Tanya, 'Pulse: A Physical Approach to Staging Text', unpublished M.A. Dissertation (held at the Lenton Parr Library, Victorian College of the Arts)

Ghose, Indira, *Shakespeare and Laughter: A Cultural History* (Manchester University Press, 2008)

Giannachi, Gabriella, *Virtual Theatres: An Introduction* (London: Routledge, 2004)

Gingrich-Philbrook, Craig, 'The Unnatural Performative: Resisting Phenomenal Closure', *Text and Performance Quarterly* 17:1 (1997), 123–29

Ginters, Laura, '"And there may we rehearse most obscenely and courageously": pushing limits in rehearsal', *About Performance* 6 (2006), 55–73

Greenblatt, Stephen, *Hamlet in Purgatory* (Princeton University Press, 2001)

Halio, Jay, 'Gloucester's Blinding', *Shakespeare Quarterly* 43:2 (1992), 221–23

Harrison, Jane, *Stolen* (Sydney: Currency Press, 1998)

Hartley, Andrew James, 'The Schrödinger Effect: Reading and Misreading Performance', in *Shakespeare Survey* 62 (Cambridge University Press, 2009), pp. 222–35

Hawkes, Terence, *Meaning by Shakespeare* (London: Routledge, 1992)

Shakespeare in the Present (London: Routledge, 2002)

Healy, Chris, *Forgetting Aborigines* (Sydney: University of New South Wales Press, 2008)

Hodgdon, Barbara, *The Shakespeare Trade: Performances and Appropriations* (Philadelphia: University of Pennsylvania Press, 1998)

'Bride-ing the Shrew: Costumes that Matter', in *Shakespeare Survey* 60 (Cambridge University Press, 2007), pp. 72–83

'Shopping in the Archives: material memories', in Peter Holland (ed.), *Shakespeare, Memory and Performance* (Cambridge University Press, 2006), pp. 135–67

Holland, Peter, 'The Lost Workers: Process, Performance, and the Archive', *Shakespeare Bulletin* 28:1 (2010), 7–18

Huggins, Jackie, 'Always was always will be', in Michelle Grossman (ed.), Blacklines: *Contemporary Critical Writing by Indigenous Australians* (Carlton: Melbourne University Press, 2003), pp. 60–65

Jackson, Shannon, *Professing Performance: Theatre in the Academy from Philology to Performativity* (Cambridge University Press, 2004)

Jones, Joni L., 'Performing Osun without Bodies: Documenting the Osun Festival in Print', *Text and Performance Quarterly* 17:1 (1997), 69–93

Joughin, John J., 'Shakespeare's Memorial Aesthetics', in Peter Holland (ed.), *Shakespeare, Memory and Performance* (Cambridge University Press, 2006), pp. 43–62

Kaye, Nick, *Site-Specific Art: Performance, Place and Documentation* (London: Routledge, 2000)

Kelly, Philippa, *The King and I* (London: Continuum, 2011)

Kennedy, Dennis, *Looking at Shakespeare: A Visual History of Twentieth-Century Performance* (Cambridge University Press, 1996)

Kerrigan, John, 'Hieronimo, Hamlet and Remembrance', *Essays in Criticism* 31:2 (1981), 105–26

Kingsley, Ben, 'Othello', in Russell Jackson and Robert Smallwood (eds.), *Players of Shakespeare 2* (Cambridge University Press, 1988)

Kirwan, Peter, 'Review of Shakespeare's *Roman Tragedies (Coriolanus, Julius Caesar, Antony and Cleopatra)* (directed by Ivo Van Hove for Toneelgroep Amsterdam) at the Barbican, London, 20 November 2009', *Shakespeare* 6:4 (2010), 478–82

Kleinert, Sylvia and Margot Neale (eds.), *The Oxford Companion to Aboriginal Art and Culture* (South Melbourne, Oxford University Press, 2000)

Knowles, Ric, *Reading the Material Theatre* (Cambridge University Press, 2003)

Langton, Marcia, *"Well, I Heard it on the Radio and I Saw it on the Television": An Essay for the Australian Film Commission on the Politics and Aesthetics of Filmmaking by and about Aboriginal People and Things* (North Sydney: Australian Film Commission, 1993)

'The Edge of the Sacred, the Edge of Death: Sensual Inscriptions', in Bruno David and Meredith Wilson (eds.), *Inscribed Landscapes: Marking and Making Place* (Honolulu: University of Hawai'i Press, 2002), pp. 253–69

Law, John, 'Pinboards and Books: Juxtaposing, Learning and Materiality', www.heterogeneities.net/publications/Law2006PinboardsAndBooks.pdf, downloaded on 18 May, 2014

Ledger, Adam J., with Simon K. Ellis and Fiona Wright, 'The Question of Documentation: Creative Strategies in Performance Research', in Baz Kershaw and Helen Nicholson (eds.), *Research Methods in Theatre and Performance* (Edinburgh University Press, 2011), pp. 162–85

Lecoq, Jacques, *The Moving Body: Teaching Creative Theatre* (London: A & C Black, 2002)

Loomba, Ania, *Shakespeare, Race and Colonialism* (Oxford University Press, 2002)

Lopez, Jeremy, *Theatrical Convention and Audience Response in Early Modern Drama* (Cambridge University Press, 2006)

Lusardi, James P. and June Schlueter, *Reading Shakespeare in Performance: King Lear* (Rutherford: Fairleigh Dickinson University Press, 1990)

MacDonald, Joyce Green, 'Black Ram, White Ewe: Shakespeare, Race, and Women', in Dympna Callaghan (ed.), *A Feminist Companion to Shakespeare* (Oxford University Press, 2000), pp. 188–207

McAuley, Gay, *Space in Performance: Making Meaning in the Theatre* (Ann Arbor: The University of Michigan Press, 1999)

Not Magic but Work: An ethnographic account of a rehearsal process (Manchester University Press, 2012)

'The National Apology Three Years Later', *Australian Studies* 3 (2011), 1–25

McConachie, Bruce, *Engaging Audiences: A Cognitive Approach to Spectating in the Theatre* (New York: Palgrave Macmillan, 2008)

McKenzie, William and Theodora Papadopoulou (eds.), *Shakespeare and I* (London: Continuum, 2011)

McMillin, Scott, 'The Sharer and His Boy: Rehearsing Shakespeare's Women', in Peter Holland and Stephen Orgel (eds.), *From Script to Stage in Early Modern England* (Basingstoke: Palgrave Macmillan, 2004), pp. 231–45

McMullan, Gordon, Lena Cowen Orlin and Virginia Mason Vaughan (eds.), *Women Making Shakespeare: Text, Reception and Performance* (London: Bloomsbury, 2014)

Merlin, Bella, *With the Rogue's Company: Henry IV at the National Theatre* (London: Oberon Books, 2005)

Miller, Daniel, *Stuff* (London: Polity, 2010)

Meehan, Katharine, Ian Graham Ronald Shaw and Sallie A. Marston, 'Political Geographies of the Object', *Political Geography* 33 (2013), 1–10

Moreira, Claudio, 'Tales of Conde: Autoethnography and the Body Politics of Performative Writing', *Cultural Studies ⇔ Critical Methodologies* 11:6 (2011), 586–95

Moses, A. Dirk, 'Genocide and Settler Society in Australian History', in A. Dirk Moses (ed.), *Genocide and Settler Society: Frontier Violence and Stolen Indigenous Children in Australian History* (New York: Berghahn Books, 2004), pp. 3–48

Mudrooroo, *Aboriginal Mythology* (London: Thorsons, 1994)

Master of the Ghost Dreaming (Sydney: Angus & Robertson, 1993)

Neill, Michael, 'Unproper Beds: Race, Adultery, and the Hideous in *Othello*', *Shakespeare Quarterly* 40 (1989), 383–412

Nelson, Robin, *Practice as Research in the Arts: Principles, Protocols, Pedagogies, Resistances* (Basingstoke: Palgrave Macmillan, 2013)

Newman, Karen, '"And wash the Ethiop white": femininity and the monstrous in *Othello*', in Jean E. Howard and Marion F. O'Connor (eds.), *Shakespeare Reproduced: The text in history and ideology* (New York: Methuen, 1987), pp. 143–62

O'Brien, J. M. S. (ed.), *The New Fortune* (Perth: University of Western Australia Press, 1964)

Palfrey, Simon, 'Ghostly Selections', in William McKenzie and Theodora Papadopoulou (eds.), *Shakespeare and I* (London: Continuum, 2011), pp. 233–57

Pearson, Mike, '*Haunted House: Staging The Persians with the British Army*', in Anna Birch and Joanne Tompkins (eds.), *Performing Site-Specific Theatre* (Basingstoke: Palgrave Macmillan, 2012), pp. 69–83

Pearson, Mike and Michael Shanks, *Theatre / Archaeology* (London: Routledge, 2001)

Pechter, Edward, 'On the Blinding of Gloucester', *English Literary History* 45:2 (1978), 181–200

Pelias, Ronald J., 'Performative Writing as Scholarship: An Apology, an Argument, an Anecdote', *Cultural Studies ⇔ Critical Methodologies* 5:4 (2005), 415–24

   'Confessions of Apprehensive Performer', *Text and Performance Quarterly* 17:1 (1997), 25–32

   Performance: An Alphabet of Performative Writing (Walnut Creek: Left Coast Press, 2014)

Pollock, Della, 'Performing Writing', in Peggy Phelan and Jill Lane (eds.), *The Ends of Performance* (New York University Press, 1998), pp. 73–103

Potter, Emily, 'Introduction: making Indigenous place in the Australian city', *Postcolonial Studies* 15:2 (2012), 131–42

Potter, Lois, *Othello*, Shakespeare in Performance (Manchester University Press, 2002)

Purcell, Stephen, *Popular Shakespeare: Simulation and Subversion on the Modern Stage* (Basingstoke: Palgrave Macmillan, 2009)

   Shakespeare and Audience in Practice (Basingstoke: Palgrave Macmillan, 2013)

Quarshie, Hugh, 'Second Thoughts About Othello', International Shakespeare Association Occasional Paper No. 7 (Chipping Campden, 1999)

Raphael, Timothy, 'Mo(u)rning in America: *Hamlet*, Reagan, and the Rights of Memory', *Theatre Journal* 59:1 (2007), 1–20

Rennie, Reko, 'Remember Me', *Creative Approaches to Research* 1:1 (2008), 73–79

Ridout, Nicholas, *Stage Fright, Animals, and Other Theatrical Problems* (Cambridge University Press, 2006)

Rippy, Marguerite Hailey, 'All our Othellos: Black Monsters and White Masks on the American Screen', in Courtney Lehmann and Lisa S. Starks (eds.), *Spectacular Shakespeare: Critical Theory and Popular Cinema* (Teaneck: Associated University Presses, 2002), pp. 25–46

Roach, Joseph, *Cities of the Dead: Circum-Atlantic Performance* (New York: Columbia University Press, 1996)

Rose, Deborah Bird, *Dingo Makes Us Human: Life and Land in an Australian Aboriginal Culture* (Cambridge University Press, 2000)

Rosenberg, Marvin, *The Masks of Othello: The Search for the Identity of Othello, Iago, and Desdemona by Three Centuries of Actors and Critics* (Newark: University of Delaware Press, 1961)

Rugg, Judith, *Exploring Site-Specific Art: Issues of Space and Internationalism* (London: I. B. Tauris, 2010)

Rutter, Carol Chillington, *Enter the Body: Women and Representation on Shakespeare's Stage* (London: Routledge, 2001)

   'Unpinning Desdemona (Again) or "Who wold be toll'd with Wenches in a shew?"', *Shakespeare Bulletin* 28:1 (2010), 111–32

   Clamorous Voices: Shakespeare's Women Today (London: The Women's Press, 1988)

Salgãdo, Gãmini, *Eyewitnesses of Shakespeare: First Hand Accounts of Performances 1590 – 1890* (London: Chatto and Windus, 1975)

Schafer, Elizabeth, *MsDirecting Shakespeare: Women Direct Shakespeare* (London: The Women's Press, 1988)

'Reconciliation Shakespeare? Aboriginal presence in Australian Shakespeare production', in Elizabeth Schafer and Susan Bradley Smith (eds.), *Playing Australia: Australian theatre on the international stage* (Amsterdam: Rodopi, 2003), pp. 63–78

Scott, Sarah K., '*Roman Tragedies*', *Shakespeare Bulletin* 28:3 (2010), 347–55

Sedgwick, Eve Kosofsky, 'Teaching "Experimental Critical Writing"', in Peggy Phelan and Jill Lane (eds.), *The Ends of Performance* (New York University Press, 1998), pp. 104–15

Selden, Raman and Peter Widdowson, *A Reader's Guide to Contemporary Literary Theory*, third edition (New York: Harvester Wheatsheaf, 1993)

Shakespeare, William, *Othello*, Arden 3, ed. E. A. J. Honigmann (London: Arden Shakespeare, 2001)

    Othello, New Penguin, ed. Kenneth Muir (London: Penguin Books, 1968)

    Hamlet, Q2 Arden 3, ed. Ann Thompson and Neil Taylor (London: Arden Shakespeare, 2006)

    King Lear, New Penguin, ed. George Hunter (London: Penguin Books, 1972)

Shaughnessy, Robert, *The Shakespeare Effect: A History of Twentieth-Century Performance* (Basingstoke: Palgrave Macmillan, 2002)

    Representing Shakespeare: England, History and the RSC (Hemel Hempstead: Harvester Wheatsheaf, 1994)

    The Routledge Guide to William Shakespeare (Abingdon: Routledge, 2011)

Simkin, Stevie, *Early Modern Tragedy and the Cinema of Violence* (Basingstoke: Palgrave Macmillan, 2006)

Simon, Eli, *The Art of Clowning* (New York: Palgrave Macmillan, 2009)

Sinfield, Alan, *Faultlines: Cultural Materialism and the Politics of Dissident Reading* (Oxford University Press, 1992)

Skantze, P. A., *Stillness in Motion in the Seventeenth-Century Theatre* (London: Routledge, 2003)

Smith, Bruce R., *Shakespeare and Masculinity* (Oxford University Press, 2000)

    The Acoustic World of Early Modern England: Attending to the O-Factor (The University of Chicago Press, 1999)

    'Speaking What We Feel about *King Lear*', in Peter Holland (ed.), *Shakespeare, Memory and Performance* (Cambridge University Press, 2006), pp. 23–42

Smith, Linda Tuhiwai, *Decolonizing Metholodologies: Research and Indigenous Peoples*, second edition (London: Zed Books, 2012)

Solga, Kim, *Violence Against Women in Early Modern Performance: Invisible Acts* (Basingstoke: Palgrave Macmillan, 2009)

States, Bert O., *Great Reckonings in Little Rooms: On the Phenomenology of Theater* (Berkeley: University of California Press, 1985)

    'The Phenomenological Attitude', in Janelle G. Reinelt and Joseph R. Roach (eds.), *Critical Theory and Performance* (Ann Arbor: The University of Michigan Press, 1992), pp. 369–79

Steggle, Matthew, 'Notes Towards an Analysis of Early Modern Applause', in Katharine A. Craik and Tanya Pollard (eds.), *Shakespearean Sensations: Experiencing Literature in Early Modern England* (Cambridge University Press, 2013), pp. 118–137

Steigerwalt, Jenna, 'Performing Race on the Original-Practices Stage: A Call to Action', *Shakespeare Bulletin* 27:3 (2009), 425–35

Stern, Tiffany, *Rehearsal from Shakespeare to Sheridan* (Oxford University Press, 2000)

Stewart, J. I. M., 'The Blinding of Gloster', *The Review of English Studies* 21:84 (1945), 266–70

Sutton, Peter, *The Politics of Suffering: Indigenous Australians and the end of the liberal consensus* (Melbourne University Press, 2009)

Tompkins, Joanne, 'The "Place" and Practice of Site-Specific Theatre and Performance', in Anna Birch and Joanne Tompkins (eds.), *Performing Site-Specific Theatre* (Basingstoke: Palgrave Macmillan, 2012), pp. 1–20

Traub, Valerie, *Desire and Anxiety: Circulations of Sexuality in Shakespearean Drama* (London: Routledge, 1992)

Ubersfeld, Anne, *Reading Theatre*, Trans. by Frank Collins (University of Toronto Press, 1999)

Vaughan, Virginia Mason, *Othello: A contextual history* (Cambridge University Press, 1994)

    Performing Blackness on English Stages, 1500–1800 (Cambridge University Press, 2005)

Walter, Harriet, *Other People's Shoes: Thoughts on Acting* (London: Nick Hern Books, 2003)

Werner, Sarah, *Shakespeare and Feminist Performance: Ideology on Stage* (London: Routledge, 2001)
    '*Audiences*', in Stuart Hampton-Reeves and Bridget Escolme (eds.), *Shakespeare and the Making of Theatre* (Basingstoke: Palgrave Macmillan, 2012), pp. 165–79

Willmot, Eric, *Pemulwuy: The Rainbow Warrior* (Moorebank: Bantam Books, 1998)

Woods, Penelope, 'Shakespeare's Globe Audiences: Old and New', in Bruce R. Smith and Katherine Rowe (eds.), *The Cambridge Guide to the Worlds of Shakespeare*, Vol. 2 'The World's Shakespeare, 1660 to the present', forthcoming

Worthen, W. B., *Shakespeare and the Force of Modern Performance* (Cambridge University Press, 2003)
    Shakespeare Performance Studies (Cambridge University Press, 2014)

Zarrilli, Phillip B., Bruce A. McConachie, Carol Fisher Sorgenfrei and Gary Jay Williams (eds.), *Theatre Histories: An Introduction* (Abingdon: Routledge, 2006)

Index